AF522662

Introduction to Human Rights

Introduction to Human Rights

Dr. Lalita Sharma

RANDOM PUBLICATIONS
NEW DELHI (INDIA)

Introduction to Human Rights

ISBN 978-93-5111-224-2

Published in 2014 in India by

RANDOM PUBLICATIONS

4376-A/4B, Gali Murari Lal, Ansari Road
New Delhi-110 002
Phone : +91-11-43580356, +91-11-23289044
e-mail: randomexports@gmail.com, sales@randompublications.com, info@randompublications.com

Reprinted 2022

Type Setting by : Keystoneprintads, Delhi-110051
Digitally Printed at: Replika Press Pvt. Ltd.

Preface

Human rights are rights inherent to all human beings, whatever our nationality, place of residence, sex, national or ethnic origin, colour, religion, language, or any other status. We are all equally entitled to our human rights without discrimination. These rights are all interrelated, interdependent and indivisible. Universal human rights are often expressed and guaranteed by law, in the forms of treaties, customary international law , general principles and other sources of international law. International human rights law lays down obligations of Governments to act in certain ways or to refrain from certain acts, in order to promote and protect human rights and fundamental freedoms of individuals or groups.

The principle of universality of human rights is the cornerstone of international human rights law. This principle, as first emphasized in the Universal Declaration on Human Rights in 1948, has been reiterated in numerous international human rights conventions, declarations, and resolutions. The 1993 Vienna World Conference on Human Rights, for example, noted that it is the duty of States to promote and protect all human rights and fundamental freedoms, regardless of their political, economic, and cultural systems. All States have ratified at least one, and 80% of States have ratified four or more, of the core human rights treaties, reflecting consent of States which creates legal obligations for them and giving concrete expression to universality. Some fundamental human rights norms enjoy universal protection by customary international law across all boundaries and civilizations. Human rights are inalienable. They should not be taken away, except in specific situations and according to due process. For example, the right to liberty may be restricted if a person is found guilty of a crime by a court of law.

All human rights are indivisible, whether they are civil and political rights, such as the right to life, equality before the law and freedom of expression; economic, social and cultural rights, such as the rights to work, social security and education , or collective rights, such as the rights to development and self-determination, are indivisible, interrelated and interdependent. The improvement of one right facilitates advancement of the others. Likewise, the deprivation of one right adversely affects the others.

Non-discrimination is a cross-cutting principle in international human rights law. The principle is present in all the major human rights treaties and provides the central theme of some of international human rights conventions such as the International Convention on the Elimination of All Forms of Racial Discrimination and the Convention on the Elimination of All Forms of Discrimination against Women. The principle applies to everyone in relation to all human rights and freedoms and it prohibits discrimination on the basis of a list of non-exhaustive categories such as sex, race, colour and so on. The principle of non-discrimination is complemented by the principle of equality, as stated in Article 1 of the Universal Declaration of Human Rights: "All human beings are born free and equal in dignity and rights."

Human rights entail both rights and obligations. States assume obligations and duties under international law to respect, to protect and to fulfil human rights. The obligation to respect means that States must refrain from interfering with or curtailing the enjoyment of human rights. The obligation to protect requires States to protect individuals and groups against human rights abuses. The obligation to fulfil means that States must take positive action to facilitate the enjoyment of basic human rights. At the individual level, while we are entitled our human rights, we should also respect the human rights of others.

I thank all members of my team who have helped in the preparation of the book. My special thanks go to "Random Publications" who have published the book.

– Dr. Lalita Sharma

Contents

1

Introduction

THE MEANING OF HUMAN RIGHTS

The term "human rights" is a relatively modern invention.

It covers under its umbrella three different types of rights:

- The fundamental freedoms or classical civil liberties,
- Ethnic and religious rights and
- Socio-economic rights.

Some constitutions have enumerated the first or the first and the second and attempted to set up judicial enforcement of such rights. The third category has not been stated in a constitution in an enforceable form, but some constitutions refer to them as directive principles of state policy.

Civil Liberties

Liberal ideas have been influential in the origins and development of the classical civil liberties. The meanings of the word "liberal" given in the Shorter Oxford Dictionary provide an indication of the context in which the word is used: "Free from restraint; free in speech or action... Free from narrow prejudice; open minded... especially open to the reception of new ideas or proposals of reform... of political opinions: favourable to changes and reforms tending in the direction of democracy". Freedom is an important value in representative democracies.

The idea of the fundamental freedoms" has been influential in all genuine representative democracies. Some constitutions contain a statement of human rights professedly in order to safeguard the freedoms of individuals and groups in society. Other constitutions may not, but freedom operates as a politically and socially persuasive doctrine. There is no agreement as to the content of such rights.

The more important rights may be said to include the right of each individual to:

- Freedom of speech and expression freedom from arrest or detention except under authority of law, freedom from cruel, inhumane or degrading punishments and the right to a fair trial by a competent and independent court

- Freedom to enjoy lawfully acquired property
- Equality of opportunity (including freedom from discrimination)
- Freedom of assembly and association (including public meeting and withdrawal of labour)
- Freedom of thought, conscience and religion freedom to contract.
- Freedom to engage in a trade, profession or occupation.
- Freedom of movement within a nation and across national borders.

ETHNIC RIGHTS

Nations with multi-linguistic, multi-cultural, multi-racial and multi-religious populations may also attempt to safeguard minorities in their charter of rights. The notion of equality before the law and equal protection of the law underlies the above rights and is generally included in constitutions which have bills of rights though in a particular-situation it may be available in conjunction with some other right. The idea of equality before the law implies that persons or groups must not be discriminated against without justification. The words "without justification" are relevant. Discrimination is inevitable in human affairs because of the differences between human beings, accidents (both natural and man induced) and many factors which affect the nurture and development of individuals.

SOCIAL WELFARE RIGHTS

Some constitutions also contain what may be called principles of state policy. These by their nature are not justifiable in the courts and are inserted for the guidance of the legislatures and government of the country. Among topics which are placed in this category are the duties of the state: to secure full employment for all people of working age, to provide adequate standards of living and education to all citizens, to rapidly develop the country, to distribute the social product equitably, to eliminate economic and social privilege and disparity, to ensure social security and welfare, to develop the culture and languages of ethnic groups, to protect the environment, to safeguard the independence, sovereignty, unity and territorial integrity of the country and to promote international peace and co-operation.

There is wide disagreement as to the nature of human rights. "Human rights", according to a marxist legal philosopher, are neither eternal truths nor supreme values. They are not valid everywhere nor for an unlimited time. They are rooted neither in the conscience of the individual nor in a God's plan of creation. They are of earthly origin... a comparatively late product in the history of human society-and their implementation does not lie in everybody's interest. In their essentials, man's interests are not the same everywhere and they cannot even be the same in any particular country under the conditions of the system of private ownership of the means of production. H Klenner, Human Rights: A Battle Cry for Social Change or a Challenge to

Philosophy of Law?, at the World Congress on Philosophy of Law and Social Philosophy, Sydney/Canberra, August 1977.

The analysis made in this stage refers to three types of rights:

- The traditional rights primarily involving protection of individuals from government,
- Ethnic and religious rights and
- Social welfare rights.

It is important to distinguish between the different historical and conceptual bases of these three categories of rights which are loosely termed "human rights". Such differences between them are often blurred or ignored, with serious consequences for the operation of fundamental freedoms. Since the second world war, there has been a great emphasis on human rights other than the classical civil liberties: on socio-economic rights, and on the rights of groups or classes or nations.

The recognition that the promotion of socio-economic rights, as rights to benefit from the state, stand in great tension with civil liberties may be often deliberately obscured, but it is nevertheless widespread and it is, of course, a correct recognition. The traditional civil liberties, many have correctly recognised, require institutional settings, historical traditions, a sense of community. The socio-economic rights can, in principle, be granted by the state, even by a state which suppresses all non-state organisations and institutions.

Very different kinds of societies may be involved.... The attempt to elevate human rights, in any particular formulation, uncritically, as urgent, unhistorical, abstract demands is not only based on intellectual error but is like most propaganda and moral indoctrination inherently unstable and unable to cope with genuine criticism. Human rights can only be understood, and therefore must be taught, in the concrete contexts in which they arise and have to be implemented. This is the social context of concrete history and real politics. There is also, in an important sense, a concrete human context. This is best portrayed by world literature, or at least by the great literature of the world, and not by shallow declarations and proclamations.

The third category commonly included within the term "human rights", namely "socio-economic rights", raises basic questions regarding the meaning and operation of human rights. The recognition of this category as rights has created certain contradictions within the concept, leading to the weakening of civil liberties. The consequences of such recognition and the conflict that arises between civil liberties and socio-economic "rights". For the present it is sufficient to state that such "rights" are not recognized as rights properly so-called by those who believe in the primacy of civil liberties. In any event such "rights" have never been incorporated in a constitution in an enforceable form and are often described as directives of state policy. There are human needs. Yet where a need exists, however compelling, a right cannot be said to automatically spring into existence.

HUMAN RIGHTS ARE NOT ABSOLUTE

Restrictions on Rights

In countries which have bills of rights there is a basic statement of freedoms subject to permitted abridgement of such freedoms. Freedoms are restricted in the public interest on grounds of national security, to preserve public order, to protect public health, to maintain moral standards, to secure due recognition and respect for the rights and freedoms of others or to meet the just requirements of the general welfare of a democratic society. The United States Supreme Court has over the years qualified the rights in the constitution. Any statement of rights is not absolute and must of necessity be subject to limitations on the above lines. The right of free speech and expression does not extend to sedition, slander, defamation and obscenity. The principle of equality before the law cannot deny a legislature the power to classify persons for legislative purposes and to legislate affecting them, provided that the classification is not arbitrary and is based on a real and substantial distinction bearing a reasonable and just relation to the objects sought to be achieved.

Thus the legislature could enact legislation regulating the activities of money lenders. This would amount to a singling out of money lenders and would be prima facie in conflict with the principle of equality before the law. But provided the classification is reasonable and there is a legitimate object to be achieved the legislation would nonetheless be valid. The on top of are instances of legitimate restrictions of rights. They are intended to illustrate that no right available to an individual or group is or can be absolute. This seems obvious but is often not appreciated.

The Clash of Rights

The reality that human rights are not absolute and are subject to reasonable restrictions does not mean that the rights can be arbitrarily curtailed according to legislative or bureaucratic discretion. The manner in which restrictions are to be determined and imposed and the criteria which apply to the formulation of restrictions are crucial. Human rights to be meaningful cannot be subject to crude majoritarian dictates. What distinguishes a human right from any other right is that a human right is available and enforceable by a minority, however small, even against the wishes of a majority. If human rights were to become subject to ordinary parliamentary control they would be no different from any other statutory right which parliament is free to confer and withdraw at its pleasure. The restriction of human rights is therefore a crucial and delicate question. They cannot be based on ideological perceptions of parliamentarians, bureaucrats or the Human Rights Commission but must be grounded on objectively ascertained and comprehended criteria.

An article in the National Times week ending 25 August, 1979 referred to "the right to march demonstrations" and by way of example: "Senator

George Georges was gaoled yet again for upholding the principle of the right to democratic protest in Brisbane streets". What are these rights? There is no absolute right to democratic protest or to march. There are rights of speech and expression and assembly. But these rights are subject to limitations. The right to freedom of association must be exercised so as not to interfere with the rights of others to move about the streets or go about their business. Where there is a clash of rights methods must be devised through rational analysis, political avenues and the courts so that the rights of all parties could be exercised so as not to inconvenience each other. If this is not possible (as it often is not) there must be a compromise or one must be restricted and give way to the other.

The clash of rights is a factor which the United States courts and citizens are very familiar with. An example of a conflict of rights is where the right of free expression of the press to coverage of news stories may clash with the right of an accused in a criminal case not to be prejudiced by adverse publicity of allegations made against him prior to trial or in a pre-trial hearing. American journalists generally would not show such an obvious lack of understanding of the basic principles underlying fundamental rights. This is just one of numerous examples in contemporary Australia where so called rights are claimed without reference to conflicting rights and basic common sense.

An example of a clash of rights which occurred in the United States is provided by the case where the Court was asked to outlaw explicit racial quotas for minority racial groups to enable them to enter universities. The idea behind the quotas was to provide a method by which underprivileged black sections of the community would be entitled to a specific number of places in a university. The rationale behind this and many other schemes which are being operated in the United States is to give some preference to blacks over whites in educational institutions and employment in order to remedy the alleged evils of past discrimination. In the case of Regents of the University of California v Bakke, 438 US 265 (1978) Bakke argued that the effect of racial quotas was that while individuals who had an inferior academic record to him had been admitted, he had as a consequence failed to gain admission. Bakke claimed that his right to equal protection before the law had been infringed. Split almost exactly down the middle, the Supreme Court offered a Solomonic compromise.

It said that rigid quotas based solely on race were forbidden, but it also said that race might legitimately be an element in judging students for admission to universities. It thus approved the principle of "affirmative action", the system by which the government is pressuring universities, corporations and other institutions in the United States to provide more places and jobs and better pay for millions of blacks, other minorities and women. Despite a wave of protests and demonstrations by militants, most observers realised that the court had made a careful and genuine effort at reconciling conflicting forces. These forces must of necessity come into conflict in the future in the actual working out of the principles stated in the judgment. The American position is that certain rights are guaranteed by law but the exercise of these rights might be restricted in various situations most notably in the public interest or where the rights of individuals or groups clash with each other. Similar qualifications are found in the law of all countries which have Bills of Rights.

In the common law system which many former British colonies have inherited there are no guaranteed rights. This is the position in Australia subject to a few not very significant exceptions. The right to freedom is residuary. One can do what the law does not forbid. The restrictions on freedom are contained in principles of English common law and English statutes which became applicable in Australia as a consequence of settlement and a mass of legislation passed by State and Commonwealth Parliaments. In a sense the common-law position is the reverse of the American in that one can do what the law does not forbid. There is no general right to free speech and expression. There is such a right subject to such limitations which the common law or legislation prescribes (defamation, sedition, conspiracy, press control and so on). It is the same with the other freedoms. The content of freedom in the common law system is residuary. A person is free to do what is not forbidden by law.

However, though the manner of treatment of rights may differ, there is one principle common to both traditions. In short, freedom must of necessity be abridged. Every society modern or ancient has recognised limitations on freedom, either of custom or law. Where human rights are respected it is not considered permissible or appropriate to restrict freedom arbitrarily or according to political expediency. Restrictions are determined by the objective evaluation of the contending interests in society and are often evolved through the process of litigation before an impartial judiciary.

Judges, Community Values and a Bill of Rights

The argument is used that a Bill of Rights would involve placing excessive power in the judges. The judges interpreting a Bill of Rights are not acting in a vacuum nor are they unfettered by public comment, as they generally are in private litigation. Controversy and comment would naturally follow judicial action or non-action.

This is very evident in the United States where there is an enforceable bill of rights and widespread comment and debate invariably follows significant fundamental rights judgments of the court. Thus judges are compelled to consider and reflect on community attitudes and values. It is significant that the United States Supreme Court handed down its epoch making civil rights decision in Brown v Board of Education 349 US 294 (1954) which outlawed racial segregation in the schools at a time when community attitudes to the issue were changing. In earlier years when community attitudes were more rigid the court had upheld racial segregation.

Community Values

This illustrates an important factor which must be borne in mind in any discussion of fundamental rights. There necessarily exists a relationship between community values and the law. The law can creep ahead of community standards (more often perhaps it might lag behind) but it cannot be entirely divorced from popular values. This is one of the many answers to those who would question why anti-discrimination legislation passed in the Australian States has not achieved much. Another answer would challenge the whole concept of discrimination in the form it is often advocated in Australia. It can be maintained that discrimination if it is based on merit, honest achievement or other rationally defensible criteria is justifiable. Such discrimination is a necessary recognition of differences between human beings.

The law operates in a social context and if the law is very much out of touch with community values, its potential to achieve change is significantly reduced. In the long term it can mould community values if community values are moving in that direction. Community sanctions and legal sanctions must necessarily work in concert to be effective. Likewise limitations on exercise of rights are brought about by law and political factors which often work in concert. There is a case for a Bill of Rights enshrining community shared values, within the framework of which the courts reacting to arguments put forward by citizens and groups, in the context of public and media discussion and analysis of the issues, can pass judgment on conflicts which arise.

In the absence of such a framework the ensuing debate, as individuals and groups are today becoming more assertive, is likely to be fragmented and lead to frustration and even violence, when the institutions provide no forum if not for redress, at least for expression of opinion and a dialogue which could lead to realisation of the existence of opposing opinions. The educative aspect of a Bill of Rights is perhaps even more important than the adjudicative function. It requires emphasis that a Bill of Rights, if it exists, should be administered by properly constituted and independent courts and not by bureaucrats or non judicial tribunals. The problems arising from non-judicial bodies determining issues relating to rights and alleged rights are demonstrated in many parts of this publication.

EXALTATION OF PARTICULAR RIGHTS

One of the real problems in the human rights arena today is the failure by the Human Rights Commission and many who profess to be concerned about human rights to appreciate that human rights are complementary to each other. The pursuit of one particular right without regard to others is self defeating and destructive of the overall framework of rights which is essential to the operation of specific rights. Human rights activists overlook this dimension. Some rights such as the right to equality of opportunity. If one right must prevail over another a rational basis must be provided. This involves an examination of the two rights, an evaluation of the importance of each and the context.

Thus for example in seeking to eliminate some forms of discrimination, damage is caused to other rights (such as freedom of speech or freedom of property) which together have progressively reduced various forms of discrimination and will continue to do so if allowed to flourish. A dispassionate look at the modern history of western civilization will reveal that these rights together with economic freedom have contributed more to the emancipation of oppressed classes than any form of governmental action.

RIGHTS WITHOUT DUTIES

Hohfeld, a legal philosopher, emphasised the relationship between rights and duties and also about the difference between right and privilege. Hohfeld emphasised that there cannot be a right without a duty. Right in one person presupposes a duty in another. The concept of a right without a duty is meaningless. Likewise he also distinguished between rights and privileges. A privilege is available on sufferance. It is a discretion vested in the person granting it. A right is an entitlement. On this analysis what are commonly called rights to employment, welfare, etc are not rights. A right to employment is meaningless because there is no person who is under a duty to employ. Welfare is not a right. It is a privilege which is given to certain persons.

Whether one agrees with this analysis or not, it is undeniable that at the commonsense level a right involves a duty in another person or institution. As an essential commonsense corollary, it must also involve an acceptance of that duty by the person who is subject to it. It is ironic in society today that while more and more people are demanding rights, fewer and fewer people are concerned about duties, least of all those who are most vocal in the assertion of rights. Governments, the Human Rights Commission and many other government agencies provide doubtful leadership in this regard. They are educating people about their rights and are attempting to make more and more rights available with no reference to logic and commonsense. But they seem unconcerned about the need to educate people about duties and the importance of a sense of responsibility.

A dangerous by-product of the welfare state and the growth of government is a profound attitudinal change in society which makes people demand more and more and contribute less and less. This transformation of the social psyche has taken place imperceptibly to the point that it unconsciously pervades the entire society. The preoccupation with rights (particularly state created social and economic rights) has become an obsession. Although this is not an intrinsic evil, the pursuit of rights becomes self defeating when it is unaccompanied by the commitment to duties. The endless cacophony of demands by interest groups has become the dominant feature of the modern Australian state. These demands come not only from the poor and the underprivileged, but also from privileged academic, bureaucratic, social and business groups. At the same time there is a deafening silence on the question of individual responsibility to society.

Surely the time has come to realise and to emphasise that rights, whether material or political, depend on the discharge of duties. Wealth and prosperity are created by effort. Only continuing effort can sustain them. Western societies through effort have achieved a level of prosperity unparalleled in history. But history has continually demonstrated that the greatest of civilizations decline and fall when they succumb to indulgence at the expense of discipline and endeavour. The fate of Egyptian and Roman civilizations are prime examples. It is not too early for Western civilization to heed this supreme lesson of human experience. The interventionist welfare state has become a super patriarchal entity from which individual members have come to expect solutions to all problems. Rights are being demanded and duties forgotten.

UNDERMINING THE JUDICIARY

A serious and disturbing recent trend in Australia in the human rights area is the process whereby Commonwealth and State Parliaments legislate in relation to what are alleged to be specific areas of human rights and invest powers, not in properly constituted courts of law, but in non-judicial tribunals and individuals. This process involves serious derogations of civil liberties. One of many examples is the Sex Discrimination Act (Cth) 1984. This trend reflects a profound lack of understanding of the theoretical and practical aspects of human rights. A major failing in the current Australian intellectual trend is the non-appreciation of the indispensable role of the judiciary in the operation of any system of human rights. An independent and impartial judicial apparatus is a prerequisite for the meaningful existence of human rights.

Human rights can be violated either by state action or by private action. Human rights were originally conceived as safeguards against oppression by rulers and their importance as such has not diminished. It need hardly be emphasised that only a wholly independent judiciary can guarantee human rights against incursions by state action. When it comes to the violation of human rights by private action, it is important to appreciate that most disputes involve a conflict of rights or claimed rights with regard to liberty. The resolution of such disputes affects not only the liberty of the complainant but also of the defendant. Judicial determination is therefore essential.

The current tendency to seek human rights goals through bureaucratic action is characteristic of the interventionist state. The Sex Discrimination Act reflects a step in this direction by making the Human Rights Commission an adjudicatory body with respect to complaints of discrimination, while retaining its promotional and investigatory functions. Although its findings of guilt are said to be non-binding (as originally drafted the Act would have made them prima facie evidence of guilt), a finding of guilt by the Commission remains a prerequisite for the institution of action in the Federal Court. In practical terms, the Commission conducts a pre-trial inquiry which can have considerable effect on the final outcome of trial.

The Commission exercises the following types of powers and/or functions: educational functions, investigative and police powers and functions of a law maker, administrator and judge. Montesquieu's warning against accumulation of power has been the basis of liberal democratic thought which has been significantly eroded in recent times in the name of human rights, discrimination, etc. The Commission further possesses an unrestrained power to delegate its functions. An important aspect of the traditional legal system is the independence, impartiality and lack of bias of the judiciary. Professor Lauchlan Chipman focuses on the anomalous position of the Commission of Human Rights: The Human Rights Commission, under the form the Sex Discrimination Act has finally taken, is still given powers and ways of proceeding which guarantee, when sex discrimination complaints get to it, that justice will never seem to be done, and which make it somewhat naive to expect it to be done in fact.

To see that this is so, let us imagine we were to deal with shoplifting in the way that sexual discrimination is to be dealt with under the new Commonwealth Sex Discrimination Act. If a person is suspected of shoplifting a complaint will be made to the newly formed Shopping Commission, which will in the first instance refer it to a newly appointed Shopping Commissioner (a shop owner who has always been passionately concerned about the harm done by shoplifting) to see if the complaint is substantial, and if so whether there is any possibility of achieving a reconciliation between the suspected shoplifter and the shop owner.

If the Shopping Commissioner fails to resolve the matter it will be referred to the full Shopping Commission (chaired by a retired distinguished judge, who now owns a shop) for a fresh enquiry. The other members of the Shopping Commission are super-market and corner store owners, and a couple of people who have never owned shops themselves, but feel very strongly that the community does not take shoplifting seriously enough. At this enquiry, the suspected shoplifter will not have the right of legal representation, except with leave of the Shopping Commission or if it, for any reason, has counsel assisting it.

The Shopping Commission will not be bound by the ordinary rules of evidence nor by legal technicalities, but must proceed expeditiously and economically for all concerned. It has no power to directly enforce its decision but may seek an order from the Federal Court if any determination it makes is not followed. Would anybody seriously recommend this as a way of dealing with shoplifters or suspected shoplifters? Presumably it would bring howls of protest from civil liberties organizations and the political Opposition. Would anybody seriously expect justice to be done? And if it were, would it seem to be done? Yet this is precisely the approach which has been so widely endorsed (and one can only hope not yet understood) for dealing with allegations and complaints to do with sex discrimination. Such a way of proceeding has more in common with the People's Courts of the Chinese Cultural Revolution or the trials of Oceania than it has with a tradition wedded to justice in and before the law.

Some of the comments made above apply to the Australian Human Rights Commission. The Human Rights Commission is noticeably silent with respect to the erosion of human rights which is taking place currently in Australia. In truth it is making a very significant contribution to such erosion. The inevitable consequence of undermining the traditional role of the judiciary as the guardian of civil liberty and entrusting that responsibility to the politicised bureaucracy, is that human rights become subjective standards capable of being used as the instruments of oppression.

SOCIAL WELFARE

It is pertinent to reiterate the extent of poverty in Zambia before examining the issue of social security and welfare assistance. In 1996, it was estimated that 69 per cent or almost 6.6 million Zambians were poor. This includes 5.1 million or 53 per cent of the population living in extreme poverty. In comparison, 70 per cent of the population lived in poverty in 1991 and 74 per cent did so in 1993. In fact, due to population growth, more Zambians are poor today than at any time during the decade.

While a decrease in the percentage of those living in extreme poverty was recorded between 1993 and 1996, the continued economic recession is likely to have seen a reversal in this trend. Indeed, latest estimates suggest a rise in poverty to effect 72 per cent of the population. The 1998 budget address is recognised as constituting the first public admission by the MMD Government that sustainable development was impossible while poverty levels were so high. The target of reducing poverty levels to less than 50 per cent by the year 2004 was set. The Government drafted a National Poverty Reduction Strategy Framework in early 1998 and has since adopted the National Poverty Reduction Action Plan 1999-2000. A national Poverty Reduction Unit has been established within the Ministry of Community Development and Social Services to coordinate the implementation of this plan.

The provision of welfare assistance is one subcomponent of the support envisaged under the action plan which spans development in agriculture, infrastructure, human resources, micro-enterprises and the informal sector, together with improved monitoring and evaluation. However, the plan must be brought to fruition before it can be characterised as a progressive step towards the alleviation of poverty in Zambia and the realisation of economic and social rights. As it is, weaknesses in existing programmes continue to render them ineffective. This applies to the Public Welfare Assistance Scheme and the National Social Safety Net which are reviewed here in the context of the right to social security. The analysis which follows is structured across four subsections. A preliminary concern is to map out the right to social security under the Covenant. In a second subsection, a brief overview is provided of the public social welfare system in Zambia. In the context of retrenchment as a result of economic reform, a third subsection details the social assistance available to retrenchees. A final subsection considers the extent of action by the World Bank to promote a social safety net in mitigation of the hardship caused by the structural adjustment programme.

THE RIGHT TO SOCIAL SECURITY

General provision for social security is made under article 9 of the Covenant:

- 'The States parties to the present Covenant recognize the right of everyone to social security, including social insurance.'

The Committee has not issued a general comment on article 9. Nevertheless, it is possible to discern some of the central elements of a right to social security. The expectation arising from a State party's obligations under the Covenant is for a formal, public social security scheme to be in operation. The range of social security envisaged under article 9 includes medical care, cash sickness benefits, maternity benefits, old-age benefits, invalidity benefits, survivors' benefits, employment injury benefits, unemployment benefits and family benefits. Moreover, it is apparent that the Committee recognises a broad right to social security under the Covenant beyond a system of social insurance available to those with a record of contributions. The universality of the rights in the Covenant is unequivocal.

In respect of the right to social security, this is underlined by the Committee's request for information on the extent to which any groups do not enjoy the right to social security at all or do so to a significantly lesser degree than the majority of the population. A Government is required to indicate the measures it has taken to realise the right for such groups, to include the adoption of timetables and benchmarks. The plight of the vulnerable and disadvantaged is singled out for special attention by the Committee. Furthermore, the Committee recognises the relevancy of a number of ILO conventions on social security to the realisation of article 9. While Zambia has not ratified the conventions referred to-and this, in itself, must be a matter of concern and regret-this does not preclude their use in interpreting the right to social security under the Covenant.

THE PUBLIC WELFARE ASSISTANCE SCHEME

The Public Welfare Assistance Scheme, run by the Ministry of Community Development and Social Services, constitutes the State social safety net in Zambia. Its coverage of is extremely limited and meagre resources are concentrated on the poorest and most vulnerable: orphans, the disabled, the elderly and unsupported children, women and dependants. Component programmes of the PWAS include the Health Care Cost Scheme, the school bursaries scheme and the Nutrition and Food National Social Safety Council.

Most payments from the scheme are for food, shelter, medical costs and educational fees. The Covenant requires a State party to use maximum available resources to achieve progressively the full realisation of the rights recognised under the Covenant. Furthermore, if essential minimum levels of each right are to be realised by the vulnerable and disadvantaged in Zambia, as required by the Covenant, then social security for such groups is essential.

The existence of user fees for health and education in Zambia reinforces the obligation on the Government to provide assistance to meet these costs to the maximum of its available resources if prima facie violations of the Covenant are to be avoided. When juxtaposed to the Government's obligations, the level of funding for the PWAS is grossly inadequate in both relative and absolute terms. In every year since 1994, payments made from the PWAS have never amounted to even 0.1 per cent of domestic expenditure. Spending in 1997 under the PWAS on assistance-support services and the health and education schemes-amounted to K517 million. This represents a fall in actual expenditure on provision of forty per cent over the previous year.

In 1998, the budget for the PWAS was doubled to K1.1 billion; however, in real terms this failed to raise spending even to the levels of 1995 and 1996. The amount spent in 1998 was the equivalent to just K217 or 13 US cents for each of the five million Zambians living in extreme poverty. The actual number assisted under the scheme during the year was 128,075 persons. Hence only 2.5 per cent of those classified as extremely poor were assisted. Payments on an average annual per capita basis were K8,800 or $4.75. To add a final perspective to this level of funding, tax concessions to the mining sector announced in the 1998 budget were worth K18 billion or sixteen times the entire budget for the PWAS. In the case of Zambia, resources targeted towards vulnerable groups to mitigate the effects of structural adjustment have.

- Been characterised by the UN ACC Task Force on Full Employment and Sustainable Livelihoods as 'far too meagre': Safety nets for vulnerable groups facing severe economic hardship can be improved and a comprehensive social security system should gradually be extended. Years of hardship and poverty have increased destitution. The worst affected are the disabled, unsupported old people, orphans and neglected children, single-headed households and the homeless. An increasing number of households are headed by children, following the early death of parents through HIV/AIDS. The effectiveness of the Public Welfare Assistance Scheme (PWAS) has been very limited.

SOCIAL SECURITY

Administration of the PWAS was decentralised in 1996 in an attempt to improve targeting. Ward Welfare Assistance Committees at the local level are responsible for identifying the most disadvantaged and vulnerable persons in a community and making a recommendation for their support to the appropriate District Welfare Assistance Committee. Furthermore, the eligibility requirements for assistance have recently been made more stringent to further focus who receives payment. The new eligibility criteria and operational guidelines are to be first tested in a pilot scheme. It will take four years to launch the revamped PWAS.

Although the emphasis upon the delivery of assistance at the community level is further reinforced, a Public Welfare Assistance Management Unit has been established in the Ministry of Community Development and Social Services to co-ordinate implementation of the PWAS. This notwithstanding, policy measures adopted by the Government in respect of the PWAS do not constitute active steps for the progressive achievement of the right to social security for the 53 per cent of the population living in extreme poverty. Instead, the attempt to focus welfare on an ever smaller subset of recipients when 5,068,000 Zambians are already classed as extremely poor is symptomatic of the utterly inadequate level of spending. While the Committee has determined that the most vulnerable must be protected by the use of targeted programmes, the underlying requirement which must be fulfilled is the use of maximum available resources. Arising out of the obligation to take steps, the Zambian Government is most certainly required to ensure the measures it adopts are deliberate, concrete and targeted towards the realisation of the right to social security.

Moreover, the requirement of progressive realisation 'imposes an obligation to move as expeditiously and effectively as possible' towards the full achievement of the right. In stark contrast, a number of organisations have been highly critical of the way in which the welfare and social safety net systems in Zambia are run. In its annual report on Zambia, Social Watch was of the view that 'above all, the capacity of the Department of Community Development and Social Services, which is charged with the responsibility of assisting persons who have been negatively affected by structural adjustment, is almost non-existent, apart from being a drain on the same meagre financial resources that are set aside for the poor.' The World Bank itself has described the PWAS as suffering from design weaknesses, limited administrative capacity and low budget allocations.

SOCIAL ASSISTANCE AIMED AT RETRENCHES

The Committee itself recognises unemployment benefits as one category of social security under article 9. As has been noted, Zambia has not ratified those ILO Conventions referred to in the Committee's reporting guideline on article 9. However, it has ratified the ILO Termination of Employment Convention 1982. This entitles a redundant worker to either terminal benefits or social security or both in combination. In the case of Zambia, where legal entitlements to terminal benefits are not honoured in practice, the obligation on the State to provide social security to retrenchees is unequivocal.

Furthermore, and this is most pertinent in a country such as Zambia where the informal economy predominates, all retrenchees have a right alongside other members of society to social assistance when they are vulnerable or disadvantaged.

A National Social Safety Net has been established in Zambia 'to co-ordinate safety net programmes for retrenched/displaced workers'. It is important to recognise that the focus is upon formal sector unemployment and the scheme does not constitute a programme of social assistance for all in Zambian society. To recap, the National Social Safety Net was set up within the Ministry of Labour and Social Security in 1993. It is managed by a Co-ordinating Committee which allows all the relevant bodies to work together. Five schemes, concerned with providing information on the social impact of privatisation, retraining, business development, resettlement, and welfare are run by the relevant Ministry or agency, but co-ordinated under the National Social Safety Net. The one component of the scheme concerned with social security *per se* is the Public Welfare Assistance Scheme.

Hence there are no dedicated measures or additional resources under the safety net to meet the welfare needs of retrenchees. On the contrary, the 80,000 redundancies in the formal sector since 1992 have increased the demands on the PWAS as former employees and their families become impoverished. However, while many retrenchees will be living in extreme poverty, many of them will not be destitute and will not therefore qualify for assistance. Overall, the National Social Safety Net Co-ordinating Committee has itself been sharply criticised for its complete lack of urgency, for spending most of its funds on its own facilities and staff, and for an almost total absence of concrete results. Despite being set up in 1993, it took four years before it even produced a policy framework in 1997. Funding from the United Nations Development Programme agreed in 1995 was spent on capacity building, staff and operational costs.

This source of funding was due to end in 1998. A direct grant of $292,000 from the World Bank was made through the Institutional Development Fund in 1996, bringing the total level of committed funds to $500,000. This money too was spent largely on staff training and equipment. Hence negligible resources were used to deliver direct measures to assist impoverished retrenchees. Given that the Government funds only the operational costs of the Safety Net to the tune of K200 million, that current donor commitments are uncertain against this background of mismanagement and inaction, it is difficult to see how the National Social Safety Net can have any impact on solving the social problems caused by retrenchment.

THE FAILURE BY THE WORLD BANK TO SUPPORT SOCIAL WELFARE MEASURES IN MITIGATION OF THE HARDSHIP CAUSED BY ADJUSTMENT

Information is sought from State parties to the Covenant about the role of international assistance in the full realisation of the right to social security. Article 22 provides a basis upon which the World Bank is required to account for the advisability or otherwise of international assistance measures. The influence of Bank action upon redundancy compensation has already been documented. The focus in this subsection is squarely upon Bank action on social assistance in mitigation of retrenchment *per se* and the wider hardship caused by structural adjustment. The Bank has also used adjustment lending to underpin reform of basic pensions and social security institutions: this action is not reviewed. The Economic Recovery Credit did little to influence pro-poor social policies, despite the fact that protecting vulnerable groups was specifically mentioned as a loan objective.

The Government was required to draw up a schedule for implementation of a Social Action Programme which the Bank has subsequently acknowledged suffered from poor implementation capacity and could not, in any case, deal with all the support required as a result of the adjustment programme. The two Privatisation and Industrial Reform Credits were orientated towards parastatal restructuring, privatisation and public sector reform. They have therefore been intrinsically linked to retrenchment. The Bank concedes that 'one of the critical aspects of privatization and other reforms envisaged under PIRC is the effect the programme will have initially on vulnerable groups' Yet the limited social actions specified under the credits have proved totally ineffective in alleviating poverty and hardship among those who have lost their jobs. PIRC I sought the development of an improved social programme. The Government agreed under PIRC I to formulate and introduce a social action plan and strengthen the national social safety net to support those most adversely affected by reform, including those made redundant as a result of rationalisation of the civil service and privatisation.

This has proved entirely inadequate. First, the planned safety net was to target only retrenchees as a subset of those adversely affected by economic reform. Second, requiring a plan of action does not guarantee the actual delivery and implementation of social support. In the context of the austerity measures simultaneously required by the Bank, the financing of an adequate safety net was always an unlikely prospect. In the event, it is unsurprising that social support has not been successfully delivered, even to the limited extent envisaged.

The Bank did earmark a small share of privatisation technical assistance to fund consultants to assist in the formulation of the social action plan and retrenchment safety net. Out of a total budget of $11m, less than 4 per cent of funds or $0.4 million were earmarked for the social action component of the technical assistance on offer. The bulk of funds under PIRTA were focused upon the hiring of long-term advisers and short-term specialists to support privatisation. The long-term posts funded through PIRTA do not include a social adviser while the hiring of short-term expertise is limited to the sale and negotiation process.

The Bank spells out terms of reference for each post, but, beyond the inclusion of the monitoring and coordination of the social action plan within the remit of the privatisation adviser at the Ministry of Finance, an explicit consideration of social issues is rarely specified. In relation to ensuring that privatisation accords with the protection of economic and social rights, this must represent a significant omission. It should also be noted that the formulation of a plan is of no use to those affected by redundancy unless it results in the actual delivery of a programme of support. The sad reality is the total inadequacy of the National Social Safety Net which has resulted. The remit of PIRC II in respect of social assistance was even more circumscribed.

It required the completion of a study on the impact of privatisation by ZPA and the exploration of ways to design and fund redundancy compensation packages. Moreover, the failure to deliver satisfactory redundancy compensation has heightened the need for an effective social safety net. Of distinctly marginal significance is the agreement with the Government to conduct an assessment of the impact of privatisation upon parastatal managers, shareholders, employees, financial institutions and the general public. In sum, both initiatives required under PIRC II, by either concealing the negative repercussions of privatisation or by engineering redundancy payments to deprive retrenchees of cash compensation, have proved to be counterproductive in terms of human rights.

One condition of second tranche release of ESAC II was the development of policy recommendations on NGO participation in the delivery of social services. In addition to specifying overall levels of social spending, loan conditions required the protection of expenditure on certain subcomponents including the PWAS. This was fixed in absolute rather than relative terms, although the sum involved was just K760 million.

In its Letter of Development Policy appended to ESAC II, the Government agreed to introduce targeting guidelines and implement a policy to deliver help through the Public Welfare Assistance Scheme to enable very poor families to pay school and medical fees. The implementation of policies developed by the Ministries of Health and Education were reliant on guidelines being drawn up by the Ministry of Community Development and Social Services under the PWAS, yet the latter had not been delivered. ESAC II was meant to foster the completion of work on a vulnerability profile in 1996 as the basis for these guidelines and implementation mechanisms. However, this was not made the subject of a specific loan condition. The vulnerability profile itself was to be designed to 'simplify and improve the identification and targeting of households qualifying under the Public Welfare Assistance Scheme for health and education payment exemptions in particular.'

In other terms, given that no extra resources were to be allocated to the PWAS, this equates as much to the exclusion of the extremely poor as it does to channelling resources to the ultra poor. As it was, already paltry expenditure on the PWAS during 1997 was decimated and the agreed reforms did not take place. Under the PSREPC (FY) there is a renewed undertaking to initiate implementation of the revamped PWAS, although clearly this should already have occurred under ESAC II. Once more, this is not made the subject of a specific loan agreement.

The Government has agreed to maintain non-personnel spending in priority areas concerned with, inter alia, social safety nets and welfare assistance. The Bank reverts to the use of relative protection 'to allow Government to adjust the absolute expenditures depending on fluctuations in revenues and domestic expenditures...' Fewer priority areas are monitored than before, although one of these is the PWAS. If the specified domestic expenditure is realised, the amount spent on the PWAS in 1999 should be K2.8 billion.

2

Human Welfare, not Human Rights

The U.S. State Department annually publishes a list of nations that violate human rights. Many NGOs do the same. These lists identify states that torture dissidents, detain people without charging them, suppress religious minorities, and commit other abuses. The reports condemn violators of human rights and urge leading states to pressure human rights abusers until they bring their conduct in line with international standards. Indeed, the United States imposes certain legal disadvantages on human rights abusing states, and the Council of Europe makes ratification of the European Convention on Human Rights a condition of membership. International organizations like the World Bank encourage recipients of aid to improve their human rights records. And by ratifying human rights treaties, even the most powerful states promise to respect the human rights of their populations.

Most states have ratified most of these treaties. The treaties bar genocide, torture, arbitrary detention, and other rights-violating activities. Although the treaties lack an enforcement mechanism, nations appear to take the treaties seriously enough to defend themselves against accusations that they have violated their treaty obligations, both in public statements and before various international and regional bodies that monitor compliance with human rights treaties.

Now consider an alternative world. Suppose that the State Department and the NGOs published annual lists of "low-welfare" states. These are states in which the public suffers from low levels of utility. The reason for the public misery could be human rights abuse, of course, but there are many other reasons for misery as well. The state might not supply a sufficiently generous social safety net. Or the state might not enforce property and contract rights, so that individual initiative is discouraged and markets fail.

The government might be inept or corrupt, and thus unable to protect people from natural disasters, insurgencies, crime, and the like. States that appear on the low-welfare lists would be subject to public criticism. Powerful states would pressure the governments of low-welfare states to improve the well-being of their populations, at least to the extent that low welfare can be attributed to the government's unwillingness to provide adequate services.

NGOs would join in. We could also imagine a parallel legal world. The human rights treaties are replaced or supplemented with human welfare treaties. The human welfare treaties oblige states to maintain a certain level of welfare among their citizens, or even to promote or maximize their welfare. The treaties would not require states to take specific steps in order to enhance welfare; states would be free to experiment and to take advantage of whatever is unique about their resources and institutions. These treaties would overlap with existing human rights treaties to the extent that respect for certain human rights also tends to maximize welfare, but the treaties would give no priority to rights; they would instead recognize that rights would be trumped when they bar government actions that advance welfarist goals.

If the proposal to replace the human rights approach with a welfarist approach seems puzzling, consider the following. First, the proposition that all people enjoy a specified set of human rights—that is, rights grounded in universal moral principles that require governments to aid, protect, and refrain from abusing their own citizens—is highly controversial among philosophers. The absence of an agreed upon philosophical justification for human rights yields well-known practical difficulties: States disagree about which rights are human rights, about which human rights should have priority, about how resources should be allocated for the purpose of correcting human rights violations, and about how much respect should be given to cultural variation. In the absence of agreement about a principled basis for human rights, these disputes cannot even in principle be resolved. Indeed, although some philosophers continue to argue that human rights have moral significance, none has offered a defence of the human rights treaty regime as it currently exists in the real world.

Second, if great controversy surrounds the question of rights, most people—even philosophers who strongly support human rights on deontological grounds—agree that the well-being of individuals is also a matter of moral concern. Philosophers who write about the importance of respecting rights agree, with few exceptions, that governments should also concern themselves with improving the well-being of citizens. The importance of well-being transcends national boundaries. In contrast to the anemic efforts to enforce human rights treaties and the controversies over the proper interpretation of the rights in those treaties, developed states have contributed massive amounts of aid to the poorest nations, though the effectiveness of that aid is questionable.

And, although governments often give aid in order to advance diplomatic goals, there seems to be a rough consensus about where aid should go when strategic interests are not paramount. Aid to victims of natural disasters is commonplace and uncontroversial. Everyone agrees that aid should go to the poorest countries. Most of the debate in the development literature is about means, not ends. Yet the commitment to aiding people who live in the poorest states is in tension with a human rights regime that envisions isolating the worst governments, because the worst governments usually govern the poorest states. Third, many of the debates about human rights are implicitly debates about the role of welfare. Developing nations often resist pressure to improve their human rights records by asserting collective rights—rights to economic development, for example. Vigorous disagreements about whether human rights are universal stand in sharp contrast with a general consensus that governments should enhance well-being by—among other things—reducing poverty and improving education: No one argues that in some countries governments should impoverish their citizens. Indeed, it is possible to believe that international human rights law has nothing to do with human rights in the philosophical sense: It refers instead to the limits on sovereignty imposed by international morality, whether or not international morality has anything to do with rights. If this is correct, then we should directly inquire as to what international morality requires rather than try to defend or rationalize the existing rights regime.

Finally, recent empirical studies suggest that states that ratify human rights treaties do not improve their human rights performance, or, at least, that improvements are small and sporadic and hard to measure, perhaps limited only to certain types of states—democracies, for example. These studies are controversial, but they raise the question whether a different type of treaty regime would produce better outcomes. We defend a welfarist alternative to international human rights law. Briefly surveys the human rights regime and its problems. It argues that the human rights treaties are both excessively rigid and excessively vague. Their rigidity consists in their refusal to allow states to trade off different values—for example, to allow states to violate political rights in order to enhance the overall well-being of the population.

Their vagueness lies in their failure to provide mechanisms for evaluating a state's allocation of resources among projects that promote the public good. We argue that rather than trying to specify the obligations of government in terms of respecting specific rights, negative and positive, the treaties should require that states enhance the public welfare. Part II sets out this welfarist alternative, including some ideas about how to implement it effectively with verifiable measures of human wellbeing. Part III discusses the relationship between the welfarist approach to human rights and foreign aid, arguing that welfarist treaties would help resolve the tension between the human rights regime and development policy.

THE HUMAN RIGHTS REGIME: A DIAGNOSIS

THE LEGAL REGIME

The Human Rights Treaties

There are seven major UN-sponsored human rights treaties. These treaties ban torture, racial discrimination, and discrimination against women, and guarantee "civil and political" rights, "economic, social, and cultural" rights, the rights of migrant workers, and the rights of the child. These treaties enjoy a large measure of support, with most obtaining participation rates ranging from 70% to nearly 100% of UN members. The UN has also recently adopted a treaty to guarantee the rights of the disabled. In addition to these treaties, several regional human rights treaties exist. The most important is the European Convention on Human Rights (ECHR), which has, uniquely, a highly developed judicial system. There are also regional treaties in Africa and the Americas.

Table. Four Major Human Rights Instruments.

Politicalaration Human	**Civil and Social, and ion Of**	**Economic sal Decl- Right**	**univer- Convent- Rights**	**European Rights Rights**	**Rights Cultural of Human**
Negative Rights					
Life	6		3	2	Torture, Cruel
	7		5	3	Punishment
Slavery	8		4	4	
Liberty/Detention	9–11		3, 9	5	
Fair Trial	14–15		8, 10–11	6–7	
Privacy	17		12	8	
Freedom of Thought,Religion, Speech	18–19		18, 19	9–10	
Assocoation	21–22		20	11	
Marriage/Family	23		16	12	
Political Participation	25		21	Protocol	
		1, Art, 3			
Equal Protection	2,26		2,7	14	
Positive Rights					
Work, Fair Wages		6–7	23		
Unionization		8	23		
Social Security		9	22		
Family Assistance		10	25		
Adequate Standard of Living		11	25		
Health Care		12	25		
Education		13-14`	26	Protocol	
		1, Art. 2			

The two most important and comprehensive of the UN treaties are the International Covenant for Civil and Political Rights and the International Covenant for Economic, Social, and Cultural Rights. The ICCPR is a charter of negative rights, whereas the ICESCR is a charter of positive rights. Negative rights are rights to be free of interference from other people and from the government; in particular, the government is prohibited from restricting the activities of the rights holders in areas such as political debate and religious worship. Positive rights are rights to receive benefits from the government; the government is required to provide benefits such as health care or education. Negative rights are associated with the classical liberal tradition of natural law, especially as embodied in the social contract theories of Locke and his successors, including the founders of the United States of America, who were particularly concerned about governmental abuse of power.

Positive rights are associated with a range of liberalism's critics, including Marxists. The Universal Declaration of Human Rights—a legally nonbinding document that was adopted by the UN General Assembly in 1948 and predated the ICCPR and ICESCR by several decades—contains both rights. The Cold War rivalry between the United States and the Soviet Union resulted in the bifurcated treaty system—with negative rights contained in the ICCPR, which the United States championed, and positive rights contained in the ICESCR, which the Soviet Union championed. Today, most countries have ratified both treaties (the United States has not ratified the ICESCR, however). Nonetheless, it is clear that states take negative rights more seriously than the positive rights of the ICESCR. The priority of negative rights takes many forms. The ECHR, which is the only human rights treaty that provides for routine adjudication of its provisions and appears to enjoy widespread compliance, is mainly a charter of negative rights.

Although many national constitutions contain positive rights as well as negative rights, for the most part only negative rights are justiciable, with the positive rights left to the vagaries of politics. NGOs recognize that they can most effectively draw attention to violations of negative rights; for that reason, the main human rights watchdogs largely ignore violations of economic, social, and cultural rights. Thus, although most developed states do provide benefits to their citizens—health care, education, a social safety net, and so forth—they refuse to place these benefits outside the realm of democratic politics. By contrast, political rights in these states are generally outside the realm of democratic politics. Justifications. Scholars have advanced two types of theories that justify or explain the human rights regimes. Moral theories argue that human rights treaties are good; political theories argue that human rights treaties are in the interest of states or most states, or the most powerful states.

Moral theories typically hold that individuals have inherent human rights, derivable from the basic postulate of equal human dignity. Some philosophers have taken a contractarian approach. Contractarians derive human rights from a Rawlsian original position argument where the veil of ignorance deprives people of knowledge of their nationality. Not knowing which nation they would belong to, people in the original position would choose international institutions that protect the rights of all human beings. Other philosophers are welfarists: They believe that human rights promote the welfare of the global population. It is an understatement to say that these theories are controversial; an enormous literature debates them. It is less well known that none of the proponents of these theories pays much attention to the actual human rights treaty regime. The debate hovers at a theoretical altitude high above the facts on the ground.

A few philosophers cite the Universal Declaration, which is a vague, hortatory document with no legal effect. Other philosophers pick and choose among provisions of national constitutions, singling out those provisions that they approve. The debate is best understood as an argument about whether states should respect some, mostly undefined, set of human rights, not about whether the existing human rights treaty regime is morally justified. Consider, for example, the work of Martha Nussbaum and Amartya Sen. Nussbaum and Sen argue that states should be required to advance the "capabilities" of their citizens, that is, their ability to enjoy various objective goods such as health, literacy, and political participation.

Their approach differs from that of traditional development economists, who believe that states should maximize economic welfare—that is, the satisfaction of subjective preferences as measured by willingness to pay. Yet Nussbaum and Sen are both "welfarists" in the broader sense that they emphasize that states should advance the well-being of people. And both scholars argue that their approach is consistent with the traditional human rights agenda. Neither scholar, however, addresses the existing human rights regime—that is, the legal regime embodied in treaties such as the ICCPR and the ICESCR.

Sen has declined to explain how exactly the capabilities approach would be implemented, arguing that "it is important to emphasize the catholicity that the approach has. The foundational affirmation of the importance of capabilities can go with various strategies of actual evaluation involving practical compromises. The pragmatic nature of practical reason demands this." This raises the question of why Sen would think that the existing human rights regime would be consistent with the capabilities approach.

That regime does not embrace catholicity but takes a specific approach to human rights in order to avoid the type of fatal indefiniteness that renders treaties unenforceable. Nussbaum similarly insists that the "language of capabilities gives important precision and supplementation to the language of rights." She argues that the capabilities approach resembles the human rights approach and concludes that therefore it "should not be seen as a rival of the human rights approach." From a legal perspective, these claims are puzzling. Either international law will continue to embody the existing human rights approach or it will be modified so as to reflect Nussbaum's alternative approach.

It cannot do both. As we have noted, the existing human rights approach, for all the talk of positive rights, gives priority to negative rights. But as Nussbaum acknowledges, the emphasis on negative rights is inconsistent with the capabilities approach. In addition, the ICESCR, though it insists on generous positive rights, allows states to take their time before satisfying them. And it provides no mechanism for allocating resources among rights, positive and negative, thus making it a highly unsatisfactory instrument for implementing the capabilities approach.

If a treaty is ambiguous, then states can easily comply with it without appreciably changing their behaviour. Unhappiness with moral theories of human rights has led to the growth of political theories of human rights. Political theories argue that states or groups within states have an interest in agreeing to human rights. The human rights treaty regime thus rests on an overlapping consensus about the obligations of states with mostly different but not wholly incompatible interests and moral and religious commitments. Consider the Universal Declaration of Human Rights, which was created in the wake of World War II. It expressed revulsion at the ideology and methods of the Nazis, but it did not express a moral consensus beyond the rejection of fascism, as was acknowledged at the time. This became unmistakable in the following years as governments attempted to reduce the ambiguous, hortatory provisions of the Universal Declaration to acceptably specific rules in legally binding treaties. Western states that initiated the treaty regime sought to publicize their commitment to liberal values, while drawing attention to the rejection of these values by the Soviet Union and its allies. They hoped that these values would appeal to people and governments around the world, who would reject the Soviet model. The Eastern Bloc championed social, economic, and cultural rights that, it claimed, were vindicated in communist, and not in Western, societies. Developing states have ratified the treaties for more diverse reasons.

Some developing states succumbed to pressure from Western states that tied aid and other benefits (such as EU membership) to treaty ratification. Other developing states may have ratified the treaties in order to show that they were "modern" or endorsed modernization or because newly empowered elites or other groups were committed to Western values. Governments of newly democratic states may have ratified the treaties in an effort to prevent future governments from reversing democratic reforms.

PROBLEMS

Many people have attributed the limited effects of human rights treaties to the absence of strong enforcement mechanisms. However, many successful treaties do not have enforcement mechanisms or have highly limited adjudication and enforcement systems. In the end, all treaties rely on the initiative of member states for enforcement. Although enforcement mechanisms can help improve compliance, the absence of effective enforcement instruments most likely reflects states' lack of enthusiasm for human rights treaties rather than inadvertence or insufficient foresight. The enforcement mechanisms theory just raises another question: Why don't states show more enthusiasm for ensuring compliance with the human rights treaties that they have negotiated?

A common answer to this question is that states are jealous of their sovereignty. But this answer is also not persuasive. States agree to all kinds of incursions on their sovereignty in return for the benefits of international cooperation. For example, states agree not to subject each other's diplomatic officials to certain legal obligations that apply to citizens. They have done so in order to obtain a reciprocal benefit—nondiscrimination against their citizens when they are on foreign territory. If states have an interest in the well-being of people in other states—and this proposition is the premise of the human rights regime—then they should be willing to accept limits on their freedom to violate the human rights of their own populations in return for other states accepting the same limits.

A more plausible explanation for the current state of affairs is that the developed nations perceive their interest in ensuring that other nations improve their human rights performance as real but limited. Developed nations refrain from pressuring human rights abusers when they have strategic, trade, or other interests in maintaining a harmonious relationship. Human rights abusing governments have no special interest in ending their human rights abuses, except in response to carrots and sticks offered by the developed nations. If the carrots are puny and the sticks are flimsy, then these governments will not improve their respect for human rights. This view is roughly consistent with the political theory of human rights treaties. An overlapping consensus holds that human rights matter. It just turns out that governments are not willing to devote substantial resources to enforcing that consensus.

However, there is another possible view, which is that human rights treaties do not reflect a political consensus, or that they reflect a consensus that is so shallow as to be practically meaningless. Nor do they reflect fundamental moral values that governments and populations support. Consider the cases where states argue that their human rights obligations do not, or should not, bind them, because other values are equally important. Typically, states argue that national security or cultural tradition or even economic growth justifies violation of rights (or alternatively argue that the rights are defeasible or limited for these reasons). The currently defunct Asian values debate and the more recent challenge from Islam are versions of this argument. Though these claims are invariably met with skepticism by the human rights community, it is worth understanding why governments make them. They argue that if "Western" human rights treaties are respected in a given situation, the public will be worse off—thrown into civil war, vulnerable to insurgents, or, alternatively, unable to engage in practices that they value. In short, human rights obligations interfere with welfare-promoting activities of the government, and these welfare-promoting activities should be given priority.

Many commentators have interpreted the Asian values challenge as a philosophical debate about the universality of human rights. On this view, the critics are cultural relativists, and one can easily refute them by pointing out the well-known philosophical difficulties with moral relativism and precedents for Western-style human rights in Confucianism, Islam, and other non-Western traditions. This critique misconceives the challenge, however. The better interpretation of the challenge is that virtually all governments concede that they have a "universal" obligation to advance the welfare of their populations, but, given local conditions and traditions, they cannot advance the welfare of their populations if they are constrained by the human rights treaties. The treaties do not allow governments to make the tradeoffs they need to make in order to advance the public interest.

The tendency has been to dismiss such arguments as pretextual or self-serving but they deserve a serious hearing. Nussbaum and Sen, for example, should agree with them in principle. A government with limited resources that seeks to enhance the capabilities of its population might correctly believe that investment in education, health, and infrastructure will do more for more people than an expensive and possibly futile crackdown on local police who detain suspected criminals without charging them. Governance unavoidably involves tradeoffs: Money spent for primary education must be taken from health clinics or police forces. Although everyone agrees that governments should spend at least some money on education, some on health clinics, and some on the police, no one agrees how much money the government should allocate among these and other activities. Nor is there any reason to think that, beyond the barest minima, there are any universally proper ways to distribute resources. For a very poor country, a government might justifiably refuse to finance education because health and security needs are so pressing.

This point is not ignored by the human rights treaties, but they recognize it only in a highly imperfect way. These treaties do, with several exceptions, give governments discretion to make legitimate tradeoffs. With respect to positive rights, the ICESCR recognizes that each state should take steps "to the maximum of its available resources, with a view to achieving progressively the full realization of those rights... by all appropriate means."

This provision implicitly recognizes that states may not have the capacity to satisfy the positive rights immediately, as the UN Economic, Social, and Cultural Rights Committee has held. Commentators agree that it is difficult to complain about states' budgetary priorities, given the difficulty for outsiders of evaluating the competing demands on the government. With respect to negative rights, the ICCPR frequently acknowledges limitations, which permit the rights to be balanced against other considerations. For example, the right to freedom of expression may be restricted "for the protection of national security or of public order... or of public health or morals." In addition, the ICCPR allows states to derogate from certain rights "in time of public emergency which threatens the life of the nation." Other human rights treaties have similar provisions. However, the treaties provide no way of evaluating the tradeoffs that governments actually make. Suppose that in two otherwise identical states, one government devotes $10 million to retraining the police so as to reduce the amount of torture. Suppose further that this amount of training would cause the total number of torture incidents per year to fall from 10,000 to 5,000. Meanwhile, another government devotes $1 million to retraining the police, and the amount of torture falls from 10,000 to 9,000 incidents per year. If each government's budget is $50 billion per year, do either or both governments violate the ICCPR? What if the government that spends only $1 million per year uses the money saved to build health clinics in poor rural areas, whereas the government that spends $10 million per year devotes much of its budget to lavish spending for the ruling class? Are these relevant considerations in evaluating the states' overall compliance with the human rights treaties?

It is possible that a state might cite its positive rights obligation to supply health care under the ICESCR as a justification for its failure to fully respect the negative rights obligation not to torture under the ICCPR. However, the treaties themselves do not permit such an argument. The ban on torture is unqualified, and although the amount of resources that states must devote to implement the ban is unspecified, any argument that a state does better by devoting resources to health care than to eliminating torture would be met with skepticism by the human rights community. If such an argument were accepted, the treaty regime would be excessively vague: It would permit states to violate human rights under the cover of pretext.

The human rights treaty regime thus commits two types of errors. First, in some places it does not permit governments that seek in good faith to advance the general welfare of the public to make reasonable tradeoffs—devoting resources to acute problems and denying resources to problems that, in local context, are less pressing. Second, in other places it allows tradeoffs without supplying a mechanism for evaluating those tradeoffs. The treaty regime manages to sail both into the Scylla of excessive strictness and the Charybdis of excessive vagueness.

AN INTERNATIONAL WELFARE FUND

One can better understand the problems with the current regime, and obtain an idea about how to reform it, by undertaking the following thought experiment about a hypothetical international welfare fund. This fund is an analytic construct only; nothing as suggested, say depends on the establishment of an actual fund.

Suppose that the populations of nations care, at least a little, about the well-being of people living in other countries. We can think of the degree or intensity of care in monetary terms as the amount that individuals would be willing to pay in taxes for the benefit of foreigners. No doubt this amount is much higher in wealthy nations than in poor nations simply because wealthy people have more money to spare. But for the sake of simplicity as suggested, imagine that most states would contribute some amount, M, to a common fund that would be used to help those in the most need of aid. M can be thought of as the monetized value of inkind contributions such as military support for an unstable government or for rebels who seek to overthrow that government; diplomatic pressure; sanctions; traditional aid; trade benefits; immigration privileges; and so forth.

Four straightforward but important points can be made about the fund. First, the more that the fund is used effectively for ends that people with diverse views and from different nations approve, the higher contributions are likely to be. The more overlapping the consensus is, the more that can be done.

Second, the fund itself is best used in a manner that is coordinated, or internally consistent, for otherwise resources will be wasted. For example, suppose that some people think that a government of a poor state should build hydroelectric dams in order to ensure a supply of electricity, while other people think that the government should not build such dams because they damage the environment, harm the fishing industry, and reduce tourism revenues. It would be a great mistake if money in the fund both financed the dam and financed local NGOs that oppose the dam. It would be much better to use the money for some other purpose to which everyone agrees.

Third, the fund should be used to pressure states that are most likely to be vulnerable to pressure. In some cases, those states will be poor and weak. In other cases, states most susceptible to pressure will be those that are eager to break out of isolation and attract trade and investment. Resources should be targeted where they can achieve the greatest results, which would most likely involve focusing on those states that are vulnerable to pressure and that have the greatest shortfalls in the welfare of their populations.

Fourth, states can often most effectively maximize M, and thereby improve the well-being of people around the world, by taking actions that are rarely associated with typical treaty enforcement practices. For example, rich state X might be reluctant to use diplomatic pressure against poor state Y for all kinds of good reasons—such as the need to cooperate with respect to some other dimension of international relations—while being willing to (for example) allow poor people in state Y to immigrate to X, or to reduce trade barriers that harm the export industry in Y.

The defects of the human rights regime can be redescribed with the help of the fund heuristic. States that seek in good faith to spend the fund in a manner dictated by the human rights treaties would withhold resources from reasonable governments that, faced with difficult choices, decide to reduce poverty rather than tackle negative rights violations committed by the police or military. At the same time, they would have no guidance as to how to treat states that allocate resources among health care, poverty relief, education, and other goods in wise or unwise ways. Hampered by the absence of a set of guiding principles, states would predictably respond inconsistently. Is there a better way?

THE WELFARIST TREATY

THE GENERAL APPROACH

The challenge, then, is to construct a treaty regime that encourages the most efficient allocation of resources towards the goal of increasing overall human welfare. A welfarist treaty would obligate states to promote the well-being of the global population. Given the constraints of the state system, which drives governments to give priority to their own populations at the expense of foreign populations, a viable welfarist treaty would not obligate states to equalize the wealth of individuals across borders—indeed, even the most egalitarian states do not go this far for their own populations. Instead, a welfare treaty might establish welfare floors or some other system of priority that identified the lowest-welfare states. These states would have a legal obligation to raise the welfare of their populations, or to try to do so, and other states would have the obligation to pressure or help low-welfare states to live up to their welfarist obligations.

As a practical matter, the effect of this treaty would be to divide the world into high-welfare states that comply with the law and low-welfare states that do not. The high-welfare states would pressure the low-welfare states to adopt better policies or reward them for doing so. Technically, the current human rights regime does not make such a clear demarcation between human rights respecters and human rights abusers. Human rights respecters violate human rights treaties if they occasionally deviate from the law, whereas high-welfare states would violate the welfarist treaty only if they adopted disastrous policies. However, the pressure brought to bear on traditional human rights respecters who occasionally deviate is small, and so the differences between the two systems in this respect would be minimal. The advantage of the welfarist approach is that it would bring the legal regime into line with practice, as well as with the pragmatic assumption that scarce international resources should be used against the worst states, not states that are generally good or marginally bad.

Consider two examples of how the welfarist approach would change our thinking about the responsibilities of states for abuses that occur on their soil. First, consider China. The Chinese government violates human rights. It suppresses political dissent, censors the press, deprives people of fair trials, and harasses religious minorities. Yet this authoritarian government is also responsible for the greatest enhancement of human welfare in recent history. From 1981 to 2001, four hundred million Chinese moved out of extreme poverty. As long as the Chinese government continues to improve the well-being of so many people, states that care about welfare should refrain from pressuring China to improve its human rights record. With respect to all the welfare indicators to be discussed shortly, including objective values such as health and education, China scores well.

Second, consider the current international controversy over the death penalty. Many countries have abolished the death penalty and criticize the United States for retaining it. Human rights organizations also pressure the United States to abolish the death penalty. In terms of the analytic framework advanced, a portion of the common fund devoted to improving human rights practices is being channeled towards American death penalty abolition. Is this a good use of these resources?

The answer is no. Capital punishment in the United States results in only a few dozen deaths per year—53 in 2006, down from a high of 98 in 1999 (over the last thirty years). These executions might deter other killings, but even assuming that they do not, the loss of life is trivial compared to the scale of other humanitarian catastrophes occurring around the world. For example, in Darfur there have been tens of thousands of deaths per year. Resources would be better used, at the margin, to set up refugee camps and provide humanitarian relief in Darfur, than to pressure the United States to abolish the death penalty.

Further, the United States appears to be impervious to pressure from foreign countries to abolish the death penalty. Most executions are carried out by state governments, which play virtually no role in American foreign relations, and have a great deal of constitutional discretion over their criminal justice systems. One state—Texas—executed 24 people in 2006, nearly five times the number in the state with the second highest rate of execution.

Texas and other states can cater to xenophobic sentiments of their citizens without worrying about the foreign relations consequences. Resources used to pressure state governments to cut back on the death penalty, or to pressure the federal government to pressure the state governments, are thus unlikely to have any effect. By contrast, resources used to pressure smaller, weaker countries where significant human rights abuses occur are more likely to have an effect. Human rights treaties do not distinguish between the United States and Sudan. Both states have an obligation to comply with human rights norms. Because the treaties do not provide a formula for limiting or balancing human rights, they give no guidance to interested states as to how to allocate resources in a manner that maximizes their effect. As a result, human rights enforcement is largely ad hoc. By contrast, a welfarist treaty directs states to focus on particular states, those with the lowest level of welfare: Sudan, not the United States. One might argue that a sufficiently specific welfarist treaty would not command universal assent because different societies have different notions of the good life.

Of course, the same argument has been made about human rights, and, as we have argued, the problem seems to be more significant for human rights than for welfare. At a minimum, it is no more of a problem for welfare than it is for human rights. The welfarist approach, however, has an advantage over the human rights approach. If welfare can be specified at a high enough level of generality, then states are free to choose whatever mechanisms they believe will best promote welfare. Such mechanisms can draw on local traditions and practices that are at variance with human rights norms—as long as the government can make the case that they improve rather than diminish welfare.

APPROACHES

Desiderata

The goal is to encourage states to pressure governments to improve well-being. This goal can be implemented in many ways.

Government Responsiveness to Pressure

States should put pressure-diplomatic, economic, military (in the extreme)-on other states that fail to adopt welfarist policies. States should not punish other states that have miserable populations when their misery cannot be attributed to government policy. However, in practice it may be difficult to determine whether the population's misery is due to government misconduct or to circumstances that are outside the government's control. To the extent that governments are responsive to pressure in general, then a strict liability approach is superior, one that looks only at the conditions of the population and not at the activities of the government. To the extent that governments cannot respond to pressure, then an approach that focuses on government behaviour and motivations is more appropriate.

How does one distinguish states that are responsive to pressure and those that are not? One possibility is that no such distinction can be made; the internal workings of states are just too difficult for the outside world to understand. If such is the case, then it may be necessary for governments to put pressure on all low-welfare states in the hope that welfare improvements in responsive states exceed welfare losses in nonresponsive states. Otherwise, it seems likely that states that seek trade and investment, cooperate with their neighbours, have relatively open political systems, have relatively effective governments that can control their population, and that are not too powerful, are most responsive. States that seek to cooperate with or obtain aid from other states will make concessions in order to obtain their goals. States with open political systems and effective governments can make promises, submit to threats, and otherwise react in a predictable way when outside states seek to influence their behaviour. These criteria exclude isolationist states like North Korea, failed states like Somalia, geopolitical giants like China and the United States, and wealthy states with crucial resources like Saudi Arabia.

To capture this point, let us distinguish between responsive governments and nonresponsive governments. Aid should flow to nonresponsive governments as long as a large enough portion reaches the population. For responsive governments, low-welfare states should be pressured and marginally higher welfare states should be rewarded. The reason is that the governments of low-welfare states must be given incentives to adopt welfare-promoting policies when officials, for personal or political reasons, or out of incompetence, are otherwise inclined. If governments know that they will receive aid (or avoid pressure) regardless of whether they adopt welfare-promoting policies, then they have no incentive to adopt such policies.

If this point seems paradoxical, one should understand that it is not special to the welfarist regime; it applies to the human rights regime as well. Governments pressure the worst human rights abusers by depriving them of aid, imposing economic sanctions, and occasionally invading them-in all of these ways usually making the population worse off rather than better off, because human rights abusing governments make sure that their populations feel the sting. As human rights improve, governments reward the country in question by extending aid, entering trade agreements, and so forth. Thus, the governments that engage in less human rights abuse, and whose populations are therefore better off from a human rights perspective, are rewarded.

Precision

It is sometimes argued that treaties with precise obligations are easier to enforce than treaties with vague obligations. If obligations are vague, then governments can easily rationalize violations. Moreover, if governments that are injured by violations have trouble agreeing among themselves as to whether the violations actually occurred, whether they were serious, and so forth, they will be unable to respond with a united front. The goal of a welfarist treaty is to promote welfare. Welfare is a contested concept. Thus, a treaty that simply required states to promote the welfare of their citizens would be vague and vulnerable to opportunistic breach. For this reason, it may be appropriate to choose more precise treaty obligations even though they do not fully capture whatever is meant by welfare.

Availability of Data

workable treaty regime requires behaviour that is verifiable. States do not enter arms control agreements unless they can verify that the other side is not producing the restricted arms. Many human rights treaties require government behaviour that is relatively easy to observe, at least in open societies. If torture occurs, witnesses and victims can come forward with testimony and evidence. A welfarist treaty suffers by comparison: Welfare is not directly observable. For a welfarist treaty to function, reliable proxies for welfare must be developed.

Welfare

A very simple treaty could provide as follows: "Each state party has the obligation to promote the welfare of its people." Two objections can be made. First, no one can agree on what "welfare" means, and therefore the obligation would be empty. Second, it is impossible to tell whether a state has satisfied its obligation because promoting welfare would be an affirmative duty, and could not be discharged simply (as in the case of negative duties) by refraining from engaging in a particular act.

As to the first objection, a large philosophical literature on welfarism suggests that welfare can be understood in three general ways. Mental state theorists, like Bentham, argue that welfare refers to hedonic affect—the felt experience of being happy, satisfied, well-off, etc. For a long time, people argued that hedonic affect cannot be measured, but recent advances in psychology and economics suggest otherwise. Desire-based theorists argue that welfare refers to the satisfaction of desires. Within this group, there is disagreement about whether satisfaction of desires improves welfare regardless of what those desires are (a view taken by most economists) or only if those desires meet further criteria—for example, being well-informed and undistorted by circumstances. Objective-list theorists, like Martha Nussbaum, argue that welfare refers to the enjoyment of certain objective goods, such as health, education, personal relationships, and recreation.

Here, too, a great deal of disagreement exists about which activities count as objective goods. Despite the disagreement between and within the camps, a consensus about, at least, the minimum requirements of welfare probably exists. Nearly everyone agrees that basic health care advances welfare—because healthier people are happier, or because people desire good health, or because health is an objective good. The same can be said about primary school education, nutrition, family life, association with friends, and so forth. The various approaches tend to come into conflict over more esoteric questions—for example, whether people who overeat and become obese should be counted as better off (they satisfy desires) or worse off (they do not satisfy informed desires, or they are not happy).

The second objection has been much discussed in the context of ordinary human rights treaties. Delicate judgments must be made as to how far a state must go in order to satisfy positive rights such as the right to work, which is contained in the ICESCR. Indeed, it is doubtful that the distinction between positive and negative rights has practical importance. Consider the negative right not to be tortured. No state can reduce the incidence of torture to zero. Local police or soldiers will always contain rogue elements who torture even when torture is not official policy. To reduce the amount of torture, a government must not only pass laws against torture. It must instruct lower-level officials not to engage in torture, train them, monitor them, and make available resources to investigate, prosecute, and punish those who violate the law. Torture will always occur, so the relevant question is how much a government must invest in reducing torture before it can be deemed to comply with a rule against torture. The inquiry is no easier than the positive right inquiry regarding how much a government must invest in promoting literacy before it complies with a right to education. Seen in this way, the distinction between negative rights and positive rights collapses. Nonetheless, the first objection is hard to quarrel with. No one, analogously, thinks that it would be better to have a single human rights treaty that required states to respect "human rights" than to have more complex treaties that spell out, the various obligations, in terms of detention, speech, freedom of conscience, and so forth.

STANDARDS OF MEASUREMENT

Gross Domestic Product

I start with per capita GDP, which is frequently used as a measure of well-being in academic research, and so provides a useful baseline for thinking about welfarist measures. The bottom forty states by per capita GDP, plus that of the United States. Treaty designers would need to make some complex choices about how a welfarist treaty would use the per capita GDP measure. It would make little sense to require that all states achieve a certain per capita GDP, such as the world median. Very poor states would have no chance to comply with the treaty. Either the median would shift over time, condemning half the states to treaty violation, or the target would need to be fixed with reference to a particular year. Both approaches seem arbitrary. A possible alternative would require states to hit certain targets that take into account their starting point—for example, a moving average growth rate for per capita GDP over a period of years. States would have an obligation to improve welfare rather than to reach a certain level of welfare.

States that comply with the treaty would eventually become wealthy enough that they could be released from further growth obligations unless per capita GDP again dips to an unacceptably low level. Further, by setting the target as an average over a period of years, one avoids penalizing states that are hit by random shocks that cause economic downturns. States would be free to choose among methods that promote economic growth, which would allow them to take into account local conditions.

Some states might find it easy to reduce trade barriers; others might prefer to invest in infrastructure or to strengthen property rights. Per capita GDP has some normative appeal and practical advantages. For the desire-based theorist who relies on raw preferences (the conventional economist's view), per capita GDP provides a rough measure of welfare. Higher per capita GDP means that more goods and services are being consumed; because people want goods and services, an increase in consumption of goods and services would seem to indicate an increase in welfare. A desire-based theorist who gives moral weight only to informed or otherwise restricted preferences would be more uneasy about per capita GDP but might be satisfied with this measure as long as laws ensure that people are sufficiently informed. Consumer protection laws, for example, might serve this function. Similarly, hedonic and objective-goods theorists might think that per capita GDP is a rough proxy for welfare as long as people spend their money on improving their happiness (in the first case) or on objective goods (in the second). Again, laws can channel people's behaviour in these directions.

An important qualification of this argument is that if marginal utility declines with wealth, overall welfare will be higher in states with greater equality of income and wealth. For per capita GDP to be an accurate measure of welfare, it should probably be adjusted using a conventional measure of equality such as the Gini coefficient. The main advantage of the per capita GDP measure is that data are readily available for most countries, which allow for easy comparison and ranking. On the other hand, uncertainty would be introduced for countries with large underground economies, which would need to be estimated. In addition, measuring equality is difficult; the Gini coefficient is only one of many possible measures; and even if it is accepted, there remains the question of how much weight would be given to it. Thus, per capita GDP turns out to be unacceptably crude or must be supplemented with data that are extremely hard to find and measure.

Another objection to the use of per capita GDP is that it would make poor states the exclusive target of international pressure, which would be unfair. But if poor states are poor because of corrupt or incompetent governments, then such pressure is justified as a way of encouraging reform. Indeed, the same thing could be said about the international human rights regime, which, in practice, focuses on poor states because poor states are usually the worst human rights violators. Human rights campaigners frequently argue that foreign aid should be withheld from human rights abusing states; as a practical matter, this would mean withholding foreign aid from very poor states that need it most. Further, the welfarist treaty would not require states to pressure poor states whose governments lack capacity to change. In such cases, a welfarist treaty would require aid, rather than pressure, as long as aid is likely to improve the well-being of the population in question.

Happiness Measures

A second approach to drafting a welfarist treaty would exploit recent social science research on the measurement of subjective well-being. Economists and psychologists have discovered that people answer happiness surveys in a consistent manner that satisfies tests of external validity. A group of scholars argues that the results of these surveys provide a useful measure of subjective happiness. A typical survey question asks the respondent how happy she is on a scale from one to five or one to ten. A random sample of the population of a country can be given the survey, and the average response provides a rough measure of the welfare level of the country as a whole. The mean score was 6.46; Denmark enjoyed the highest score (8.38). The United States had a score of 7.57.

As a generalization, happier countries tend to be wealthier, but exceptions abound. Nigeria (6.87), for example, is very poor but has an average happiness greater than that of Greece (6.78), Poland (6.37), and Portugal (5.97)—all relatively wealthy countries. Bangladesh (5.77) is happier than Ukraine (5.67) and Egypt (5.36), even though both countries have more than twice the per capita GDP of Bangladesh. Thus, Bangladesh and Nigeria would probably be in compliance with a welfarist treaty that used happiness measures but not a welfarist treaty that used per capita GDP; the opposite could be true for Ukraine and Egypt.

Tanzania is unhappy and poor and would be in violation of either type of welfarist treaty. The United States, wealthy and happy, would violate neither type of treaty. A happiness treaty, like a per capita GDP treaty, would need to have targets. States that have happiness levels above a certain level would be in compliance with the treaty; other states would be required to achieve a designated growth rate over a period of years. Happiness studies are controversial and raise numerous questions. Some critics argue that self-reported happiness is not the same as real happiness; people's survey responses might reflect cultural norms rather than subjective well-being. There is also a great deal of controversy about the moral status of happiness or life satisfaction.

Still, the happiness measure has advantages. For the mental state theorist, happiness measures surely approximate welfare better than per capita GDP does. Even the desire-based theorist might endorse the happiness measure, especially if she fears that per capita GDP reflects distorted rather than restricted or ideal preferences. Although people with informed desires might prefer other things besides happiness, the happiness measure might be a sufficient approximation of desire-based welfare. For the objective-list theorist, the value of the happiness measure depends on whether people who enjoy objective goods tend to be happier than other people. If they do, a happiness measure might suffice; if not, it will not. The evidence suggests that happiness is correlated with many items on standard objective lists, including health, education, and life expectancy.

Objective Social Goods

Martha Nussbaum lists the following objective goods: life; bodily health; bodily integrity; senses, imagination, and thought; emotions; practical reason; affiliation (including the goods of both friendship and self-respect); play; other species; and control over one's environment (including both political rights and property rights). Others have provided similar lists. For our purposes, the most significant challenge posed by such lists is that of converting them into standards against which a state's activities can be measured. Arguably, the ICESCR is a welfarist treaty: It requires states to promote health, education, literacy, and other aspects of human well-being. But if so, it is poorly designed. It fails the challenge to provide a basis for evaluating allocations of resources that governments make to achieve these goals. Should a government spend its last million dollars on a health clinic or a school? How should the government balance the lifesaving effects of the clinic and the school's impact on practical reason, self-esteem, and economic growth?

This challenge has two elements. First, each objective good must be converted into a scale. In some cases, this is not difficult. "Life" becomes mortality or life expectancy; "bodily health" can be captured with measures of morbidity or health care expenses. "Play" poses more difficult challenges, but could conceivably be approximated with measures of leisure time. Second, the goods need to be placed on a single metric. Otherwise, we have no way to compare a state that scores well on life expectancy and poorly on control over one's environment and a state that scores poorly on life expectancy and well on control over one's environment. Various scholars and organizations have made progress with both these problems. Development agencies gather cross-country statistics on longevity, infant mortality, health, education, and other variables related to objective goods. Some of these development indicators for the forty poorest countries, ten middle income countries, and ten rich countries.

Reduction. There is now a large literature on social indicators with its own journal entitled Social Indicators Research. United Nations Dev. Programme, Human Development Report 2006 (2006). All data are from 2004 except health expenditure per capita and GDP, which are from 2003. GDP data are taken from Heston *et al*, supra note 89. Cells are blank where data were not collected by the cited sources. Life expectancy, infant mortality, literacy, enrollment, and health expenditure per capita are all reasonable measures of life, health, practical reason, and other objective goods. But none can serve on its own as a measure of objective well-being and thus an aggregative index would need to be developed. The Human Development Index is a weighted average of per capita GDP, life expectancy, and enrollment in primary, secondary, and tertiary schools. Some poor states, such as Cambodia and Madagascar, have higher scores for objective indicators than wealthier states, such as Benin and Mauritania—and so Cambodia and Madagascar could be in compliance with an objective list welfarist treaty that Benin and Mauritania would violate.

Other combinations and weightings can be imagined, leading to the fear that any such index would be arbitrary. However, there is a great deal of consistency across categories of objective indicators, which creates hope that a reasonable index can be identified. It would then be necessary to establish a treaty obligation in terms of a state's location on the index or its progress towards a higher level. As we have discussed this point in connection with the per capita GDP and happiness measures, further discussion here is unnecessary.

Democracy

One might choose not to focus on indicators of a population's well-being and instead focus on indicators of government quality. Some states might be poor because of bad governments while others are poor because of natural disadvantages, including a history of civil conflict or bad government, which the current government cannot overcome. Pressure should be put only on the governments of the first type of state. Thus, the human welfare treaty should oblige the world to pressure bad governments of low-welfare states (or perhaps bad governments of any state), while tolerating or aiding states that have relatively good governments, even if they have low welfare levels. What might such a treaty look like? A simple approach would be a democracy treaty, one that required all states to be democracies. Although we do not think that this approach has much to recommend it, it provides a useful baseline for examining more complex approaches.

The theory of such a treaty has two premises. First, democracy reliably leads to welfare improvements for the population. The argument for such a view is that democratic governments need the support of most of the population, whereas authoritarian governments rely on only the support of an elite group or tribe or other small segment of the population. Therefore, democracies distribute welfare broadly, whereas authoritarian states distribute welfare narrowly. However, the empirical evidence for this argument is slim. Second, pressure on authoritarian states reliably results in transitions to democracy. Although this proposition seems intuitively plausible, the evidence is even weaker than it is for the first proposition. The experience with Iraq provides a cautionary tale. Economic sanctions on Iraq during the 1990s did not weaken the authoritarian system; and the recent war in Iraq has not delivered a stable democracy. For these reasons, a welfarist treaty that required states to pressure authoritarian states with the view of encouraging democracy would probably be ill-advised.

Nonetheless, it is worth looking at the data. Political scientists have classified states according to their degree of democratization, with a score of 0 signifying an authoritarian state and a score of 10 signifying the highest level of democracy. The United States and other western countries receive a score of 10; North Korea receives a 0. Among the forty poorest countries, many—including North Korea—lack democracy: Eritrea, Gambia, Bhutan, and Sudan also receive 0; many others receive 1 or another low score. Yet there are some democracies, including Mongolia (10), Kenya (8), Madagascar (7), and Malawi (6). An approach that stresses democracy, then, would require western states to provide aid to Mongolia and the other democracies, while denying aid to, and imposing pressure on, Eritrea and the other authoritarian states. Presumably wealthy democracies would receive no aid, but they would also receive no pressure even if they violate human rights. Other authoritarian states would receive pressure regardless of whether they are rich or poor, and regardless of whether they respect or violate human rights.

Government Corruption

Democratic states often have bad governments and authoritarian states can have good governments. A treaty regime might thus focus not on the type of government but the quality of governance. Relevant indicators of quality might include the ratio of tax revenues to the value of government services, the speed and integrity of the legal system, and the level of government corruption. As suggested, focus on this last indicator here.

The Corruption Perception Index (CPI) measures "the degree of public sector corruption as perceived by business people and country analysts." The score ranges from 0 (highly corrupt) to 10 (clean). A welfarist treaty would require states to pressure highly corrupt states, regardless of whether they are democracies (such as Mongolia (10 on democracy, 3 on CPI)) or authoritarian regimes (such as Eritrea (0 and 2.6)); whether they are relatively wealthy (such as Belarus (3.3)) or poor; whether their people are happy (such as Nigeria (1.6)) or unhappy. If the world turned its attention from the twenty poorest countries to the twenty most corrupt countries, then Madagascar and Mali (among others) would be removed from the list, and Bangladesh, Azerbaijan, and Paraguay (among others) would be added to it. The theory is that corruption prevents welfare gains; so if countries were forced or encouraged to reduce corruption, welfare would increase.

Although many scholars believe that corruption interferes with development and hence well-being, this view is controversial. Indeed, it seems perverse to pressure corrupt countries that do well on the various welfare indicators. At least for some countries, corruption might not interfere excessively with the delivery of public services to the population. A compromise approach would be to target only countries that are both corrupt and low in welfare.

Aggregative Indices

If no single one of the measures described seems satisfactory, they could be combined into an aggregate index. Doing so would be extremely difficult, however, as we would need to decide how much weight to give each measure. There is no a priori reason, for example, to give equal weighting to, say, corruption and happiness. And a person who believes that the happiness measure is the philosophically correct approach would reject weighting any of the objective measures, unless they happen to correlate with happiness. The Human Development Index, which gives weight to per capita GDP, life expectancy, and schooling, seems similarly arbitrary. Still, this problem can potentially be evaded. Suppose, for example, that we can identify a group of states that do poorly on all of our measures. These states might justifiably be considered the worst offenders against human well-being, and the governments of other states ought to pressure or help them to improve their performance.

Which are the lowest-welfare states in this sense? To compile a list, we examined the twenty poorest states, and among them chose those that appear in the bottom twenty (or more if there are ties) of the following indicators:

democracy, corruption, life expectancy, and adult literacy. Six nations were in the bottom twenty on three or more lists: Bhutan, Central African Republic, Chad, Democratic Republic of the Congo, Niger, and Sierra Leone. We would need to consider further issues such as whether these governments are susceptible to pressure, and how many people in these countries are likely to benefit from such pressure. Nonetheless, we might agree—in the sense of developing an overlapping consensus—that these states are plausible candidates for foreign pressure on welfarist grounds. They have low-welfare populations and they have bad governments. A welfarist treaty, then, might require states to pressure these states, or a larger group of low-welfare states.

Summary

The various welfare measures are offered as a thought experiment rather than as a definite proposal for reform. If one or more of them seem plausible, then a case can be made for replacing human rights treaties with welfare treaties or (more realistically) amending the human rights treaties or construing them in a manner that allows states to maximize the welfare of their populations when formulating policy. If the welfare measures instead strike one as absurd or perplexing, then the prospects of a welfare treaty may be dim. However, by the same token, the ICESCR and other treaties that advance positive rights would need to be discarded. Treaties that require behaviour that cannot be measured against a standard of conduct are empty vessels. And if we are correct that the negative right is just a species of the positive right, because complying with negative rights requires states to allocate resources to specific programmes rather than simply refraining from doing some act, then the absence of such measures should discredit the negative rights treaties as well. For the ICCPR to function, for example, it must be possible for states to be able to complain that other states have not devoted enough resources to stamping out unlawful detentions. But to be able to make that complaint, states must be able to prove that those resources do not have a better use.

A PRAGMATIC DEFENCE OF THE WELFARIST APPROACH

Human rights advocates, especially those committed to vindicating negative rights, will not easily be persuaded that a welfarist approach could be desirable. The notion that a government could legitimately put resources into economic growth, health care, or security rather than eliminating torture is highly controversial. However, there is another argument in favour of the welfarist approach to which they should be more open, which is that a welfarist approach will have the indirect effect of promoting respect for negative rights. The argument rests on a political science chestnut that people in wealthier societies have the means to demand that their government respect negative rights. Whether the government approves or not, wealth brings education, literacy, familiarity with practices in foreign lands, better ability to organize, the development of civil society, and so forth—and these factors contribute to a rights-respecting culture.

The evidence is consistent with this claim. Ratings states have received for political rights and civil liberties (Freedom House) and political terror (Amnesty International and U.S. State Department). The political and civil rights scores range from one to seven, with lower numbers representing greater freedoms. The political terror scores range from one to five, with lower numbers referring to less political terror. These extremely crude ratings are the best approximation that we have of a state's compliance with human rights norms in the area of civil and political rights. The lesson of this isolated albeit important exceptions, wealthier states have stronger political and civil rights and lower levels of political terror. Indeed, all of the welfare measures are highly correlated, and so wealth, happiness, objective measures of well-being, and democracy are also correlated with respect for human rights. By contrast, ratification of human rights treaties does not appear to lead to improvement in human rights.

The limited empirical research that has been conducted establishes correlation, not causation. Suppose that some omitted variable—"culture" or favourable geography or some such thing—causes some states both to become wealthy and to respect rights. If so, an international policy of pressuring states to improve welfare will have no effect on wealth, welfare, and human rights.

The tentative case for focusing on economic growth and other welfare measures as a means for improving human rights, then, rests on a theory that:

- Aid and pressure can cause other states to become wealthier, and
- Increasing wealth causes populations to demand that their governments respect human rights. The case has not yet been made, but it may well be sound.

THE RELATIONSHIP WITH FOREIGN AID

Most poor states, and many middle-income states, receive significant foreign aid—much of it intended to improve the well-being of the poor, and much of it designed to serve strategic or political interests of the donors. At one time, donor nations did not expect that recipient nations would necessarily comply with human rights treaties, but in recent years there has emerged a norm of "rights-based development" that insists that aid must be sensitive to the human rights practices of the recipient state. When an aid recipient abuses human rights, advocates frequently argue that aid should be withheld.

This response has been institutionalized: Many international agencies, such as the IMF, condition assistance on adequate human rights performance. Many countries take this position as well. The Millennium Challenge Corporation, a U.S. government entity, sends aid to countries that score above the median on a group of indicators for political rights, educational investment, economic freedom, and corruption. This approach is in tension with the usual justification for foreign aid, which is to help the worst-off populations. Most of the poorest people in the world live in states that violate human rights. When states withdraw aid from human rights abusing governments, they risk further impoverishing the people whose rights are being violated.

This policy can be given two justifications. First, one might hope that the withdrawal of foreign aid will hurt government officials rather than the public. Unfortunately, it is very difficult to ensure that aid flows reach their intended recipients; they must usually go through government intermediaries who can skim off a portion of the proceeds. Thus, except in unusual circumstances, reducing aid will hurt populations and not (or not just) officials. Second, one might argue that states will improve their human rights practices only if their governments believe they will be rewarded for doing so. If aid is given to poor states regardless of their human rights practices, then states will have no incentive to stop abuse. As an unfortunate but necessary consequence, poor people in at least some states will have to suffer both human rights abuse and a loss of foreign aid.

For example, a sanctions regime imposed on Iraq between the first and second Gulf Wars was designed to pressure Saddam Hussein to step down or cooperate with other countries but mainly had the effect of immiserating the Iraqi people. Even when foreign pressure works, people must suffer in the short term so that improvements will occur in the long term. However, it may sometimes be unrealistic to expect that the threat to withhold aid will cause a state to improve its compliance with human rights norms. The government may be too weak or corrupt to change. In such cases, the decision to grant aid requires a delicate tradeoff. On the one hand, aid will help alleviate the misery of the population. On the other hand, it will likely increase the power of a human rights abusing government and extend its hold on power. At least in some cases, the tradeoff will favour foreign aid. Yet such an approach is in tension with a human rights regime that makes no concessions to welfarist considerations except in extreme cases. The result is that the human rights community and the foreign aid community work at cross purposes. One arm of a government scolds a state for violating human rights law while another arm continues to dole out aid. One NGO places the state on its list of human-rights violators, while another sets up clinics and provides other benefits to the population that may reduce internal pressure on the government to reform. This tension between the human rights and foreign aid regimes threatens to derail progress towards the overlapping goal of both—to improve the well-being of people around the world.

By contrast, a welfarist treaty would involve no such tension. The treaty could be drafted to oblige developed states both to pressure states that fail to deliver adequate welfare to their populations and to provide aid to states that show progress. When potential aid recipients have responsive governments, donor states should condition aid on welfare improvement, and should threaten sanctions or other penalties if welfare does not improve, regardless of whether the government accepts aid. When potential aid recipients do not have responsive governments (and are unlikely to obtain responsive governments), then aid should be unconditional, as long as it reaches the intended beneficiaries among the population of the recipient state. Sanctions would be avoided.

This approach works best if responsive and unresponsive governments can be distinguished. If they cannot be distinguished, then either the treaty would require all high-welfare states to put pressure on all low-welfare states, or else no treaty would be justified. The desirability of the treaty would depend on whether the welfare gains to the subset of states with responsive governments are greater than the welfare losses to the subset of states with unresponsive governments. If not, a welfarist treaty would simply reduce welfare, and would not be justified. It seems likely, however, that a rough distinction can be made. Failed states such as Somalia, isolationist states like North Korea, and giants like China are impervious to pressure. When no government exists, one cannot threaten to withhold aid from that government unless it changes its behaviour.

When the government has committed itself to isolation, it will be unlikely to respond to bribes and threats. And when the government controls a vast and powerful state, then efforts to pressure that government will backfire, as it can retaliate by reducing trade, threatening military action, and doing other things that harm pressuring states more than they are willing to tolerate for the sake of improving welfare elsewhere. Currently, high-welfare states have no legal obligations to provide aid to low-welfare states. States nonetheless do provide such aid. Most wealthy states have foreign aid programmes. Although much aid, perhaps the majority of aid, is used to promote strategic interests, at least some of it is used to help impoverished people in foreign countries, frequently the victims of natural disasters or civil war. Aid from different states or organizations is not coordinated, and for this reason it is probably not distributed optimally. Recognizing this problem, states from time to time enter nonlegal agreements to coordinate the aid with a view of reaching a particular goal.

Under the current system, then, states have no obligation to give foreign aid (though they do), but they do have an obligation to pressure states that violate human rights. The aid regime and the human rights regime work at cross purposes: Much aid goes to human rights violators precisely because their populations are so miserable. And states put under diplomatic or public pressure to condemn the human rights violations of strategic allies can, in effect, compensate the allies for the diplomatic costs they incur by increasing foreign aid. In addition, some evidence suggests that aid can weaken government institutions and even exacerbate civil war—with predictably unfortunate effects on human rights. A better system would coordinate aid and pressure—the carrot and the stick.

Whether a welfare treaty that contains obligations to give aid is possible is not a question we can answer here. Certainly, the obstacles would be significant; it may be impossible to write a treaty that directs aid flows in a manner that all donor states found acceptable. In addition, foreign aid has so far been largely unsuccessful at promoting economic growth. It would be a mistake to freeze by treaty the amount or nature of foreign aid before academics understand how aid is optimally allocated (if at all). Still, the literature does not show that foreign aid has no short term positive welfare effects. This means that minimal treaty provisions requiring high-welfare states to offer aid in coordinated fashion to states that improve their welfare levels might be appropriate.

CONCLUSION

The inevitable objection to a welfarist treaty is that it would permit a state to commit atrocities while claiming that overall welfare will increase because the public benefits more than the victims lose—the kind of objection familiar from the endless dispute between utilitarians and deontologists. One can just as well point out that human rights treaties require governments to risk civil war rather than detain a potentially dangerous person. Both types of approaches are vulnerable to the risk of a catastrophic scenario. The superior value of the welfarist approach lies in its insistence that the government would have to prove that its policies enhance public welfare.

A more important objection is that a welfarist treaty implicitly declares victory on behalf of welfarism in the long-running debate with critics who point out that welfarism, or certain versions of welfarism, has not been able to deal with certain persistent complaints: that welfarism does not take seriously the difference between persons; that welfarism assumes that values are commensurable when they are not; that welfarism fails to recognize that some values are more important than others; and many more. We have argued that some of these objections will influence how a welfarist treaty will be designed. But the more important point is that a treaty is just a means to an end, and a treaty that is sufficiently general about how states may advance welfare, while being sufficiently precise about how to measure overall welfare, need not take a strong position among these competing positions. Of course, it is possible that no welfarist treaty would satisfy all reasonable conceptions of the good, but if that is the case, it is hard to believe that any human rights treaty could. People who use the language of human rights find that they cannot agree on such diverse topics as the death penalty, the role of religion in public life, female genital cutting, the treatment of women and criminal defendants under Sharia, regulation of hate speech and subversive political parties, and human rights limitations on military action—leading to religious-wars style impasses that excite violent emotions and interfere with essential forms of international cooperation. If states can agree to respect the laws and practices of other states as long as those laws and practices are broadly consistent with maintaining and promoting the welfare of the local population, when measured against historic norms, then much would be accomplished.

Not only would welfare improve; human rights probably would as well, as people obtain the means to demand that their rights be respected.

Another objection is that arguments based on rights have stronger motivating force than arguments based on well-being. It is easier for a person to complain that the government has violated her right to a trial than to argue that by failing to grant her a trial, the government failed to take seriously her well-being. However, the force of this objection depends on rights actually either having intrinsic deontological value or promoting well-being in a rule-utilitarian sense. Otherwise, rights talk just plays off misunderstandings. And it is not clear that the objection is correct on its own terms. People in the West spontaneously offer aid in response to natural disasters such as the recent tsunami in South Asia; they seem less motivated by reports of ordinary human rights violations such as the imprisonment of political dissenters than by reports of famine, natural disaster, and civil war.

These objections aside, the welfarist treaty has two advantages over human rights treaties. It would advance an undeniable value—promoting the well-being of people in poor countries—rather than a controversial and philosophically suspect commitment to a bevy of rights. And after the hard work of adjudicating among the competing metrics has been done, it would use a common, simple, and transparent metric for evaluating states, rather than a set of incommensurable and ambiguous standards. As a result, it would create a system of priorities and ease coordination among states, and, at the same time, it would give each state a great deal of flexibility, allowing it to experiment with different approaches for advancing welfare, and to take advantage of whatever is unique about its resources and institutions. Diplomatic pressure would be directed against low-welfare states like Zimbabwe, Sudan, and Chad, and not against high-welfare states, such as the United States and China, which are in any event much more resistant to pressure. And foreign aid could be better coordinated so as to help those who need it most.

3

Human Rights and Welfare Conditionality

Over the last 10 to 15 years, talk about economic and social rights has become part of social policy debates in developed countries. Rights-based approaches emphasise participation, yet the debate around economic and social rights is largely driven. This object examines the extent to which the values which underpin rightsbased approaches are consistent with the values of those whom such an approach is designed to help. The values underlying rights-based approaches and those with experience of poverty are identified and then compared in three ways: in general; in relation to the specific issue of welfare conditionality; and as prescriptions for action. The comparative analysis is facilitated by linking the discussion of values to discussion of the forms of power relationships involved in rights-based approaches and what is valued by those with experience of poverty. While there is considerable overlap between rights-based approaches and what is valued by those with experience of poverty, there are also subtle differences which should not be ignored.

Introduction

Towards the end of the 20th century, talk about rights, particularly economic and social rights, entered social policy discourse. Even in Australia, where all attempts to establish guarantees of rights within the legal system have failed, the influence of UN treaties or conventions can be seen in policy statements and documents in specific policy sectors. For example, one of the most important elements of the Convention on the Rights of the Child is set out in Art 12, which calls on state parties to 'assure the child who is capable of forming his or her own views the right to express those views freely in all matters affecting the child'.

While consultation with children can be tokenistic or undermined by bureaucratic structures, the principle of seeking children's views has become part of policy rhetoric, if not practice. For example, one of the four rights set out in the South Australian Charter of Rights for Children and Young People in Care is 'the right to understand and have a say in decisions that affect you'. Rights-based approaches differ from past practice in the emphasis on obligation, in particular the obligation of the state to ensure its citizens are able to exercise their economic and social rights and by acknowledging that all citizens are entitled to exercise such rights.

Thus the Office of the High Commissioner for Human Rights defines a rights-based approach as one that 'links poverty reduction to questions of obligation rather than welfare or charity'. Governments become 'duty-holders' who are obliged to guarantee the rights of all citizens, including those who are marginalised or disadvantaged. Welfare recipients become rights-holders who are assisted by the state, not as an act of paternalistic benevolence, but as an entitlement. As with any normative framework, rights talk has generated a mixed response.

For some, rights-based approaches provide a powerful social instrument for challenging the sites and uses of power. Others point to the fact that institutionalising human rights is a social process which itself involves the use of power. Compared to civil and political rights, economic and social rights require a much greater level of active intervention by government before such rights can be realised.

The International Covenant on Economic, Social and Cultural Rights recognises that the adoption of legislative measures may be highly desirable in many instances, but leaves it up to individual states to determine whether legislation is necessary. The belief that legislation, though important, is not sufficient to ensure a full realisation of rights is reflected in the covenant, which for some rights lists the steps to be taken by state parties in order to achieve full realisation of a particular right. In all cases, the steps refer to broad policy goals and programmes rather than specific legislative measures. For example, in relation to the right to work, the covenant lists 'technical and vocational guidance and training programs' and 'policies and techniques to achieve steady economic development and full and productive employment' as some of the steps to be taken.

Furthermore, guidelines governing the type of reporting required under the covenant clearly indicate that states should provide details of non-legislative measures such as policies, programmes or techniques, as well as all relevant laws. In establishing the principle of progressive achievement,1 the covenant also recognises that full realisation of economic and social rights requires a significant amount of resources and state parties are given considerable discretion in determining the level of financial resources devoted to policies and programmes designed to achieve realisation of economic and social rights. Thus, economic and social rights are contingent on available resources and progressively realised through a range of measures, not all of which will be based on legislation and give rise to enforceable rights.

Cox notes that governments are increasingly relying on activities which are not codified in law, citing the example of aged care in Denmark, where elderly people enjoy the right to be cared for in their own home, but this right is not stated in law and its realisation is dependent on the amount of money local communities, which fund home care activities, allocate to aged care. Carney argues that a similar process is underway in Australia, where recent welfare-to-work reforms have converted rule-based norms into discretionary powers under the control of government departments. Increasing levels of conditionality applied to welfare entitlements are seen to further erode the 'rights' of social security clients. Given the debate around rights-based approaches and, in particular, the claim that rights-based approaches have the potential to challenge existing power structures, it is worth considering the extent to which the values which underpin rights-based approaches are consistent with the values of those whom such an approach is intended to help.

In this object, we have taken the views of people with experience of poverty about what they want from government and service providers as indicative of what they value. The remainder of this object is organised as follows. First, four general principles or values underlying all rights-based approaches are identified. This is followed by a discussion of what is valued by those with experience of poverty. The values underlying rights-based approaches are then compared to the values of those with experience of poverty, first in general, then in relation to a specific issue—welfare conditionality—and finally as a prescription for action. Linked to the discussion of values is discussion of the forms of power involved in rights-based approaches and what is valued by those with experience of poverty.

Rights-based approaches

As noted earlier, the realisation of economic and social rights requires a range of different forms of intervention by government, and under the ICESCR governments have considerable discretion in how they choose to institutionalise such rights. While there is no single agreed rights-based approach, all rights-based approaches derive from the international human rights framework from which a set of common principles or values can be identified. The first of these is that the inherent dignity of the human person is the basis of all rights.

The second is that participation is the way in which individuals are able to live with dignity. Consequently, the Office of the High Commissioner for Human Rights has suggested that in terms of the policymaking process, this principle obliges governments to facilitate participation by affected groups at all stages of the policy process, from initial conception through to implementation and evaluation. Thus, empowering rights-holders to be active participants in decision-making processes that affect their lives is a key component of rights-based approaches, with some political theorists arguing that participation is a basic right upon which all other rights rest. From a rights-based perspective, participation should not be confined to decision-making at the local level, but should encompass broader decision-making forums that impact on policy-making at the national and international level.

In addition, duty-holders have an obligation to encourage right sholders to pursue the legal defence of their rights within national and international jurisdictions. While the ICESCR provides for gradual realisation of economic and social rights, taking into account the level of financial resources available to individual governments, the third principle underlying rights-based approaches is that realisation of economic and social rights must start from the bottom up. That is, governments are obliged to concentrate their efforts on the most vulnerable or disadvantaged groups in society.

The fourth principle concerns governmental accountability. Geiringer and Palmer argue that the stipulation in Art 2(1) of the ICESCR that state parties use 'all appropriate means' in moving towards full realisation of economic and social rights requires some degree of governmental accountability to its own citizens in addition to its periodic reports to the United Nations. These principles illuminate the type of power relationships involved in rights based approaches.

Larmour identifies seven types of power relationships, of which five are relevant to this discussion of human rights approaches—that is, first dimensional or coercive power, where one party has the power to force another to do something that they would rather not do; second dimensional or agenda setting power; infrastructural power, which involves the transfer of resources in order to empower the recipient; disciplinary power, where one party tries to make the other party want what they want so that the second party takes responsibility for achieving the desired outcome; and, finally, the form of power that is linked to knowledge and expertise. Clearly, the most important type of power relationship involved in rights-based approaches is infrastructural power. Governments exercise infrastructural power when they provide resources that enhance the capacity of rights-holders to participate in decision-making processes that affect their lives.

However, genuine participation, which equates to the top three rungs of Arnstein's ladder of citizen participation,2 involves a rebalancing of second dimensional power. In addition, the principle of governmental accountability has the potential to shift the balance of second dimensional power slightly from governments towards rights-holders as governments are forced to report on progress towards full realisation of economic and social rights.

WHAT DO PEOPLE WITH EXPERIENCE OF POVERTY WANT FROM GOVERNMENT AND SERVICE PROVIDERS?

When asked about their life experiences and what they want from government and service providers, the desire for dignity and respect is almost always mentioned—regardless of the age of respondents, their gender or where they live. For example, the UK Commission on Poverty, Participation and Power noted that 'the lack of respect for people living in poverty was one of the clearest and most heartfelt messages which came across to us'. The same message was received by the Hume City Council when they talked to people from Indigenous communities, people from culturally diverse communities, women, those not in the workforce, people with a disability, older people and younger people:

- The desire for respect was by far the most important theme that emerged from discussions with those people who are experiencing, or who belong to particular community groups that are at a higher risk of experiencing poverty.

Clients of a range of welfare services in NSW and Victoria identified dignity and respect as two essential ingredients of a decent life, the desire for which was fuelled by the demeaning nature of interactions with government officials, an experience shared by people in the United Kingdom:

- Complaints were not about the quantity of payments … the problem was punitive and disrespectful treatment. Governments were not just at fault because they didn't deliver but because what they delivered came at such a heavy price in terms of self-respect and dignity.
- You shouldn't have to be made to feel as though you are useless. We feel very angry sometimes that people are ignorant of the fact that we are humans as well and we do need to be respected.

Being treated with dignity and respect means being recognised as a person rather than a 'problem' and being listened to without being judged. Clients of welfare services clearly identify the importance of this form of emotional support:

- People often think it is all about money. We don't necessarily need money, we need help dealing with being on welfare, we need help with all the shit about being worthless and useless and doing nothing. We need someone who knows what I'm going through, to sit down with me and sort all of this crap out.

While being accepted and being listened to are important, people with experience of poverty want more than a passive form of listening. People living in poverty want their expertise to be acknowledged and heard. For example, in the many conversations Mark Peel had with people living in Inala in Brisbane, in Broadmeadows in Melbourne and in Mount Druitt in Sydney, this desire came through very strongly:

- Justice was about being respected, trusted and listened to because what you had to say was important … What mattered to them was acknowledgment of capacity and intelligence.
- If they wanted one thing to change, it was that they be treated as knowledgeable, that outsiders should expect to learn and to listen.

Being listened to because what you have to say is considered valuable is a sign of respect and an acknowledgment of competency, both of which are valued by those with experience of poverty. For example, for participants in a personal loan pilot in Melbourne run by the Brotherhood of St Laurence and Community Sector Banking:

- ... obtaining a loan was more than just money, dignity, inclusion, trust and respect. It was an opportunity to not be just a passive recipient of welfare, but to gain some self-esteem by taking a positive active role in the process.

Thus, agency—the ability to take control of your life—is clearly linked to dignity and respect, and being treated with dignity and respect can increase feelings of selfrespect and a sense of agency. As one participant in the personal loan pilot explained, having a relationship with a mainstream bank:

- ... gave me the confidence to go ask somewhere else for credit ... this time I walked in with my head high and I said I want this and that.

People with experience of poverty often identify feelings of powerlessness and a lack of control over their lives. Choice is therefore important, because in choosing individuals are able to exercise control and agency. Thus, pensioners living in residential care in Melbourne experience greater financial stress than do pensioners living in rental accommodation, because they retain control over much less of their pension.

Access to services, such as affordable public transport, is valued because being able to use these services increases people's choices. When people with experience of poverty talk about receiving resources, they do so in instrumental terms—that is, the resources are valued because they increase agency. For example, clients of welfare services in New South Wales and Victoria are critical of the lack of access to dental services, because having bad teeth makes it harder to compete for jobs.

The desire of many welfare recipients for information and assistance before their lives reach a crisis point is further evidence of the value placed on agency:3 People with experience of poverty often identify feelings of powerlessness and a lack of control over their lives. Choice is therefore important, because in choosing individuals are able to exercise control and agency. Thus, pensioners living in residential care in Melbourne experience greater financial stress than do pensioners living in rental accommodation, because they retain control over much less of their pension. Access to services, such as affordable public transport, is valued because being able to use these services increases people's choices. When people with experience of poverty talk about receiving resources, they do so in instrumental terms—that is, the resources are valued because they increase agency. For example, clients of welfare services in New South Wales and Victoria are critical of the lack of access to dental services, because having bad teeth makes it harder to compete for jobs. The desire of many welfare recipients for information and assistance before their lives reach a crisis point is further evidence of the value placed on agency:3

- I know what has happened and I know what I want to do, I just need someone to help me get the right information ... what I need to do to get there.

The high priority placed on receiving information and getting access to resources which will increase agency indicates that those with experience of poverty are happy with governments exercising infrastructural power—power which is exercised in order to 'empower' the powerless. However, individuals with experience of poverty place an even higher priority on being able to exercise power that is linked to knowledge and expertise. Those with experience of poverty want their knowledge and expertise to be recognised; they want to be able to exercise the form of power linked to knowledge and expertise, because exercising this form of power is a powerful symbol of their worth as a human being, as well as a means of exercising second dimensional power. However, the desire to exercise second dimensional power is not absolute. Those with experience of poverty are not seeking to dominate or control negotiations to the exclusion of all other interests. What is important is a rebalancing of second dimensional power.

As Mark Peel observed:

- People did not expect to receive the world on a platter. As they said only the rich presume that as their right. They did not expect immediate changes in their situation but they did expect to be listened to, to play some part in defining what they needed and to be treated with respect.

Children and young people also want to exercise this nuanced form of second dimensional power. Few young people and fewer children want to be given sole decision-making responsibility, but most want to have their say and have their wishes taken into account when decisions are being made, rather than being asked to endorse a course of action decided by others. As a 12-year-old boy who had experienced the care and protection system put it:

- I might want to see my grandma. I might want to see my cousins. I might want to see my uncles or my aunties. I should be able to say 'yes, I do' or 'no, I don't'. I should have some say.

COMPARING THE TWO

It is clear from the considerable overlap between the values underpinning rights-based approaches and what is valued by those with direct experience of poverty. Rights-based approaches recognise the dignity of the human person as the basis of all rights and, for people with experience of poverty, being treated with dignity and respect is more important than anything else:

- You can put up with the struggle, you know, just get by, if you get respect and if you're treated right.

Similarly, the principle of governmental accountability is consistent with the desire of people with experience of poverty for:

- … 'someone to make and keep a promise'. In their version of social justice, powerful people should be held to account in the same way they were … 'You see, the difference is we pay for our mistakes. They don't. We have to understand limitations and forgive them and be reasonable and make the best of it. They don't. That's not fair.'

Participating in decision-making processes that affect their lives is clearly important to those with experience of poverty who value choice and agency, but the emphasis on encouraging rights-holders to pursue a legal defence of their rights is not necessarily shared by those with experience of poverty. Indeed, the language of rights seems to be largely confined to the non-poor. People with experience of poverty do not talk about claiming a legally defensible 'right' to a job, accessible public transport or health services; they talk instead about 'fair' access to resources and opportunities, which more closely equates to the principle that realisation of economic and social rights must start from the bottom up.

Those with experience of poverty place greater emphasis on receiving information or accessing resources which will increase agency—for example, receiving information about services which may help them get a job—than claiming their 'right' to a job. For example, in a 1997 telephone survey of 6897 jobseekers which gathered information about jobseekers' needs and expectations of service quality, as well as those aspects of service most valued by jobseekers, the desire for dignity and respect and the desire for information that would help them gain employment were all valued highly. Of much less importance was information about rights and information about rules and regulations.

So far, discussion of rights-based approaches and what is valued by those with experience of poverty has been confined to general principles. But these general principles are only ever given force in specific contexts. Discussion now turns to a specific issue, that of welfare conditionality, which is regarded by many as incompatible with rights-based approaches but is a defining characteristic of Australia's welfare system.

In residualist systems, welfare conditionality is used as a rationing device—a way of ensuring that benefits and payments go to those in greatest need. Using welfare conditionality in this way is consistent with the principle that, when faced with resource constraints, realisation of economic and social rights has to begin with those most in need. However, more recently a second layer of conditionality has been added to residualist welfare systems, with conditionality being used as a way of modifying behaviour—that is, some welfare payments have become dependent on an individual accepting their responsibility to undertake certain activities deemed socially desirable, such as actively looking for paid employment or ensuring their children attend school. The legitimacy of linking rights and responsibilities in this way has been widely debated with many arguing that rights-holders have a right to health, employment or an adequate standard of living simply by virtue of their humanity, and consequently do not have to do anything to 'earn' such rights.

Others argue that conditionality imposes additional burdens on the most vulnerable and disadvantaged, such as the homeless or those with multiple disabilities, or on 'third parties', particularly the children of those who are penalised for not meeting benefit requirements, such as applying for jobs or attending job interviews. While it is not the intention of this object to resolve the debate about whether welfare conditionality is a legitimate part of rights-based approaches, it is clear that in imposing conditionality with the aim of modifying behaviour, governments are exercising different forms of power from those associated with the key elements of rights-based approaches. When governments introduce conditions, such as participation in the Work for the Dole programme, as a requirement for receipt of unemployment benefits, they are exercising a disciplinary form of power—that is, governments want welfare recipients to take responsibility for themselves for ensuring that they are 'work ready'.

This disciplinary power can be exercised through first dimensional power—as, for example, when those deemed to have demonstrated a pattern of work avoidance are obliged to undertake 'full-time' Work for the Dole—or it can be exercised in a non-coercive way—as, for example, when individuals volunteer to have a portion of their welfare payments managed on their behalf by Centrelink. Justifications for conditionality fall into three main camps. Contractualist justifications centre on the belief that there is an implied contract between citizens and the state, where the state agrees to support its citizens in times of need if the citizen accepts their responsibilities, of which the most important is the responsibility to work. On the other hand, paternalistic justifications are based on the belief that imposing conditions is in the best interests of those in receipt of welfare payments because such individuals are so defeated by poverty and disadvantage that they are incapable of fulfilling their own desire to work or to look after their family without the threat of penalties or sanctions. Unlike contractualist arguments, paternalistic justifications do not emphasise the reciprocal obligations of the state—that is, welfare recipients are obliged to meet the conditions imposed upon them by the state because doing so will improve their lives, not because the state has already provided services and programmes that will enable welfare recipients to overcome poverty and disadvantage.

The third justification for welfare conditionality, derived from the writings of communitarian theorists, is based on the belief that people have a responsibility to be good parents, neighbours or citizens—not because the state has provided certain benefits or support, but because of the responsibility individuals owe to each other.

But what do recipients of social welfare services believe? For a sample of welfare service users living in Bradford in the north of England, the legitimacy of welfare conditionality is dependent on the specific policy sector. While accepting that individual behaviour could be a contributing factor to the need for health care, the overwhelming majority of respondents believed access to health care should be unconditional:

- I feel there are just too many different criteria on which to apply a value judgment, it would be impractical to apply it. You can't just take an isolated thing whether it be smoking, weight or age or nice person/bad person ... The universal thing is the only real way out of it. You could say that people who do dangerous sports or whatever are endangering their health so there is nowhere to draw the line really.

On the other hand, conditionality in the housing sector was considered appropriate, particularly in situations where individuals repeatedly reneged on agreements, ignored warnings and continued to engage in behaviour which had a negative impact on their neighbours:

- If they have been notified of the rule and they are a nuisance, yes I think that the council or housing association has got a right to evict them ... I think they should get a warning first, not just throw them out. There should be a procedure like.

Support for conditional unemployment payments fell between the two, with more than half believing it was reasonable to expect those receiving unemployment benefits to accept specific work or training responsibilities because this would increase their chance of finding a job, or because respondents believed it was desirable that those in receipt of a benefit contribute in some way to the community.

However, a substantial minority, who tended to see unemployment in terms of structural rather than individual failings, did not believe it was appropriate to make the receipt of unemployment benefits conditional on fulfilling certain duties or obligations:

- If there are no jobs people should be paid unemployment benefits.

This nuanced approach to conditionality is consistent with Australian studies of community attitudes. For example, Eardley, Saunders and Evans found that support for conditionality was high when applied to young unemployed people, but only 36 per cent of those surveyed believed an unemployed parent should be forced to undertake mutual obligation activities and only 25 per cent of those surveyed believed it was appropriate to impose obligations on unemployed people who had a disability. While elements of contractualist, paternalist and mutualist justifications can be found in the views of welfare service recipients, what these studies indicate is that users of social welfare services would agree with White's conclusion that:

- ... there is nothing intrinsically objectionable about welfare contractualism ... legitimacy ... is difficult to assess in isolation from the character of the rest of the welfare system, indeed of the rest of the economic system as a whole.

In other words, those who are often subject to the exercise of coercive power as part of the provision of assistance do not automatically condemn the use of such power. Indeed, criticisms of the compulsory nature of mutual obligation in workfare schemes such as the Work for the Dole programme are largely confined to commentators, advocacy and service delivery agencies.

Participants are more concerned with the lack of flexibility in programme design and implementation, which means the programme is unable to meet individual needs. For example, some older job seekers want access to accredited training so that they can move into new areas of employment while others do not, preferring wage subsidy schemes that would enable them to work in a real workplace in the private sector where they could demonstrate their skills and abilities to employers. Once again, the emphasis of those with experience of poverty is centred on the ways in which the programme can help them achieve their goal—getting a job—rather than concern about the exercise of first dimensional power.

Rights-based approaches can be seen both as an international system of treaties, visionary statements and commitments and as a conceptual framework that allows policy-makers to 'recharacterise and guide what we do and how we do it'. The remainder of this part of the object considers what would need to change in 'what we do and how we do it', if the values of those with experience of poverty are taken as a conceptual framework.

The biggest challenge facing policy-makers and service providers lies in allowing those with experience of poverty to exercise the form of power that is linked to knowledge and expertise. Policy-makers and service providers are comfortable with the exercise of infrastructural power, but allowing service users to exercise the form of power that is linked to knowledge and expertise cuts across the strong streak of paternalism that still exists in the social welfare sector. In other words, it challenges the belief of all professionals involved in delivering social welfare programmes that they know what is best for their clients, just as it challenges the belief of academics and policy experts that their ideas or the latest policy fad will solve particular policy problems. Allowing those with experience of poverty to exercise the form of power that is linked to knowledge and expertise means policy-makers and professionals involved in the delivery of social welfare services must at times surrender control over outcomes, even if placing power in the hands of individuals means that outcomes are less than what policy-makers and welfare professionals believe they could be.

There are agencies already doing this, in spite of the ongoing frustration experienced by their staff when clients choose not to make changes that the staff believes would be beneficial. For example, staff involved in Anglicare Tasmania's Acquired Injury and Home Support Service are committed to the principle of treating their clients with dignity and respect, which means giving them choice—choice over who is employed as their personal support worker and choice over how allocated hours are used. Even when staff members see clients who choose to make goal-oriented plans for how allocated hours are used improve their quality of life while others do not do so well, they remain committed to the principle of letting clients decide.

As the preceding example illustrates, clients want different things. Some clients want personal support workers who are trained to care for people with spinal cord injuries; others are more concerned about the personality of the support worker—whether they 'hit if off'. Therefore, making assumptions about what clients want is dangerous. As Renee, a young Aboriginal woman who was interviewed for Judith Brett and Anthony Moran's book Ordinary People's Politics, explains, even well-meaning assumptions which incorporate sessions from past policy failures do not always hold true:

- My sister doesn't want to be part of the Aboriginal community any more. She thinks it is destructive, and that the violence and abuse has caused all her problems ... [M]y sister's happy to be removed. She'd rather be in care because she's getting all the things Mum couldn't provide. It's not that she doesn't like Mum, but she'd rather be out of there.

For Renee, the answer lay in treating each person as an individual and listening to what they wanted for their life:

- Renee ... stressed repeatedly that people trying to help should talk with the children and have more faith in their resilience, and that the current situation should not just be seen in terms of the previous generation's experience.

Treating everyone as an individual and allowing them to choose means that services have to be flexible—flexible in terms of both what is provided and how long assistance is provided. This level of flexibility is often difficult to achieve in an environment where services are under-resourced and accountability frameworks emphasise upward accountability, rather than downward accountability. But, as noted earlier, for those with experience of poverty, exercising the form of power that is linked to knowledge and expertise is a means of rebalancing, not dominating, the exercise of second dimensional power.

Therefore, finding a balance between the demands of upward and downward accountability should not be impossible.4 Re-orienting service provision to fully reflect the values of those whom the service is designed to assist would require greater emphasis on the provision of information to clients or programme participants about available services, and how to access these services as a way of strengthening the exercise of infrastructural power.

As noted earlier, individuals want this sort of information and the success of service models based on care in the community requires it. Unfortunately, clients and programme participants often report difficulties in accessing relevant information:

- Unless you actually enquire about what services are available then people are not normally keen to tell you. So you actually have to

> do a lot of prying and literally ask specific questions about what is available and what is not. There is never one person. It is always several people and you will find a lot of people will do a lot of buck passing and say 'we don't handle that' and they will say you need to speak to this person or that and before you know it you have spoken to fourteen different people and you still don't have the answers you need.

Giving clients choice, providing flexible services which are responsive to individual needs and placing greater emphasis on the provision of information are all consistent with rights-based approaches. This indicates that, far from being yet another imposition on 'the poor' by experts who believe that they know best, rights-based approaches provide a conceptual framework that allows policy-makers and those involved in the delivery of social welfare services to recharacterise what they do and how they do it in ways that are largely consistent with the values of those whom they are trying to help.

CONCLUSION

In setting forth arguments for the development of an Australian system for the protection of human rights, Hilary Charlesworth characterises human rights as 'a framework for debate over basic values and conceptions of a good society'. Recognising that this debate should be conducted by all groups in society, not just those with the power to influence what is done and how it is done, this object asked: To what extent are the values which underpin rights-based approaches consistent with the values of those such an approach is intended to help? A comparison of the general principles underlying all rights-based approaches to what is valued by those with experience of poverty reveals considerable overlap.

Those with experience of poverty value dignity and respect above all else and place a high priority on choice and agency and on receiving information which will enhance their capacity to exercise choice and agency, all of which is consistent with rights based approaches, where the inherent dignity of the human person is seen as the basis of all rights and participation in decision-making processes is seen as the way in which individuals are able to live with dignity. However, as Arnstein noted in her analysis of forms of citizen participation, genuine participation involves a redistribution of power, and when the forms of power involved in rights-based approaches and what is valued by those with experience of poverty are compared, slight differences emerge. For those with experience of poverty, it is important to participate in decisionmaking processes through the exercise of power that is linked to knowledge and expertise. In other words, those with experience of poverty want to be treated as knowledgeable and to participate in decision-making processes because their knowledge and expertise are respected, rather than—as would be the case under rights-based approaches—because they have a 'right' to participate.

While the outcome—participation—is the same, the basis for that participation is different. This difference is also evident when attitudes to welfare conditionality are examined. For many advocates of rights-based approaches, welfare conditionality is not consistent with such an approach because individuals have a right to health or employment and therefore should not have to do anything to earn what is theirs by right. On the other hand, with the exception of health, those with experience of poverty are less concerned about claiming something by right and more concerned about enhancing their capacity to achieve their goals.

But what are the practical implications of this difference? The discussion of what would need to change if the values of those with experience of poverty are taken as a conceptual framework revealed that the recommended actions are entirely consistent with rights-based approaches. The considerable overlap between the values which underpin rights-based approaches and what those with experience of poverty value means that those committed to a human rights framework for the development of social policy do not have to make major changes to what they do and how they do it if they wish to fully reflect the values of those with experience of poverty. What is needed, however, is an awareness of the sources of second dimensional power and an increased understanding of what is already being done, as well as what could be done, to incorporate the knowledge and expertise of those with experience of poverty into the process of policy-making, implementation and evaluation.

4

Elements of a Theory of Human Rights

THE NEED FOR A THEORY

Few concepts are as frequently invoked in contemporary political discussions as human rights. There is something deeply attractive in the idea that every person anywhere in the world, irrespective of citizenship or territorial legislation, has some basic rights, which others should respect. The moral appeal of human rights has been used for a variety of purposes, from resisting torture and arbitrary incarceration to demanding the end of hunger and of medical neglect. At the same time, the central idea of human rights as something that people have, and have even without any specific legislation, is seen by many as foundationally dubious and lacking in cogency. A recurrent question is, Where do these rights come from? It is not usually disputed that the invoking of human rights can be politically powerful. Rather, the worries relate to what is taken to be the "softness" of the conceptual grounding of human rights. Many philosophers and legal theorists see the rhetoric of human rights as just loose talk—perhaps kindly and well meaning forms of locution—but loose talk nevertheless.

The contrast between the widespread use of the idea of human rights and the intellectual skepticism about its conceptual soundness is not new. The U.S. Declaration of Independence, in 1776, took it to be "selfevident" that everyone is "endowed by their Creator with certain inalienable rights," and thirteen years later, the French declaration of "the rights of man" asserted that "men are born and remain free and equal in rights." But it did not take Jeremy Bentham long, in his Anarchical Fallacies written during 1791 and 1792 to propose the total dismissal of all such claims. Bentham insisted that "natural rights is simple nonsense: natural and imprescriptible rights, rhetorical nonsense, nonsense upon stilts." That suspicion remains very alive today, and despite persistent use of the idea of human rights in practical affairs, there are many who see the idea of human rights as no more than "bawling upon paper," to use another of Bentham's barbed portrayals of natural right claims. The dismissal of human rights is often comprehensive and is aimed against any belief in the existence of rights that people can have unconditionally, simply by virtue of their humanity. Some critics, however, propose a discriminating rejection: they accept the general idea of human rights but exclude specific classes of proposed rights, in particular the so-called economic and social rights, or welfare rights. These rights, which are sometimes referred to as second generation rights, such as a common entitlement to subsistence or to medical care, have mostly been added relatively recently to earlier enunciations of human rights, thereby vastly expanding the claimed domain of human rights. These additions have certainly taken the contemporary literature on human rights well beyond the eighteenth-century declarations that concentrated on a narrower class of "rights of man," including such demands as personal liberty and political freedom.

These newer inclusions have been subjected to more specialized skepticism, with the critics focusing on their feasibility problems and their dependence on specific social institutions that may or may not exist. Human rights activists are often quite impatient with such critiques. The invoking of human rights tends to come mostly from those who are concerned with changing the world rather than interpreting it. It is not hard to understand their unwillingness to spend time trying to provide conceptual justification, given the great urgency to respond to terrible deprivations around the world. This proactive stance has had its practical rewards, since it has allowed immediate use of the colossal appeal of the idea of human rights to confront intense oppression or great misery, without having to wait for the theoretical air to clear. However, the conceptual doubts must also be satisfactorily addressed, if the idea of human rights is to command reasoned loyalty and to establish a secure intellectual standing. It is critically important to see the relationship between the force and appeal of human rights, on the one hand, and their reasoned justification and scrutinized use, on the other.

There is, thus, need for some theory and also for some defence of any proposed theory. The object of this object is to do just that, and to consider, in that context, the justification of the general idea of human rights and also of the includability of economic and social rights within the broad class of human rights. For such a theory to be viable it is necessary to clarify what kind of a claim is made by a declaration of human rights, and how such a claim can be defended, and furthermore how the diverse criticisms of the coherence, cogency and legitimacy of human rights can be adequately addressed. That is the aim of this object.

However, before going into this investigation, we should make a clarificatory point. The rhetoric of human rights is sometimes applied to particular legislations inspired by the idea of human rights. There is clearly no great difficulty in seeing the obvious judicial status of these already legalized entitlements. No matter what they are called ("human rights laws" or any other appellation), they stand shoulder to shoulder with other established legislations. The present inquiry on the foundations and cogency of human rights does not have any direct bearing on the obvious legal status of these "human rights laws," once they have been properly legislated. As far as these laws are concerned, the relevance, if any, of this study would lie, rather, in the motivation that leads to the enacting of such laws, which builds on the pre-legislative standing of these claims.

Indeed, a great many acts of legislation and legal conventions (such as the "European Convention for the Protection of Human Rights and Fundamental Freedoms") have been clearly inspired by a belief in some pre-existing rights of all human beings. This applies even to the adoption of the U.S. Constitution, including the Bill of Rights, linked to the normative vision of the U.S. Declaration of Independence. The difficult questions regarding the status and standing of human rights arise in the domain of ideas, before such legalization occurs. We also have to examine whether legislation is the pre-eminent, or even a necessary, route through which human rights can be pursued.

HUMAN RIGHTS: ETHICS AND LAW

What kind of an assertion does a declaration of human rights make? we would submit that proclamations of human rights are to be seen as articulations of ethical demands. They are, in this respect, comparable with pronouncements in utilitarian ethics, even though their respective substantive contents are, obviously, very different. Like other ethical claims that demand acceptance, there is an implicit presumption in making pronouncements on human rights that the underlying ethical claims will survive open and informed scrutiny. Indeed, the invoking of such an interactive process of critical scrutiny, open to information (including that about other societies) as well as to arguments coming from far as well as near, is a central feature of the theory of human rights proposed here.

It differs both from trying to justify the ethics of human rights in terms of shared—and already established—universal values (the uncomplicated "non-partisan" view), and from abdicating any claim of adherence to universal values (and in this sense, eschewing any claim to being "non-partisan") in favour of a particular political conception that is suitable to the contemporary world. But the point to note for the moment, in answer to the first question, is that pronouncements of human rights are quintessentially ethical articulations, and they are not, in particular, putative legal claims, despite considerable confusion on this point, generated not least by Jeremy Bentham, the obsessive slayer of what he took to be legal pretensions.

A pronouncement of human rights includes an assertion of the importance of the corresponding freedoms—the freedoms that are identified and privileged in the formulation of the rights in question—and is indeed motivated by that importance. For example, the human right of not being tortured springs from the importance of freedom from torture for all. But it includes, furthermore, an affirmation of the need for others to consider what they can reasonably do to secure the freedom from torture for any person. For a would-be torturer, the demand is obviously quite straightforward, to wit, to refrain and desist.

The demand takes the clear form of what Immanuel Kant called a perfect obligation. However, for others too (that is, those other than the would-be torturers) there are responsibilities, even though they are less specific and come in the general form of "imperfect obligations". The perfectly specified demand not to torture anyone is supplemented by the more general, and less exactly specified, requirement to consider the ways and means through which torture can be prevented and then to decide what one should, thus, reasonably do. The relations between human rights, freedoms.

Even though recognitions of human rights (with their associated claims and obligations) are ethical affirmations, they need not, by themselves, deliver a complete blueprint for evaluative assessment. An agreement on human rights does involve a firm commitment, to wit, to give reasonable consideration to the duties that follow from that ethical endorsement. But even with agreement on these affirmations, there can still be serious debates, particularly in the case of imperfect obligations, on

- The ways in which the attention that is owed to human rights should be best paid,
- How the different types of human rights should be weighed against each other and their respective demands integrated together,
- How the claims of human rights should be consolidated with other evaluative concerns that may also deserve ethical attention, and so on.

A theory of human rights can leave room for further discussions, disputations and arguments. The approach of open public reasoning, which is central to the understanding of human rights as proposed here, can definitively settle some disputes about coverage and content (including the identification of some clearly sustainable rights and others that would be hard to sustain), but may have to leave others, at least tentatively, unsettled. The admissibility of a domain of continued dispute is no embarrassment to a theory of human rights.

In practical applications of human rights, such debates are, of course, quite common and entirely customary, particularly among human rights activists. What is being argued here is that the possibility of such debates—without losing the basic recognition of the importance of human rights—is not just a feature of what can be called human rights practice, they are actually part of the general discipline of human rights including the underlying theory (rather than being an embarrassment to that discipline). An acknowledgment of the necessity to pay ethical attention to human rights, far from obliterating the need for such deliberation, actually invites it. A theory of human rights can, therefore, allow considerable internal variations, without losing the commonality of the agreed principle of attaching substantial importance to human rights (and to the corresponding freedoms and obligations) and of being committed to considering seriously how that importance should be appropriately reflected.

Variability of this kind is not only not an embarrassment, it tends to be standardly present in all general theories of substantive ethics. Indeed, a similar diversity can be found within utility-centered ethics, even though this feature of that large ethical discipline often receives little or no recognition. In the case of utility-based reasoning, variations can arise not only from the different ways in which utilities can be interpreted (as pleasures, fulfillment of desires, or realization of choices), nor only from the acknowledged heterogeneity of utilities themselves (well recognized by both Aristotle and John Stuart Mill). They can also arise from the diversity of ways in which utilities can be used, whether by mere addition, or by multiplication (after suitable normalization), or through the addition of concave transformations of utility functions, all of which have been proposed and pursued, within the discipline of utility-based evaluation.

Further, the discipline of interpersonal comparison of utilities may itself allow alternative procedures of quantification of utilities and go comfortably with accommodating permissible variations within specified classes of "partial comparability." The existence of different ways of making use of utility-based reasoning and alternative utilitarian procedures does not invalidate or even undermine the general approach of utility-centered ethics. And, similarly, the ethics of human rights is not nullified or thwarted by internal variations that it allows and incorporates.

Thus, the analogy between articulations of human rights and utilitarian pronouncements has considerable perspicacity, even though the great founder of modern utilitarianism, Jeremy Bentham, managed to miss that connection altogether in his classic hatchet job on natural rights in general and on the "rights of man" in particular.

Bentham took the appropriate comparison to be that between the legal significance, respectively of:

- Declarations of human rights, and
- Actually legislated rights.

Not surprisingly, he found the former to be essentially lacking in legal status in the way the latter, obviously enough, would have.

Bentham's dismissal of human rights came, thus, with amazingly swiftness.

- Right, the substantive right, is the child of law; from real laws come real rights; but from imaginary laws, from "law of nature" [can come only] "imaginary rights."

It is easy to see that Bentham's rejection of the idea of natural "rights of man" depends substantially on the rhetoric of privileged use of the term of "rights," seeing it in its specifically legal interpretation. However, insofar as human rights are meant to be significant ethical claims, the pointer to the fact that they do not by themselves have legal or institutional force is obvious enough, but also quite irrelevant to the discipline of human rights.

The appropriate comparison is, surely, between:

- A utility-based ethics (championed by Bentham himself), which sees intrinsic ethical importance in utilities but none in human rights or human freedoms (any role that the latter can have in the utilitarian system is, thus, entirely instrumental), and an ethics that makes room for the fundamental significance of human rights (as the advocates of "rights of man" did), linked with a diagnosis of the basic importance of human freedoms and the obligations generated by that diagnosis.

Just as utilitarian ethical reasoning takes the form of insisting that the utilities of the relevant persons must be taken into account in deciding on what should be done, the human rights approach demands that the acknowledged human rights must be given ethical recognition. The relevant comparison lies in this contrast, not in differentiating the legal force of legislated rights (for which Bentham's phrase "the child of law" is an appropriate description) from the absence of any legal standing generated by an ethical recognition of rights (without any legislation or legal reinterpretation). Indeed, even as Bentham was busy in 1791 and 1792 writing down his dismissal of "rights of man," the reach and range of ethical interpretations of rights were being powerfully explored by Thomas Paine's Rights of Man, and by Mary Wollstonecraft's A Vindication of the Rights of Woman: with Strictures on Political and Moral Subjects, both published during the period 1791 to 1792 (though neither seemed to arouse Bentham's curiosity).

An ethical understanding of human rights goes not only against seeing them as legal demands (and against taking them to be, as in Bentham's view, legal pretensions), but also differs from a law-centered approach to human rights that sees them as if they are basically grounds for law, almost "laws in waiting." Ethical and legal rights do, of course, have motivational connections. In a rightly celebrated article "Are There Any Natural Rights?" Herbert Hart has argued that people "speak of their moral rights mainly when advocating their incorporation in a legal system." He added that the concept of a right "belongs to that branch of morality which is specifically concerned to determine when one person's freedom may be limited by another's and so to determine what actions may appropriately be made the subject of coercive legal rules." Whereas Bentham saw rights as a "child of law," Hart's view takes the form, in effect, of seeing some natural rights as parents of law: they motivate and inspire specific legislations.

Although Hart does not make any reference whatever to human rights in his article, the reasoning about the role of natural rights as inspiration for legislation can be seen to apply to the concept of human rights as well. There can, in fact, be little doubt that the idea of moral rights can serve, and has often served in practice, as the basis of new legislation. It has frequently been utilized in this way, and this is indeed an important use of human rights. That, for example, is precisely the way the diagnosis of inalienable rights was invoked in the U.S. Declaration of Independence and reflected subsequently in the Bill of Rights, a route that has been well-trodden in the legislative history of many countries in the world. Providing inspiration for legislation is certainly one way in which the ethical force of human rights has been constructively deployed.

However, to acknowledge that such a connection exists is not the same as taking the relevance of human rights to lie exclusively in determining what should "appropriately be made the subject of coercive legal rules." It is important to see that the idea of human rights can be, and is, actually used in several other ways as well. Indeed, if human rights are seen as powerful moral claims, indeed as "moral rights" (to use Hart's phrase), then surely we have reason for some catholicity in considering different avenues for promoting these claims. The ways and means of advancing and implementing human rights need not, thus, be confined only to making new laws (even though sometimes legislation may indeed turn out to be the right way to proceed). For example, monitoring and other activist support, provided by such organizations as Human Rights Watch or Amnesty International or OXFAM or Médicins Sans Frontièrs, can themselves help to advance the effective reach of acknowledged human rights. In many contexts, legislation may not, in fact, be involved.

RIGHTS, FREEDOMS AND SOCIAL INFLUENCE

Why are human rights important? Since declarations of human rights are ethical affirmations of the need to pay appropriate attention to the significance of freedoms incorporated in the formulation of human rights, an appropriate starting point must be the importance of freedoms of human beings to be so recognized. Note that while rights involve claims (specifically, claims on others who are in a position to make a difference), freedoms, in contrast, are primarily descriptive characteristics of the conditions of persons. By starting from the importance of freedoms as the appropriate human condition on which to concentrate, rather than on utilities, we get a motivating reason not only for celebrating our own rights and liberties, but also for our taking an interest in the significant freedoms of others, not just in their pleasures and desirefulfillment. Bentham's insistence on choosing utility as the basis of ethical evaluation can be contrasted with the reasons for focusing instead on freedoms.

We have discussed elsewhere why those reasons are weighty and how the focus on freedoms can avoid some of the major pitfalls of concentrating only on utility in the form of pleasure or desire fulfillment. For example, the utilitarian calculus can suffer from valuational distortions resulting from the neglect of substantive deprivation of those who are chronically disadvantaged but who learn, by force of circumstances, to take pleasure in small mercies and get reconciled to cutting down their desires to "realistic proportions" (thereby appearing to be not particularly deprived in the special metric of pleasures or desire-fulfillment). Before going into the difficult issue of duties related to rights, some exploration of the connection between rights and freedoms is necessary, to which we devote the rest of this part. Freedoms can vary in importance and also in terms of the extent to which they can be influenced by social help. For a freedom to count as a part of the evaluative system of human rights, it clearly must be important enough to justify requiring that others should be ready to pay substantial attention to decide what they can reasonably do to advance it. It also has to satisfy a condition of plausibility that others could make a material difference through taking such an interest.

There have to be some "threshold conditions" of:

- Importance and
- Social influence ability for a freedom to figure within the interpersonal and interactive spectrum of human rights.

Insofar as the idea of human rights demands public discussion and engagement, the agreement that would be sought is not only on whether some specific freedom of a particular person has any ethical importance whatsoever (that condition can be easy to satisfy), but also whether its significance and its influenceability meet the threshold conditions for inclusion among the human rights on which the society should focus. The threshold conditions may prevent, for a variety of reasons, particular freedoms from being an appropriate subject matter of human rights.

To illustrate, it is not hard to argue that some importance should be attached to all four of the following freedoms:

- A person's freedom not to be assaulted;
- Her freedom to receive medical care for a serious health problem;
- Her freedom not to be called up regularly by her neighbours whom she detests;
- Her freedom to achieve tranquillity.

However, even though all four may be important in one way or another, it is not altogether implausible to argue that the first (freedom not to be assaulted) is a good subject matter for a human right, and so is the second (freedom to receive necessary medical care), but the third (freedom not to be called up by detested neighbours) is not, in general, important enough to cross the threshold of social significance to qualify as a human right. Also, the fourth, while quite possibly extremely important for the person, is too inward-looking—and too hard to be influenced by others—to be a good subject matter for human rights. The exclusion of a "right to tranquillity" relates not to any skepticism about the possible importance of tranquillity and the significance of a person's being free to achieve it, but to the difficulty of guaranteeing it through social help. There can be fruitful debates on the thresholds and their use, and in particular on whether a specific case of freedom meets the threshold conditions or not. The analyses of thresholds, related both to the seriousness and to the social influence ability of particular freedoms, cannot but have a significant place in the discipline of human rights.

PROCESSES, OPPORTUNITIES AND CAPABILITIES

I turn now to a closer scrutiny of the contents of freedom and its multiple features. We have argued elsewhere that "opportunity" and "process" are two aspects of freedom that require distinction, with the importance of each deserving specific acknowledgment. An example can help to bring out the separate (though not necessarily independent) relevance of both substantive opportunities and freedom of processes. Consider an adult person, let us call her Rima, who decides that she would like to go out in the evening. To take care of some considerations that are not central to the issues involved here (but which could make the discussion more complex), it is assumed that there are no particular safety risks involved in her going out, and that she has critically reflected on this decision and judged that going out would be the sensible, indeed the ideal, thing to do.

Now consider the threat of a violation of this freedom if some authoritarian guardians of society decide that she must not go out in the evening ("it is most unseemly"), and if they force her, in one way or another, to stay indoors. To see that there are two distinct issues involved in this one violation, consider an alternative case in which the authoritarian bosses decide that she must—absolutely must—go out ("you are expelled for the evening: just obey"). There is clearly a violation of freedom here even though Rima is being forced to do exactly what she would have chosen to do anyway, and this is readily seen when we compare the two alternatives "choosing freely to go out" and "being forced to go out." The latter involves an immediate violation of the process aspect of Rima's freedom, since an action is being forced on her (even though it is an action she would have freely chosen also).

The opportunity aspect may also be affected, since a plausible accounting of opportunities can include having options and it can inter alia include valuing free choice. However, the violation of the opportunity aspect would be more substantial and manifest if she were not only forced to do something chosen by another, but in fact, forced to do something she herself would not otherwise choose to do. The comparison between "being forced to go out" (when she would have gone out anyway, if free) and, say, "being forced to polish the shoes of others at home" (not her favourite activity) brings out this contrast, which is primarily one of the opportunity aspect, rather than the process aspect. In being forced to stay home and polish the shoes of others, Rima loses freedom in two different ways, related respectively to,

- Being forced with no freedom of choice, and
- Being obliged in particular to do something she would not choose to do.

Both processes and opportunities can figure in human rights. A denial of "due process" in being, say, imprisoned without a proper trial can be the subject matter of human rights (no matter what the outcome of the fair trial might be), and so can be the denial of the opportunity of medical treatment, or the opportunity of living without the danger of being assaulted (going beyond the exact process through which these opportunities are made real).

For the opportunity aspect of freedom, the idea of "capability" (that is, the opportunity to achieve valuable combinations of human functionings: what a person is able to do or be) can typically provide a helpful approach.

It allows us to distinguish appropriately between:

- What she values doing or being, and
- The means she has to achieve what she values.

By shifting attention, in particular, towards the former, the capability-based approach resists an overconcentration on means (such as incomes and primary goods) that can be found in some theories of justice (for example, in the Rawlsian Difference Principle). The capability approach can capture the fact that two persons can have very different substantial opportunities even when they have exactly the same set of means: for example, a disabled person can do far less than an ablebodied person can, with exactly the same income and other "primary goods." The disabled person cannot, thus, be judged to be equally advantaged—with the same substantive opportunities—as the person without any physical handicap but with the same set of means (such as income and wealth and other primary goods).

The capability perspective concentrates on what actual opportunities a person has, not the means over which she has command. More particularly, the capability perspective allows us to take into account the parametric variability in the relation between the means, on the one hand, and the actual opportunities, on the other. The capability perspective can also help in bringing out the need for transparent valuational scrutiny of individual advantages and adversities, since the different functionings have to be assessed and weighted in relation to each other, and the opportunities of having different combinations of functionings also have to be evaluated. The richness of the capability perspective broadly interpreted, thus, includes its insistence on the need for open valuational scrutiny for making social judgments, and in this sense, it fits in well with the importance of public reasoning. This openness of transparent valuation contrasts with burying the evaluative exercise in some mechanical, and valuationally opaque, convention (for example, by taking market-evaluated income to be the invariable standard of individual advantage, thereby giving implicit normative priority to institutionally determined market prices).

There has, however, been some serious criticism of describing these substantive opportunities—to live one kind of a life or another—as "freedoms," and it has been argued that this makes the idea of freedom too inclusive. For example, in her illuminating and sympathetic critique of my

Development as Freedom, Susan Okin has presented arguments to suggest that we tend "to overextend the concept of freedom." She argues: "It is hard to conceive of some human functionings, or the fulfillment of some needs and wants, such as good health and nourishment, as freedoms without stretching the term until it seems to refer to everything that is of central value to human beings".

There is indeed scope for argument on how broadly the concept of freedom should be used. But the particular example considered in Okin's counterargument is, we think, based on a misinterpretation of the idea of freedom underlying the concept of capability. It has not been suggested at all that a functioning (for example, being in good health or being well-nourished) should be seen as freedom of any kind. Rather, freedom, in the form of capability, concentrates on the opportunity to achieve combinations of functionings (including, inter alia, the opportunity to be well-nourished or in good health, as in this particular case): the person is free to use this opportunity or not. A capability reflects the alternative combinations of functionings over which the person has freedom of effective choice.

It is, therefore, not being suggested at all that being well-nourished or in good health is to be seen as a freedom in itself. Capability, as a kind of freedom, refers to the extent to which the person is able to choose particular combinations of functionings (including, inter alia, such things as being well-nourished), no matter what the person actually decides to choose. Mahatma Gandhi famously did not use that opportunity to be well-fed when he chose to fast, as a protest against the policies of the British Raj in India. In terms of the actual functioning of being well-nourished, the fasting Gandhi did not differ from a starving famine victim, but the freedoms and opportunities they respectively had were quite different. The freedom to have any particular thing can be distinguished from actually having that thing. What a person is free to have, not just what he or she actually has, is relevant, we have argued, to a theory of justice. A similar point can be made about the relevance of substantive freedoms in a theory of human rights.

The fact that many of the terrible deprivations in the world seem to arise from a lack of freedom to avoid those deprivations (rather than from choice, including choosing to be "indolent": a classic issue in the historical literature on poverty) is an important motivational reason to emphasize the role of freedom. This led Marx to argue passionately for the need to replace "the domination of circumstances and chance over individuals by the domination of individuals over chance and circumstances." The general idea of freedom, with its many distinct components, seems particularly relevant to normative social choice theory, in general, and to the theory of justice, in particular. The argument here is that it can also figure powerfully in the normative foundations of human rights.

To take a different type of example, consider the freedom of new immigrants to West Europe or North America to conserve the ancestral cultural customs and life-styles from their countries of origin. This complex subject cannot be adequately assessed without distinguishing between doing something and being free to do that thing. A strong argument can be constructed in favour of an immigrant's having the freedom to retain at least parts of her ancestral life-style, but this must not be seen as an argument in favour of her pursuing her ancestral life-style whether she chooses to do this or not. The central issue, in this argument, is the freedom to choose how she should live, including the opportunity to pursue ancestral customs, and it cannot be turned into an argument for her specifically pursuing those customs in particular, irrespective of the alternatives she has and the choices she would make. The importance of capability, reflecting opportunities, is central to this distinction.

We have been concentrating on what the capability perspective can do for a theory of justice or of human rights in the immediately preceding discussion, but we now to turn to what it cannot do. Although the idea of capability has considerable merit in the assessment of the opportunity aspect of freedom, it cannot possibly deal adequately with the process aspect of freedom, since capabilities are characteristics of individual advantages, and they fall short of telling us enough about the fairness or equity of the processes involved, or about the freedom of citizens to invoke and utilize procedures that are equitable.

Let me illustrate the contrast of perspectives with a somewhat harsh example. It is now fairly well established that given symmetric care, women tend to live longer than men. If one were concerned only with capabilities (and nothing else), and in particular with equality of the capability to live long, it would have been possible to construct an argument for giving men more medical attention than women to counteract the natural masculine handicap. But giving women less medical attention than men for the same health problems would clearly violate an important requirement of process equity, and it seems reasonable to argue, in cases of this kind, that demands of equity in process freedom could sensibly override a single-minded concentration on the opportunity aspect of freedom (and the requirements of capability equality in particular).

While it is important to emphasize the relevance of the capability perspective in judging people's substantive opportunities (particularly in comparison with alternative approaches that focus on incomes, or primary goods, or resources), that point does not, in any way, go against seeing the simultaneous relevance also of the process aspect of freedom in a theory of human rights, or, for that matter, in a theory of justice.

Related to this issue, we should perhaps take the opportunity here to correct a misinterpretation of the place of the capability perspective in a theory of justice. A theory of justice, or more generally an adequate theory of normative collective choice, has to be alive both to the fairness of the processes involved and to the equity and efficiency of the substantive opportunities that people can enjoy. In dealing with the latter, capability can indeed provide a very helpful perspective, in comparison with, say, the Rawlsian concentration on "primary goods." But capability can hardly serve as the sole informational basis for the other considerations, related to processes, that must also be accommodated in normative collective choice theory. Perhaps the point can be seen most easily by considering the different components of Rawls's theory of justice. His "first principle" of justice involves the priority of liberty, and the first part of the "second principle" involves process fairness, through demanding that "positions and offices be open to all." Even though the concerns that lead Rawls to these particular formulations can be dealt with in different ways, not only in the way that Rawls himself addresses them, the force and cogency of these Rawlsian concerns can neither be ignored nor be adequately addressed through relying only the informational base of capabilities.

In contrast, capability comes into its own in dealing with the remainder of the second principle, *viz.* "the Difference Principle" (with its concentration on "primary goods"). The territory that Rawls reserved for the accounting of primary goods, as used in his Difference Principle, would indeed be, we argue, better served by the capability perspective. That does not, however, obliterate in any way the relevance of the rest of the territory of justice, in which process considerations, including liberty and procedural equity. The same plurality of informational base links with the multiplicity of considerations that can be invoked in a theory of human rights. Capabilities and the opportunity aspect of freedom, important as they are, have to be supplemented by considerations of fair processes and the lack of violation of the individual's right to invoke and utilize them.

DUTIES, REASONABLE CONSIDERATION AND IMPERFECT OBLIGATIONS

I turn now from rights to correlative duties. We can, again, proceed from the importance of freedoms and their different aspects. Since freedoms are important, people have reason to ask what they should do to help each other in defending or promoting their respective freedoms. Since violation, or non-realization, of the freedoms underlying significant rights are, in this evaluative system, bad things to happen, even others who are not themselves responsible for causing the violation have a good reason to consider what they should do to help. Nevertheless, the move from a reason for action to help another person, which is easy to see in a consequence-sensitive ethical system, to an actual duty to give reasonable consideration to undertaking such an action might appear, at least at first sight, to be a rather gigantic jump.

However, that sense of distance is largely illusory. The difference would indeed involve an immense escalation if the duty in question were not one of giving reasonable consideration to a possible action, but an absolute obligation to undertake that action, no matter what other values one has and what other commitments one has reason to consider. But that way of seeing one's duties—as compulsory action—is not only at some distance from the acknowledgment of reasons for action, but it also lacks cogency, and even internal coherence. There are many fine deeds for each of which a reason for action exists, but it would typically be impossible to carry out the totality of all those deeds. There is a need for the assessment of priorities and for discrimination in the way the obligation to give reasonable consideration may be followed up by sensible choices of action.

To accept that one has a duty to give reasonable consideration to many different types of actions is not an agreement to tie oneself up in hopeless knots. And it is particularly important in the present context to emphasize the converse: the determination not to get into a pandemonium of practical reasoning is not a ground for denying that one does have a duty to give reasonable consideration to what one can sensibly do for the rights, and the underlying significant and influenceable freedoms, of others.

The demands of reasonable consideration would vary with a great many parameters that may be relevant to a person's practical reasoning. Even though the acknowledgment that certain freedoms qualify as human rights already reflects an assessment of their general importance and their possible influenceability, a person has to go beyond these pervasive features into more specific circumstances in giving reasonable consideration to what he or she, in particular, should do in a specific case. The person has to judge, for example, how important the freedoms and rights are in the case in question compared with other claims on the person's possible actions (involving other rights and freedoms, but also altogether different concerns that a person may, inter alia, sensibly have). Furthermore, the person has to judge the extent to which he or she can make a difference in this case, either acting alone or in conjunction with others.

It will be relevant also to consider what others can be expected to do, and the appropriateness of how the required supportive actions may be shared among possible agents. A great many parametric considerations of these and other kinds will inescapably figure in the reasoned evaluation of what a person should do, even after the need to undertake such an evaluation has been fully accepted. Also, since detailed reflection on what one should do is itself time consuming (and cannot even be actually undertaken for all the ills of the world), the duty of reasonable consideration will not, in a great many cases, translate into an obligation to take on an elaborate scrutiny—only a willingness to do just that, when it seems relevant and appropriate.

The recognition of obligations in relation to the rights and freedoms of all human beings need not, thus, be translated into preposterously demanding commands. And yet, despite the parametric variability of the reach and force of reasonable consideration, the requirement to give such consideration is not by any means vacuous. The basic general obligation is that one must be willing to consider seriously what one should reasonably do, taking note of the relevant parameters of the cases involved. The necessity to ask that question (rather than proceeding on the assumption that we owe nothing to others, unless we have actually harmed them) can be the beginning of a more comprehensive line of ethical reasoning.

The territory of human rights firmly belongs there. The reasoning cannot, however, end there. Given one's limited abilities and reach, and the need for priorities involving different types of obligations as well as the demands of other moral concerns, there are serious exercises of practical reasoning to be undertaken, in which one's various obligations (including "imperfect obligations") must figure, in an explicit or implicit form.

The recognition of human rights is not an insistence that everyone everywhere rises to help prevent every violation of every human right no matter where it occurs. It is, rather, an acknowledgment that if one is in a plausible position to do something effective in preventing the violation of such a right, then one does have an obligation to consider doing just that. It is still possible that other obligations or non-obligational concerns may overwhelm the reason for the particular action in question, but that reason cannot be simply brushed away as being "none of one's business." Loosely specified obligations must not be confused with no obligations at all. Rather, they belong to the important category of duties that Immanuel Kant called "imperfect obligations" (and to which he attached great importance).

It is to be noted that, in this understanding, imperfect obligations are ethical requirements that stretch beyond the fully delineated duties, "the perfect obligations," that specific persons may have to perform particular acts. They involve the demand that serious consideration be given by anyone in a position to provide reasonable help to the person whose human right is threatened.

These "imperfect obligations" firmly correlate, in the same way as fully specified "perfect obligations" do, with the recognition of rights. The difference lies in the nature and form of the obligations, not in the general correspondence between rights and obligations, which apply in the same way to imperfect as well as perfect obligations.

It may be useful to illustrate, with a concrete example, the distinction between different kinds of obligations that, despite their differences in content, relate in a similar way to human rights. Consider a real-life case that occurred in Queens, New York, in 1964, when a woman, Kitty Genovese, was fatally assaulted in full view of many others watching the event from their apartments, who did nothing to help her.

It is plausible to argue that three terrible things happened here, which are distinct but interrelated:

- The woman's freedom—and right—not to be assaulted and killed was violated (this is clearly the principal nastiness in this case);
- The murderer violated the immunity that anyone should have against assault and killing (a violation of a "perfect obligation").

- The others who did nothing whatever to help the victim also transgressed their general—and "imperfect"—obligation to seriously consider providing the help which they could reasonably be expected to provide.

These distinct failings bring out a complex pattern of rights–duties correspondence in a structured ethics, which can help to explicate the evaluative framework of human rights, which yields imperfect as well as perfect obligations. The presumed precision of legal rights is often contrasted with inescapable ambiguities in the ethical claims of human rights. This contrast, however, is not in itself a great embarrassment for ethical claims, including those of imperfect obligations, since a framework of normative reasoning can sensibly allow variations that cannot be easily accommodated in fully specified legal requirements. As Aristotle remarked in the Nicomachean Ethics, we have "to look for precision in each class of things just so far as the nature of the subject admits."

As it happens, however, in the laws of some countries, there is even a legal demand, which can hardly have extreme precision, for providing reasonable help to third parties. For example, in France there is provision for "criminal liability of omissions" in the failure to provide reasonable help to others suffering from particular types of transgressions. Not surprisingly, ambiguities in the application of such laws have proved to be quite large and have been the subject of considerable legal discussion in recent years. The ambiguity of duties of this type, whether in ethics or in law, would be difficult to escape if third-party obligations of others in general are given some room, and this cannot be avoided for an adequate theory of human rights.

RECOGNITION, AGITATION AND LEGISLATION

While the preceding analysis has been concerned with giving reasonable consideration to actions in general that people can undertake in defending or advancing the human rights of others, it is the legislation of human rights, along with their institutionalization, that has tended to receive the lion's share of attention in the theoretical literature in this field. It is this legislative outlook that has also been firmly incorporated in much of the institutional understanding of human rights. However, while legislation is an important domain of public action, there are other ways and means which are also important and often effective in advancing the cause of recognized human rights.

First, under what can be called the "recognition route" (to be distinguished from the "legislative route"), there is acknowledgment but not necessarily any legalization or institutional enforcement of a class of claims that are seen as fundamental human rights. The Universal Declaration of Human Rights, sponsored by the United Nations in 1948, which was perhaps the most important move that promoted global activities on human rights in the last century, falls solidly into this category (even though, as was discussed earlier, the framers of the Declaration had also hoped that it would lead to specific bills of rights in different countries). Subsequently, there has been a sequence of other international declarations, often through the United Nations, giving recognition, rather than a legal and coercive status, to various general demands, for example the "Declaration on the Right to Development," signed in 1986. This approach is motivated by the idea that the ethical force of human rights is made more powerful in practice through giving it social recognition and an acknowledged status, even when no enforcement is instituted.

A second line of advance goes beyond recognition to active agitation. There can be organized advocacy urging compliance with certain basic claims of all human beings that are seen as human rights, and there can also be monitoring of violations of these rights and attempts to generate effective social pressure. The global NGOs have increasingly been involved in advancing human rights, through public discussion and support, on the one hand, and publicizing and criticizing violations, on the other.

These efforts have come not only from dedicated human rights organizations, such as Human Rights Watch and Amnesty International, but also from broader organizations, such as OXFAM, Médicins Sans Frontièrs, the Red Cross, Save the Children, and Action Aid. The rights invoked in this "agitation route" may or may not have any legal status in the country in question, but advocacy and support are not necessarily rendered useless by the absence of legal backing. Furthermore, even when some identified human rights have legal status, good enforcement of the relevant legislation may also call for public activism, which is to be distinguished from the process of legislation itself.

The third approach is, of course, that of "legislation." Even though the ethics of human rights must not be seen merely as "parents" of "human rights laws," it is certainly the case that many such legislations have been encouraged or inspired by considerations of human rights. Many actual laws have been enacted by individual states, or by associations of states, which gave legal force to certain rights seen as basic human rights. For example, the European Court of Human Rights, established in 1950 following the European Convention, can consider cases brought by individuals from the signatory states against violations of human rights. This has been supplemented by the Human Rights Act of 1998, aimed at incorporating the main provisions of the European Convention into domestic law, with an overseeing role of the European Court to see "just satisfaction" of these provisions in domestic judgments. Many other examples can be given from different parts of the world. The "legislative route" has had much active use.

There is an interesting question about the appropriate domain of the legislative route. It would be a mistake, we would argue, to presume in general that if a human right is important, then it must be ideal to legislate it into a precisely specified legal right. For example, recognizing and defending a wife's moral right to be consulted in family decisions, even in a traditionally sexist society, may well be extremely important, and can plausibly satisfy the threshold conditions needed to qualify as a human right. And yet the advocates of this human right, who emphasize, correctly, its far-reaching ethical and political relevance, can quite possibly agree that it is not sensible to make this human right into, in Herbert Hart's language, a "coercive legal rule" (perhaps with the result that a husband would be taken in custody if he were to fail to consult his wife). The necessary change would have to be brought about in other ways. Because of the importance of communication, advocacy, exposure and informed public discussion, human rights can have influence without necessarily depending on coercive legislation.

Similarly, the moral or political entitlement, which can easily be seen as a human right, of a somewhat slow speaker not to be snubbed in an open public meeting by a rudely articulate sprinter may well be important both for the self-respect of the leisurely speaker and for public good, but it is not likely to be a good subject for punitive legislation. The protection of that human right would have to be sought elsewhere. The effectiveness of the human rights perspective does not rest on seeing them invariably as putative proposals for legislation.

ECONOMIC AND SOCIAL RIGHTS

I turn now to criticisms that have been particularly aimed against extending the idea of human rights to include economic and social rights, such as the right not to be hungry, or the right to basic education or to medical attention. Even though these rights did not figure in the classic presentations of rights of human beings in, say, the U.S. Declaration of Independence, or French "rights of man," they are very much a part of the contemporary domain of what Cass Sunstein calls the "rights revolution." The legitimacy of including these claims within the general class of human rights has been challenged through two specific lines of reproach, which we shall call, respectively, the institutionalization critique and the feasibility critique.

The institutionalization critique, which is aimed particularly at economic and social rights, relates to the general issue of the exact correspondence between authentic rights and precisely formulated correlate duties. Such a correspondence, it is argued, would exist only when a right is institutionalized. Onora O'Neill has presented this line of criticism with force:

- Unfortunately much writing and rhetoric on rights heedlessly proclaims universal rights to goods and services, and in particular "welfare rights," as well as to other social, economic and cultural rights that are prominent in international Charters and Declarations, without showing what connects each presumed right-holder to some specific obligation-bearer(s), which leaves the content of these supposed rights wholly obscure.... Some advocates of universal economic, social and cultural rights go no further than to emphasize that they can be institutionalized, which is true. But the point of difference is that they must be institutionalized: if they are not there is no right.

In responding to this significant criticism, we have to invoke the understanding, already discussed, that obligations can be both perfect and imperfect. Even the classical "first generational" rights, like freedom from assault, can be seen as yielding imperfect obligations on others, as was illustrated with the example of the case of assault on Kitty Genovese in public view in New York. Depending on institutional possibilities, economic and social rights may similarly call for both perfect and imperfect obligations. There is a large area of fruitful public discussion and possibly effective pressure, concerning what the society and the state, even an impoverished one, can do to prevent violations of certain basic economic or social rights (associated with, say, the prevalence of famines, or chronic undernourishment, or absence of medical care).

Indeed, the supportive activities of social organizations are often aimed precisely at institutional change, and these activities can be seen as part of imperfect obligations that individuals and groups have in a society where basic human rights are violated. Onora O'Neill is right to emphasize the importance of institutions for the realization of "welfare rights" (and even for economic and social rights in general), but the ethical significance of these rights provide good grounds for seeking realization through institutional expansion and reform. This can be helped through a variety of approaches, including demanding and agitating for appropriate legislation, and the supplementation of legal demands by political recognition and social monitoring. To deny the ethical status of these claims would be to ignore the reasoning that motivates these constructive activities.

The feasibility critique proceeds from the argument that even with the best of efforts, it may not be feasible to arrange the realization of many of the alleged economic and social rights for all. This would have been only an empirical observation (of some interest of its own), but it is made into an allegedly powerful criticism of the acceptance of these claimed rights on the basis of the presumption, largely undefended, that recognized human rights must, of necessity, be wholly accomplishable. If this presumption were accepted that would have the effect of immediately putting many so-called economic and social rights outside the domain of possible human rights, especially in the poorer societies. Maurice Cranston puts the argument thus:

- The traditional political and civil rights are not difficult to institute. For the most part, they require governments, and other people generally, to leave a man alone.... The problems posed by claims to economic and social rights, however, are of another order altogether. How can governments of those parts of Asia, Africa, and South America, where industrialization has hardly begun, be reasonably called upon to provide social security and holidays with pay for millions of people who inhabit those places and multiply so swiftly?

In assessing this line of rejection, we have to ask: why should complete feasibility be a condition of cogency of human rights when the objective is to work towards enhancing their actual realization, if necessary through expanding their feasibility? The understanding that some rights are not fully realised, and may not even be fully realizable under present circumstances, does not, in itself, entail anything like the conclusion that these are, therefore, not rights at all. Rather, that understanding suggests the need to work towards changing the prevailing circumstances to make the unrealised rights realizable, and ultimately, realised.

It is also worth noting in this context that the question of feasibility is not confined to economic and social rights only; it is a much more widespread problem. Even for liberties and autonomies, to guarantee that a person is "left alone," which Cranston seems to think is simple to guarantee, has never been particularly easy. That elementary fact, easily seen always, cannot but be rather clearly recognized now, at least since September 11, 2001 (and more recent events). If the current feasibility of guaranteeing complete and comprehensive fulfillment were made into a necessary condition for the cogency of every right, then not only economic and social rights, but also liberties, autonomies and even political rights may well fall far short of cogency.

THE REACH OF PUBLIC REASONING

How can we judge the acceptability of claims to human rights and assess the challenges they may face? How would such a disputation—or a defence—proceed? we would argue that like the assessment of other ethical claims, there must be some test of open and informed scrutiny, and it is to such a scrutiny that we have to look in order to proceed to a disavowal or an affirmation. The status of these ethical claims must be dependent ultimately on their survivability in unobstructed discussion. In this sense, the viability of human rights is linked with what John Rawls has called "public reasoning" and its role in "ethical objectivity." Indeed, the connection between public reasoning and the formulation and use of human rights is extremely important to understand.

Any general plausibility that these ethical claims, or their denials, have is dependent, on this theory, on their survival and flourishing when they encounter unobstructed discussion and scrutiny, along with adequately wide informational availability. The force of a claim for a human right would be seriously undermined if it were possible to show that they are unlikely to survive open public scrutiny. But contrary to a commonly offered reason for skepticism and rejection, the case for human rights cannot be discarded simply by pointing to the fact (even when that is the case) that in politically and socially repressive regimes, which do not allow open public discussion, many of these human rights are not taken seriously at all. Uncurbed critical scrutiny is essential for dismissal as well as for defence. Even as far as use is concerned, the fact that monitoring of violations of human rights and the procedure of "naming and shaming" can be so effective (at least in putting the violators on the defensive) is some indication of the reach of public reasoning when information becomes available and ethical arguments are allowed rather than suppressed.

However, it is important not to confine the domain of public reasoning to a given society only, especially in the case of human rights, in view of the inescapably non-parochial nature of these rights, which are meant to apply to all human beings. This is in contrast with Rawls's inclination, particularly in his later works, to limit such public confrontation within the boundaries of each particular nation (or each "people," as Rawls calls this regional collectivity), for determining what would be just, at least in domestic affairs. We can demand, on the contrary, that the discussion include, even for domestic justice (if only to avoid parochial prejudices and also to examine a broader range of counterarguments), views also from "a certain distance."

The necessity of this was powerfully identified by Adam Smith:

- We can never survey our own sentiments and motives, we can never form any judgment concerning them; unless we remove ourselves, as it were, from our own natural station, and endeavour to view them as at a certain distance from us. But we can do this in no other way than by endeavouring to view them with the eyes of other people, or as other people are likely to view them.

The universalist nature of Adam Smith's approach raises the question whether distant people can, in fact, provide useful scrutiny of local issues, given what are taken to be "uncrossable" barriers of culture. One of Edmund Burke's criticisms of the French declaration of the "rights of man" and its universalist spirit was concerned with disputing the acceptability of that notion in other cultures. Burke argued that "the liberties and the restrictions vary with times and circumstances, and admit of infinite modifications, that cannot be settled upon any abstract rule." The argument that, for this, or some similar, reason, the universality that underlies the notion of human rights is profoundly mistaken can be found in many other writings as well.

For example, Rosa Luxemburg, a leading Marxist thinker and political leader in the early twentieth century, invoked a similar line of criticism of what she called the "metaphysical cliché of the type of 'rights of man' and 'rights of the citizen'." However, a scrutiny of Rosa Luxemburg's real concerns brings out the remarkable fact that she persistently invoked universalist principles herself, as is quite standard in the Marxist tradition (consider: "from each according to his ability, to each according to his needs"). Rather, Luxemburg was keen on emphasizing that the substantiation of these principles must depend on specific circumstances that obtain. Shorn of the rhetoric, there is, in fact, no particular difficulty in using basic universalist principles in general, while taking note of Luxemburg's pointer to the relevance of local circumstances and regional conditions in appropriately contingent, or parametric, specification of the exact demands of human rights.

However, a belief in uncrossable barriers between the values of different cultures has surfaced and resurfaced repeatedly over the centuries, and they are forcefully articulated today. The claim of magnificent uniqueness, and often of superiority, has sometimes come from critics of "Western values," varying from champions of regional ethics (well illustrated by the fuss in the 1990s about the peerless excellence of "Asian values"), or religious or cultural separatists (with or without being accompanied by fundamentalism of one kind or another). Sometimes, however, the claim of uniqueness has come from Western particularists.

A good example is Samuel Huntington's insistence that the "West was West long before it was modern," and his claim that "a sense of individualism and a tradition of individual rights and liberties" are "unique among civilized societies." Similarly, no less a historian of ideas than Gertrude Himmelfarb has argued that ideas of "justice," "right," "reason" and "love of humanity" are "predominantly, perhaps even uniquely, Western values." We have discussed these diagnoses elsewhere. Contrary to cultural stereotypes, the histories of different countries in the world have shown considerable variations over time as well as between different traditions within the same country. The championing of open public discussion, tolerating and encouraging different points of view, has a long history in many countries in the world.

Indeed, some of the earliest open general meetings aimed specifically at settling disputes between different points of view took place in India in the so-called Buddhist councils, the first of which was held shortly after Gautama Buddha's death twenty-five hundred years ago. The grandest of these councils, the third, occurred under the patronage of Emperor Ashoka in the third century bce. Ashoka also tried to codify and propagate what must have been among the earliest formulations of rules for public discussion, a kind of ancient version of the nineteenth-century Robert's Rules of Order. He demanded, for example, "restraint in regard to speech, so that there should be no extolment of one's own sect or disparagement of other sects on inappropriate occasions, and it should be moderate even in appropriate occasions." Even when engaged in arguing, "other sects should be duly honoured in every way on all occasions."

To consider another historical example, in early seventh-century Japan, the Buddhist Prince Shotoku, who was regent to his mother, Empress Suiko, produced the so-called constitution of seventeen articles, in 604 ad. The constitution insisted, much in the spirit of the Magna Carta to be signed six centuries later in 1215 ad: "Decisions on important matters should not be made by one person alone. They should be discussed with many."

When, in the twelfth century, the Jewish philosopher Maimonedes had to flee an intolerant Europe to try to safeguard his human right to stick to his own religious beliefs and practice, he sought shelter in Emperor Saladin's Egypt (via Fez and Palestine), and found an honoured position in the court of this Muslim emperor. Several hundred years later, when, in Agra, the Moghul emperor of India, Akbar, was arguing, and legislating, on the government's duty to uphold the right to religious freedom of all citizens, the European Inquisitions were still going on, and Giardino Bruno was burnt at the stake in Rome, in 1600. In his autobiography, Long Walk to Freedom, Nelson Mandela describes how he learned about democracy and individual rights, as a young boy, by seeing the proceedings of the local meetings held in the regent's house in Mqhekezweni:

- Everyone who wanted to speak did so. It was democracy in its purest form. There may have been a hierarchy of importance among the speakers, but everyone was heard, chief and subject, warrior and medicine man, shopkeeper and farmer, landowner and laborer.

Not only are the differences on the subject of freedoms and rights that actually exist between different societies often much exaggerated, but also there is, typically, little note taken of substantial variations within each local culture—over time and even at a point of time (in particular, right now). What are taken to be "foreign" criticisms often correspond to internal criticisms from non-mainstream groups. If, say, Iranian dissidents are imprisoned by an authoritarian regime precisely because of their heterodoxy, any suggestion that they should be seen as "ambassadors of Western values" rather than as "Iranian dissidents" would only add serious insult to manifest injury.

This issue is particularly important in determining what may be taken to be culturally "partisan" in a world of many cultural differences. Charles Beitz rejects, rightly, the plausibility of seeing the use of human rights as emanating from a "supposedly symmetrical relationship to the conception of political justice or legitimacy to be found in the world's cultures," and he goes on to seek their justification in terms of "the role they play in international relations." But how should this "role" be judged in terms of its acceptability, and in what sense should such an evaluation be culturally "partisan"?

If the reasoning presented here is right, then we must distinguish between:

- The values that are dominantly favoured in a society (no matter how repressive it is), and
- The values that could be expected to gain wider adherence and support when open discussion is allowed, when information about other societies becomes more freely available, and when disagreements with the established views can be expressed and defended without suppression and fear.

Being "non-partisan" requires respecting the participation of people from any corner of the earth, which is not the same thing as accepting the prevailing priorities in existing societies when information is extremely restricted and discussions and disagreements are not permitted. Widespread acceptability, which must be distinguished from pre-existing ubiquitous acceptance, is an important issue in any social evaluation, even in dealing with the role that human rights play in international relations.

There does, of course, exist considerable variation in the balance of manifest opinions and observed preconceptions in different countries and different societies. These opinions and beliefs often reflect, as Adam Smith noted in a powerfully illuminating analysis, strong influence of existing practices in different parts of the world, along with a lack of broader intellectual engagement. The need for open scrutiny, with unrestrained access to information (including that about practices elsewhere in the world and the experiences there), is particularly great because of these connections. Which is precisely why Adam Smith's insistence on the necessity of viewing actions and practices from a "certain distance" is so important for substantive ethics in general and the understanding of human rights in particular. In a stage entitled "On the Influence of Custom and Fashion upon the Sentiments of Moral Approbation and Disapprobation," Smith illustrated his contention:

- ... the murder of new-born infants was a practice allowed of in almost all the states of Greece, even among the polite and civilized Athenians; and whenever the circumstances of the parent rendered it inconvenient to bring up the child, to abandon it to hunger, or to wild beasts, was regarded without blame or censure.... Uninterrupted custom had by this time so thoroughly authorized the practice, that not only the loose maxims of the world tolerated this barbarous prerogative, but even the doctrine of philosophers, which ought to have been more just and accurate, was led away by the established custom, and upon this, as upon many other occasions, instead of censuring, supported the horrible abuse, by far-fetched considerations of public utility. Aristotle talks of it as of what the magistrates ought upon many occasions to encourage. Plato is of the same opinion, and, with all that love of mankind which seems to animate all his writings, no where marks this practice with disapprobation.

What are taken to be perfectly "normal" and "sensible" in an insulated society may not be able to survive a broad-based and less limited examination once the parochial gut reactions are replaced by critical scrutiny, including an awareness of variations of practices and norms across the world. Scrutiny from a distance may have something to offer in the assessment of practices as different from each other as the stoning of adulterous women in Taliban's Afghanistan and the abounding use of capital punishment (sometimes with mass jubilation) in parts of the United States. This is the kind of issue that made Smith insist that "the eyes of the rest of mankind" must be invoked to understand whether "a punishment appears equitable." Ultimately, the discipline of critical moral scrutiny requires, among other things, "endeavouring to view [our sentiments and beliefs] with the eyes of other people, or as other people are likely to view them." The need for interactions across the borders can be as important in rich societies as they are in poorer ones. The point to note here is not so much whether we are permitted to make cross-boundary scrutiny, but that the discipline of critical assessment of moral sentiments, no matter how locally established they are, demands that such scrutiny be undertaken.

A CONCLUDING REMARK

I have tried to present, the elements of a theory of human rights, which sees them as pronouncements in social ethics, sustainable by open public reasoning. They may or may not be reflected in a legal framework through, say, specific "human rights legislation," but there are also other ways of implementing human rights (including public recognition, agitation and monitoring). Since the main themes developed in this object were specifically, we shall not try to provide a further summary in this concluding part. we should, however, emphasize that the understanding and viability of human rights are, in this perspective, intimately linked with the reach of public discussion, between persons and across borders. The viability and universality of human rights are dependent on their ability to survive open critical scrutiny in public reasoning. The methodology of public scrutiny draws on Rawlsian understanding of "objectivity" in ethics, but the impartiality that is needed cannot be confined within the borders of a nation.

The fact that authoritarian orders are typically quite afraid of uncensored news media and of uncurbed public discussion, which make them resort often enough to suppression (including censorship, intimidation, incarceration, and even execution), provides some indirect evidence that the influence of public reasoning can indeed be quite large. That influence also lies behind the effectiveness of the interactive ways and means, including social recognition, informational monitoring and public agitation, which human rights activists tend to use. There is certainly a need for a fuller understanding of the associative nature of the acceptability of values, and this requires us to go well beyond lazy reliance on the given mores of the dominant social groups in the respective societies.

To conclude, despite their practical preoccupations, human rights activists have reason enough to pay attention to the skepticism that the idea of human rights generates among many legal and political theorists. These doubts have to be—and can be—addressed. But it is also important to note that the conceptual understanding of human rights, in turn, can benefit substantially from considering the reasoning that moves the activists and the range and effectiveness of practical actions they undertake, including recognition, monitoring and agitation, in addition to legislation. Not only is conceptual clarity important for practice, the richness of practice, we have argued, is also critically relevant for understanding the concept and reach of human rights. There is, we must conclude, no great deficit in the balance of trade between theory and practice.

5

Social and Human Rights Budgeting

TRANSLATING HUMAN RIGHTS INTO THE NATIONAL BUDGET

If you want to protect human rights, you need to engage in economic and fiscal policies. This insight is at the origin of human rights budgeting initiatives. Democratisation and decentralisation after the end of the Cold War as well as a stronger emphasis on good governance by policy actors have resulted in an increased integration of human rights perspectives into macroeconomic policy.

Yet it remains an open question as to how human rights such as the right to food or the right to education can be translated into something tangible like the national budget. First, it is difficult to integrate a specific human right into a budget because human rights are interdependent and relate to each other. Second, it is controversial to conceptualise a minimum core content of a human right for practical purposes because there is a risk of reducing the original broadness this particular right implies. Third, it is problematic to define maximum available resources for the realisation of a human right.

Fourth, you need to develop suitable indicators and benchmarks since not every aspect of a human right can be quantified. Fifth, CSOs must be able to dig into the budget processes. Moreover, in some countries the budget cycle is on the verge of becoming more and more affected by donor interests. With an increasing share of Official Development Assistance provided in form of budget support, governments in many Southern countries are no longer only accountable to their own parliaments, but to foreign donors as well. In the case of Honduras, the government even pleaded with the parliament not to propose changes to its budget plan because it had taken months to find an agreement with international donors. Thus, it is questionable whether human rights budgeting represents an effective tool for making governments accountable–an enormous challenge for human rights budgeting initiatives.

Nevertheless, the Social Watch Report 2008 stimulated national coalitions to stand up to this challenge and analyse the relation between the economy and human rights in their respective countries. They did it from very different angles. Some civil society initiatives focused on the regulatory framework; others addressed policy incoherence between trade policies and human rights. Various initiatives sought to enhance the transparency of the budgeting process while others focused more on participatory budgeting, gender budgeting or the budgeting of specific rights. An important approach discussed was frontloading, *i.e.* to look at the draft budget Ex-ante instead of analysing the adapted budget ex-post. How much should be allocated *e.g.* to primary education in order to meet human rights criteria? Civil society experiences from India, the Philippines, South Africa and Argentina illustrate how budget analysis and advocacy from a human rights perspective can be done in practice.

INDIA: TAKING IN THE POOR AND MARGINALISED

In India, the 'center of budget and Governance engages in budgeting initiatives for marginalised groups in society: Dalits, *i.e.* people of low caste still discriminated against, tribals, women, children and inhabitants of the isolated North-Eastern region. The main role of Indian CSOs is to demystify available budget information. Knowledge is power in a political system in which most people are not able to understand the budgeting process. While data from primary sources is the foundation for good budget work, many important ministries like the Ministry of Finance are not reporting. Thus, CBGA is often forced to rely on secondary data.

Despite the lack of data, CBGA clearly identifies a large gap between aspiration and reality. India's national budget actually provides for 16% of the total allocation of every ministry in the central government to be spent on Dalits and 8% on tribals. However, there are serious doubts behind the implementation of these schemes. In reality, only half of these percentages are allocated. Therefore, 'CBGA supported Dalit groups in a coordinated boycott of the national budget 2008/9 under the slogan "The Government has stolen our 8%" which attracted significant media attention.

Moreover, the concept of gender budgeting has already been part of the national budget since 1985. However, 'CBGA demonstrated that allocations had been decreasing in recent years to merely 3.6% of the total budget in 2008/9. Besides, of these low gender allocations only 44.7% had actually been spent. Public expenditures thus only reach 7% of the most marginalised women. CGA attempts to bring about change by research, budget tracking, capacity building, and advocacy measures. Until now, it primarily engages in ex-post analysis, not in ex-ante analysis. Thus, it monitors how much is spent for marginalised groups in the actual budget. Projecting how much should be spent in future budgets is a new challenge ahead.

PHILIPPINES: THE ALTERNATIVE BUDGET INITIATIVE

CSOs in the Philippines are frontrunners with regard to human rights budgeting. Within two years only, the Alternative Budget Initiative of Social Watch Philippines has become a serious and important player in the budgeting process.

Based on the Millennium Development Goals, it has addressed five major concerns in a comprehensive alternative budget proposal to the government: Education, environment, food and agriculture, health, macroeconomics and debt. As soon as the President of the Philippines submits the proposed budget to the two houses of Parliament, ABI crafting process gets underway. ABI analyses the budget and redistributes expenses according to the five concerns. For example: When two helicopters were allocated to the President's office, ABI reduced this number to one and reallocated the rest of the expenses to educational purposes. After the end of the crafting process, legislators are briefed.

Then, contact with the media is established and a press conference convened in which the alternative budget is presented to the public. In many cases, ABI is in direct contact with the legislators who negotiate the President's budget proposal in parliament. The ultimate control of the budget process, however, lies with the President who can use his veto power. Then, ABI's main challenge is to ensure that the concessions made by Parliament throughout the budget cycle are not revoked.

In 2008, ABI was able to present its alternative budget to the Committee on Appropriations which has jurisdiction over all discretionary spending legislation. Since then a resolution has been filed which institutionalises the participation of CSOs in public hearings in the annual budget deliberations–a milestone for human rights budgeting initiatives in the Philippines. The nongovernment organizations making up the ABI consult their constituents, which are people's organizations working at the ground level, to come up with critical data and comprehensive analyses on what is most needed in the budget. For instance, the education cluster's proposals for more school buildings and allocations for teachers' benefits are based on actual research results where serious lack of school facilities as well as poverty experienced by many teachers who do not receive their wages and benefits cause grave implications to the quality of education. The consultation with constituents provide basis for the Alternative Budget Initiative's call that government should increase allocations for social development to address underspending on the Millennium Development Goals.

SOUTH AFRICA: CHILDREN RIGHTS RESEARCH

The Imali Ye Mwana Net-work monitors government policies, the national budget and its implementation commitments in eight different southern African countries. Its objective is to increase public resources and their efficient use for the fulfilment of children's socio-economic rights. For this purpose Imali Ye Mwana relies on two key human rights principles as laid down in the Child Rights Convention. It calls upon governments to achieve progressively the full realization of the rights of the child and to undertake measures to the maximum extent of their available resources. One of the major challenges for the network is the lack of reliable and disaggregated information on children and budgetary expenditures. The existing mistrust between civil society initiatives and government officials makes it difficult for Imali Ye Mwana to get access to information law and practices. Furthermore, many CSOs still think that rights budgeting is a very scientific approach and fail to identify a link to their own programmes.

Consequently, it is difficult for Imali Ye Mwana to promote child rights budgeting when it is not even mainstreamed in other civil society initiatives. Imali Ye Mwana experience shows that child rights budgeting is far more successful when linked to a broader advocacy campaign. For example, strong advocacy work in Zambia resulted in the prioritisation of children's programmes in the national budget and the access to information on disaggregated budget allocations in education, health and welfare and community development. Child rights clubs were established throughout Zambian schools. Thus, even if the members of Imali Ye Mwana use different methodologies, they are aware of the importance of networks and alliances for their advocacy work.

The activities of the network also prove that sustainable capacity building initiatives should target both decision makers and beneficiaries. On the one hand, this unveils the potential of children and ensures their ownership; on the other hand, policy makers become aware of children's needs. This is also one reason why Imali Ye Mwana plans to focus increasingly on the right to education in its future work.

ARGENTINA: THE USE OF LEGAL INSTRUMENTS

In Buenos Aires the right to education is far from being granted to all children. Through its budget work, the Civil Association for equity and justice (ACIj) fights for a better access of the poor to public education. The programme aims to investigate the socio-economic discrimination and empowerment of the civil society in the slums of Argentina's capital. In 2006, (ACIj) discovered that more than 6000 children were not going to school because of a lack of vacancies. Further investigation proved that Buenos Aires was a staging ground for socio-economic discrimination. More than 70% of the violations of the right to education occurred in the poorest districts of the municipality.

An analysis of the city's budget further revealed that the government was allocating and expending less money in the poorest districts. This provoked (ACIj) to file a legal suit, using media and video advocacy as well as intense community work. At first, ACIJ used the procedure of budget analysis only to obtain a proper diagnosis of the situation. But it quickly developed into a powerful tool, contributing decisively to win the court case. (ACIj) was so successful with its advocacy work that it was ultimately allowed to participate in the annual budget law discussions of the municipality. Since September 2008 it has been involved in the budgeting process on a regular basis. But there are huge challenges ahead.

Access to the information necessary for budget work remains critical. Public officials must become more aware of the interconnectedness of the budget and human rights. For this purpose interdisciplinary work and creative advocacy strategies are needed in order to raise even more awareness. Additionally, socio-economic discrimination must also be addressed outside of Buenos Aires, where the situation is probably worse, and the inclusion of children into the budgeting process has not yet been realised.

LEARNING FROM THE SOUTH

Concerning human rights budgeting, CSOs in the South are way ahead of those in the North. But there is a growing awareness of the need to analyse budget from a human rights perspective in the North as well. Feasibility studies both in Europe and Germany clearly confirm the importance of budgeting as a development tool for the inclusion of human rights in the national budget.

However, there still exists a certain "paternalistic bias" in the North according to which human rights budgeting is only needed in the South and not in the North. This bias is well reflected in the fact that both the European Union (EU) and Germany actually demand human rights budgeting from EU accession states as well as from development partners such as Afghanistan without doing it at home.

In order to build up a human rights budgeting initiative in Germany, this practice clearly needs to change. German federal states such as Berlin, in which gender budgeting is already seen as an integral element of the budget process, are good examples of what is possible if there is a clear political will. Marginalised groups have to be given the chance to take part in human rights budgeting initiatives in order to talk with them and not only about them. A German human rights budgeting initiative could possibly function as role model for others. Therefore, it was considered to be important to initiate such a project in Germany.

If implemented, a German human rights budgeting initiative must draw upon the lessons learned in other countries such as India, the Philippines, South Africa or Argentina. Their experiences show that a German budgeting initiative should not just focus on economic, social and cultural rights, but also take into account civil and political rights. It should empower the beneficiaries of its initiative, particularly the marginalised groups in society. Furthermore, it would be indispensable to actively cooperate with people in the ministries and to closely involve the media.

Beyond questions of access, a human rights budgeting initiative would need to build up its own capacity to dig into the budget processes. CSOs would probably have to rely on the expertise of researchers and legal experts to be able to identify human rights violations in their own countries. In this respect, the budget analysis project of Queen's University of Belfast is one initiative that provides excellent groundwork. It has undergone the ambitious attempt to map comparative and international efforts in relation to budget analysis and economic and social rights. Human rights budgeting groups are eagerly anticipating its first report.

6

The Scope of Human Rights

INTRODUCTION

In their contemporary manifestation, human rights are a set of individual and collective rights that have been formally promoted and protected through international and domestic law since the 1948 Universal Declaration of Human Rights. Arguments, theories, protections, and violations of such rights, however, have been in existence for much longer but since the Universal Declaration, the evolution of their express legal protection has grown rapidly. Today, the numerous international treaties on human rights promulgated since the Universal Declaration to which an increasingly large number of nation states are a party define the core content of human rights that ought to be protected across categories of civil, political, economic, social, and solidarity rights.

CATEGORIES OF HUMAN RIGHTS

The collection of human rights protected by international law draws on a longer of tradition of rights from philosophy, history, and normative political theory and now includes three sets, or categories of rights that have become useful shortcuts for talking about human rights among scholars and practitioners in the field, and will be used throughout the remainder of this thesis.

These three categories are:

- Civil and political rights,
- Economic, social, and cultural rights, and
- Solidarity rights.

It has been typically understood that individuals and certain groups are bearers of human rights, while the state is the prime organ that can protect and/or violate human rights. The political sociology of human rights argues that historical struggles by oppressed groups have yielded a greater degree of protection for larger sets of individuals and groups whose rights have not always been guaranteed while the state itself, in attempt to construct a national identity and fortify its capacity to govern, has extended various rights protections to increasingly larger sectors of society. The struggle for human rights and contemporary arguments about their continued promotion and protection have extended beyond exclusive attention on the legal obligations of nation states and have started focussing on how non-state actors, such as guerrilla movements, terrorist organisations, warlords, multi-national corporations, and international financial institutions, may be conceived as responsible for human rights violations and how such entities may carry an obligation for their protection. These different categories of human rights are considered in turn.

Civil and political rights uphold the sanctity of the individual before the law and guarantee his or her ability to participate freely in civil, economic, and political society. Civil rights include such rights as the right to life, liberty, and personal security; the right to equality before the law; the right of protection from arbitrary arrest; the right to the due process of law; the right to a fair trial; and the right to religious freedom and worship. When protected, civil rights guarantee one's 'personhood' and freedom from state-sanctioned interference or violence. Political rights include such rights as the right to speech and expression; the rights to assembly and association; and the right to vote and political participation.

Political rights thus guarantee individual rights to involvement in public affairs and the affairs of state. In many ways, both historically and theoretically, civil and political rights have been considered fundamental human rights for which all nation states have a duty and responsibility to uphold. They have also been seen as so-called 'negative' rights since they merely require the absence of their violation in order to be upheld. Social and economic rights include such rights as the right to a family; the right to education; the right to health and well being; the right to work and fair remuneration; the right to form trade unions and free associations; the right to leisure time; and the right to social security. When protected, these rights help promote individual flourishing, social and economic development, and self-esteem.

Cultural rights, on the other hand, include such rights as the right to the benefits of culture; the right to indigenous land, rituals, and shared cultural practices; and the right to speak one's own language and 'mother tongue' education. Cultural rights are meant to maintain and promote sub-national cultural affiliations and collective identities, and protect minority communities against the incursions of national assimilationist and nation-building projects.

In contrast to the first set of rights, this second set of social, economic, and cultural rights is often seen as an aspirational and programmatic set of rights that national governments ought to strive to achieve through progressive implementation. They have thus been considered less fundamental than the first set of rights and are seen as 'positive' rights whose realisation depends heavily on the fiscal capacity of states.

Solidarity rights, which include rights to public goods such as development and the environment, seek to guarantee that all individuals and groups have the right to share in the benefits of the earth's natural resources, as well as those goods and products that are made through processes of economic growth, expansion, and innovation. Many of these rights are transnational in that they make claims against wealthy nations to redistribute wealth to poor nations, cancel or reduce international debt obligations, pay compensation for past imperial and colonial adventures, reduce environmental degradation, and help promote policies for sustainable development. Of the three sets of rights, this final set is the newest and most progressive and reflects a certain reaction against the worst effects of globalization, as well as the relative effectiveness of 'green' political ideology and social mobilization around concerns for the health of the planet.

DIMENSIONS OF HUMAN RIGHTS

The distinction between these sets of rights follows the historical struggle for them, the appearance of the separate international instruments that protect them, the philosophical arguments concerning their status, and the methodological issues surrounding their measurement. But significant sections of the human rights community have challenged these traditional distinctions between 'generations' of human rights and have sought to establish the general claim that all rights are indivisible and mutually reinforcing, a sentiment that found formal expression in the 1993 Vienna Declaration and Programme of Action.

Such a challenge suggests that it is impossible to talk about certain sets of human rights in isolation, since the protection of one right may be highly contingent on the protection of other rights. For example, full protection of the right to vote is largely meaningless in societies that do not have adequate health, education, and social welfare provision, since high rates of illiteracy and poverty may mean the de facto disenfranchisement of large sectors of the population. Equally, those interested in combating torture need to examine possible underlying socio-economic, cultural, and organizational reasons for the practice of torture, which themselves may rely on the variable protection of other human rights.

This human rights challenge also suggests that there is a false dichotomy between negative and positive rights that tends to privilege civil and political rights over economic and social rights, since the protection of the former appears less dependent on state resources than the latter. One response to this false dichotomy is to claim that 'all rights are positive' since the full protection of all categories of human rights ultimately relies on the relative fiscal capacity of states. In this view, the protection of property rights requires a well-funded judiciary, police force, and fire service, as well as a well-developed infrastructure that can relay information, goods, and services in the event that property is under threat in some way. A similar argument can be made about guaranteeing the right to vote. Beyond prohibiting intimidation and discrimination at the polls, running a free and fair election requires a tremendous amount of financial support, technology, and infrastructure, the need for which has been illustrated dramatically by the highly contested process and result of the 2000 Presidential Election in the United States. The prevention of torture involves training and education within police and security forces, which entails the need for significant financial resources from the state.

Another response to the traditional division between positive and negative human rights is to view them has having positive and negative dimensions, the full delineation of which is essential for human rights measurement. By claiming that all rights are positive, we may lose sight of significant negative characteristics of human rights. While it is clearly possible to see how civil and political rights have positive characteristics, it is equally possible to see how economic and social rights have significant negative characteristics. For example, just like torture by the state is seen as preventable if only the state refrained from torturing, discrimination in public education and healthcare is equally preventable if only the state refrained from so discriminating. In this way, it is equally possible to have a 'violations approach' to studying the promotion and protection of economic, social, and cultural rights as it is to studying the promotion and protection of civil and political rights.

A conceptualisation of human rights looks if we are to include their positive and negative dimensions. The table is a 2 × 3 matrix resulting from three categories of human rights, each with corresponding positive and negative dimensions. Positive dimensions include those actions that states can take to provide resources and policies for improving the protection of human rights while negative dimensions are those actions that states do that deliberately violate human rights. Certain cells in the matrix have been well covered in the theory and practice of human rights. For example, the negative dimensions of civil and political rights in Cell II are the traditional focus of human rights international standards, systems, and mechanisms for reporting and redress; monitoring, advocacy, and campaigns from human rights non-governmental organisations; and much of the academic scholarship in political science. Equally, the positive dimensions of economic, social, and cultural rights in Cell III have been the traditional focus of human rights international standards, mechanisms for reporting and redress, non-governmental organisations working on social justice and minority rights issues and academic scholarship primarily in sociology, developmental economics, and anthropology.

Outside these two areas of human rights that have received wide attention and debate, there have been varying degrees of attention paid to the positive and negative dimensions of human rights depicted in the remaining cells. For the positive dimensions of civil and political rights in Cell I, the work on 'good governance' has sought to examine the ways in which investment in judiciaries, prisons, and police forces can improve the foundations of governance and so deliver better economic prosperity, while those interested in the administration of justice see such positive aspects of civil and political rights as essential to addressing problems of the '(un)rule' of law.

For the negative dimensions of economic, social, and cultural rights in Cell IV, there has been much focus on general patterns of gender, ethnic, racial, linguistic, and religious discrimination, but perhaps less attention on how these practices may constitute violations to economic, social, and cultural rights. Since the debt crisis in the 1980s, there has been an increase in social mobilization and attention around the transnational issues of debt relief, developmental assistance and distribution of global income, and 'post-colonial' reparations for past practices made most vocally at the 2001 World Conference Against Racism. Since the 1970s, groups have been mobilizing for transnational solutions to the global environmental problems and have focussed on the negative dimensions of 'offending' states such as the United States but there has been less of a focus on the rights issues associated with such solutions. Finally, from a human rights perspective, the work on globalization and trade has focussed on the 'violation' represented by unfair trade agreements hammered out in the World Trade Organisation which is seen to be disproportionately influenced by the United States and the European Union as well as unsavoury manufacturing and production techniques used by multinational corporations.

Table. Positive and Negative Dimensions of Human Rights Categories

	Dimensions	
	'Positive' (*i.e.* provision of resources and outcomes of policies)	**'Negative' (*i.e.* practices that deliberately violate)**
Civil and political	I Investment in judiciaries, prisons, police forces, and elections intimidation,	II Torture, extra-judicial killings, disappearance, arbitrary detention, unfair trials, electoral disenfranchisement
Economic, social, and cultural	III Progressive realisation Investment in health, education, and welfare	IV Ethnic, racial, gender, or linguistic discrimination in health, education, and

		welfare
Solidarity	V Compensation for past wrongs Debt relief Overseas development and technical	VI Environmental degradation CO_2 emissions Unfair trade assistance

FROM CONCEPTS TO INDICATORS

The various examples outlined in the previous part show how human rights measurement can benefit from such a conceptual delineation, since it disaggregates the concept of human rights into different categories across different dimensions and facilitates the process of operationalizing human rights for systematic analysis. The different dimensions and categories provide the content for developing 'events-based', 'standards-based', 'survey based' and other measures of human rights. But what are the operational steps that allow us to move from these conceptual distinctions of human rights to the provision of valid, meaningful, and reliable measures? At an abstract methodological level, the process of measurement converts well-defined and well-specified concepts into meaningful quantitative measures or qualitative categories, and has four main steps. The first level concerns the background concept that is to be measured, which is the broad constellation of meanings and understandings associated with the concept.

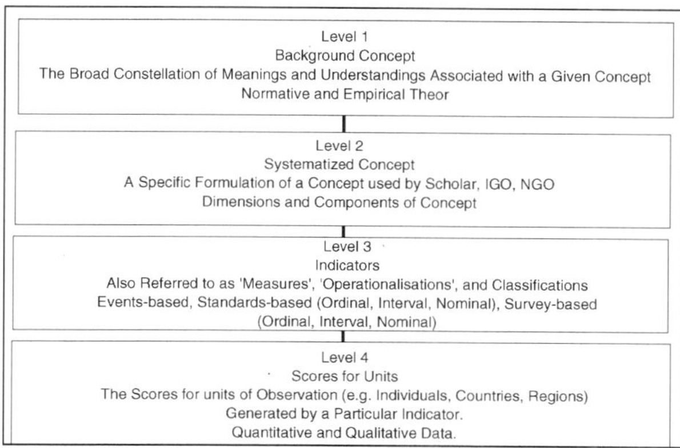

The scope of human rights summarises what comprises such a broad constellation of meanings and understandings in the field of human rights. The second level develops the systemised concept, which specifies further the concept that is to be measured, such as a specific right (*e.g.* the right not to be tortured) or a group of rights (*e.g.* civil rights). The third level operationalizes the systematised concept into meaningful, valid, and reliable indicators, such as events-based, standards-based, survey-based, or other measures. The final level provides scores on indicators for the units of analysis being used. Figure depicts these four levels graphically. Consider a concrete example. The background concept to be measured is human rights, the scope of which has been systematically across its different categories (civil, political, economic, social, cultural, and solidarity) and dimensions (positive and negative). The international community of human rights scholars and practitioners have spent the years in the lead up to and the years since the 1948 Universal Declaration of Human Rights 'constructing' and 'justifying' human rights in conceptual and legal terms. While there have not been agreed philosophical foundations for the existence of human rights, the extant international law of human rights provides a general consensus on the core content of those human rights that ought to be protected. Such a core content comprises Steps 1 and 2 in the levels of measurement.

The matrix representing the intersection between the categories and dimensions of human rights is a systematic way of organising the first step to measurement. Consider the right not to be tortured, which is a systematised concept of human rights that has been identified most notably in the Universal Declaration of Human Rights (UDHR), the International Covenant on Civil and Political Rights (ICCPR), and the Convention Against Torture (CAT). The systematised concept is susceptible to operationalization at Level 3. But given the two dimensions of human rights, the right not to be tortured can be measured at Level 3 both positively (*i.e.* resources a state is investing in procedures, policies, reforms, and training for the prevention of torture) and negatively (formal commitment to international standards on torture and actual incidence of torture).

At Level 4, the right not to be tortured is measured for a unit (*e.g.* Brazil) at a particular time, across its positive dimension (*e.g.*% GDP spent on torture reform, number of police in receipt of torture training, cases of reprimand for torture) and its negative dimension (*e.g.* incidence of torture revealed through events counting, a scale of torture, or survey estimations on popular experiences of torture). In this way, the right not to be tortured may have several indicators that measure its core content across its two dimensions.

EXTANT MEASURES

The burgeoning literature on human rights measurement comprises. Extant approaches have measured human rights in principle (*i.e.* as they are laid out in national and international legal documents), in practice (*i.e.* as they are enjoyed by individuals and groups in nation states), and as outcomes of government policy that has a direct bearing on human rights protection. Measurement of human rights can take the form of coding country participation in regional and international human rights regimes, coding national constitutions according to their rights provisions, qualitative reporting of rights violations, survey data on perceptions of rights conditions, quantitative summaries of rights violations, abstract scales of rights protection based on normative standards, and individual and aggregate measures that map the outcomes of government policies that have consequences for the enjoyment of rights.

RIGHTS IN PRINCIPLE

International and domestics law enshrines norms and principles of human rights, which can be coded using protocols that reward a country for having certain rights provisions in place. van Maarseveen and van der Tang set an important precedent by coding constitutions for 157 countries across a multitude of institutional and rights dimensions for the period 1788-1975. The study compares the degree to which national constitutions contain those rights mentioned in the UN Declaration for Human Rights by examining their frequency distributions across different historical epochs before and after 1948. Their study is broadly descriptive in nature, but their data allow for global patterns and processes of change in the formal protection of rights at the domestic level to be mapped, while secondary and more advanced statistical analysis could be conducted on the patterns within the data while exploring possible relationships with other indicators. For example, Foweraker and Landman use an 'institutional procedural index' to code rights in principle for Brazil, Chile, Mexico, and Spain using the various national constitutions and constitutional amendments during the years of political liberalization and democratic transition. In similar fashion, Poe and Keith code national constitutions to measure their ability to suspend rights protection during states of emergency. At the global level, Keith, Landman and Hathaway code the regional and international human rights regimes by scoring countries for signing and ratifying major human rights instruments. Rather than code individual rights provisions, these authors code the degree to which countries are parties to human rights treaties over time. since it translates qualitative legal information into quantitative information that can be used to track the formal commitment of countries to rights protection against which their actual practices can be compared.

Foweraker and Landman use regression techniques to gauge the relative 'gap' between rights in principle and Coding rights in principle, either at the national or international level is important rights in practice in Brazil, Chile, Mexico, and Spain. Their analysis demonstrates that during the process of political liberalization, authoritarian states can deny rights that they proclaim are protected, protect rights they proclaim are protected, or protect rights that they proclaim are not protected (a positive gap).

Poe and Keith (2004) use their state of emergency variable to examine the relationship between the law and practice of human rights while controlling for the independent effects of democracy, wealth, and warfare. Using the notions of principle and practice for global analysis shows that regimes frequently make formal commitments to human rights treaties, but continue to violate human rights. This difference is captured by weak positive or even negative correlation and regression co-efficients between ratification and rights variables. Carrying out such analyses, however, requires measurement of rights in practice to which the discussion now turns.

RIGHTS IN PRACTICE

Rights in practice are those rights actually enjoyed and exercised by groups and individuals regardless of the formal commitment made by a government. While there ought to be a correspondence between formal rights commitments found in national constitutions and international human rights instruments and those enjoyed on the ground, it is often the case that individuals and groups do not enjoy the full protection of their rights. Ideally, there ought to be in place a legal appeals procedure, mechanisms for seeking domestic and international remedies, and a subsequent 'correction' in national practices to uphold the rights to which regimes have made formal commitments.

In the absence of such systems or in the face of weak systems, the role of many human rights practitioners is to provide meaningful and accurate information on the degree to which human rights are being violated. Indeed, greater concerns over humans rights since World War II has led to an explosion in the number of domestic and international human rights NGOs collecting information on violations. Such NGOs have been given greater status in international governmental organizations, and their activities include setting standards, providing information, lobbying, and giving direct assistance to those suffering abuse of their rights.

The increase in the salience of human rights as an issue combined with organizations dedicated to documenting human rights violations means that there is greater availability of comprehensive information on actual practices of states and the conditions under which individuals live. But this information necessarily will be lumpy and incomplete, since reporting of human rights violations is fraught with difficulties, including fear within victims, power of the offenders, comprehensive evidence, quality of communications technology, among others.

In recognising this problem, Bollen argues that there are six levels of information on human rights violations:

- An ideal level with all characteristics of all violations (either reported or unreported), followed by
- Recorded violations,
- Known and accessible violations,
- Locally reported violations (nation-state),
- Internationally reported violations, and
- The most biased coverage of violations, which may include only those reported in US.

Indeed, the early behaviourist attempts to measure political violence used the New York Times Index only for its source of information, while new approaches on dissent and repression use multiple newswire sources that are machine coded. Other work in this area seeks to obtain lower levels of information in much greater detail. For example, the Torture Reporting Handbook and Reporting Killings as Human Rights Violations are manuals that define specific rights, outline the legal protections against their violation, and provide ways in which testimony and evidence from victims can be collected. The Human Rights Information and Documentation System, founded in 1982, provides standards for human rights violations reporting, and now represents a vast network of human rights groups.

While such increased information at all levels is helpful for systematic human rights research, there remains a trade-off or tension between micro levels of information gathering and the ability to make systematic comparative inferences about human rights. In order for equivalent measures to 'travel' for comparative analysis, there will necessarily be some loss of information, while the comparability of measures allows for stronger generalizations about human rights violations to be drawn. These issues about levels of information and the commensurability for cross-national analysis delineate the three types of data available for measuring human rights in practice:

- Events-based,
- Standards-based, and
- Survey-based.

Events-based data chart the reported acts of violation committed against groups and individuals. Events-based data answer the important questions of what happened, when it happened, and who was involved, and then report descriptive and numerical summaries of the events. Counting such events and violations involves identifying the various acts of commission and omission that constitute or lead to human rights violations, such as extra-judicial killings, arbitrary arrest or torture. Such data tend to be disaggregated to the level of the violation itself, which may have related data units such as the perpetrator, the victim, and the witness. Standards-based data establish how often and to what degree violations occur, and then translate such judgements into quantitative scales that are designed to achieve commensurability. Such measures are thus one level removed from event counting and violation reporting, and merely apply an ordinal scale to qualitative information.

Finally, survey-based data use random samples of country populations to ask a series of standard questions on the perception of rights protection. Such measures track individual level perceptions or rights violations. These different types of data map overall human rights practices within a country in different ways. The HURIDOCS project, handbooks such as those on torture and unlawful killings and the work of nationally based human rights commissions collect events-based data, which can provide time-series and continuous indicators on human rights violations. Standards-based scales such as the 'political terror scale', the 'index of political freedom', the torture scale, 'the minorities at risk' project, and the 'state failure project' use available information on human rights practices of states to generate global indices.

Finally, general survey-based data on rights can be found in such studies as the Eurobarometer series and the World Values Survey. Governments themselves have begun conducting mass public opinion surveys on individual perceptions of human rights. For example, the Home Office in the United Kingdom commissioned a citizenship survey, which contains a series of questions on the Human Rights Act of 1998 and general questions about rights and duties of UK citizens. Finally, NGOs such as Physicians for Human Rights have begun using household surveys of 'at risk' populations to capture the degree to which particular groups suffer disproportionate human rights violations.

Figures provide examples of the three different types of data depicting rights in practice. An example of events-based data on political killings collected and analysed by the Commission for Truth and Reconciliation in Peru. The abstract measures of civil and political rights from Freedom House, personal integrity rights, and torture in the world between 1976 and 2000. Freedom House has a standard checklist it uses to code civil and political rights based on press reports and country sources about state practices and then derives a scale that ranges from 1 to 7.

The personal integrity rights measures are abstract scales that range from 1 (full protection) to 5 (full violation) for state practice that include torture, political imprisonment, unlawful killing, and disappearance. Information for these scales comes from the US State Department and Amnesty International country reports. In similar fashion, Hathaway measures torture on a 1 to 5 scale using information from the US State Department. Finally, Figure summarises the results of household surveys on sexual violence in Sierra Leone during the worst years of the armed conflict.

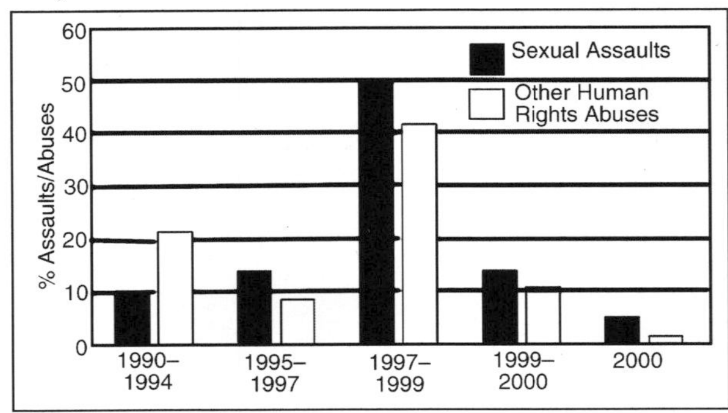

Fig. Occurance of Sexual Assaults Among Respondents and other Human Rights Abuses Among Household Members

While these three examples of human rights measures focus on civil and political rights, This thesis argued that it is possible to extend the methodological discussion to include the measurement of economic, social, and cultural rights. Indeed, if the denial of economic, social, and cultural rights is the product ofparticular government practices, then it is seems equally possible to use qualitative information to summarize such practices into ordinal scales similar to those used for civil and political rights violations.

Overt, institutionalised, or implicit discrimination against individuals or groups that prevents their access to education or adequate health constitutes a practice that violates a right. In theory, such a violation can be reported and coded using events-based, standards-based, and/or survey-based data. The minorities at risk project codes the degree to which 224 different minority and communal groups experience discrimination using such ordinal scales.

Despite their development and increasingly wider use these three types of data are fraught with methodological problems. Events-based data are prone to either under-reporting of events that did occur or over-reporting of events that did not occur, creating problems of selection bias and misrepresentative data. It is impossible to document every last human rights violation and those organisations collecting such information tend to concentrate on conflict-stricken societies during discrete periods of time and thus cross-country comparisons using such measures is problematic. In contrast, standards-base data establish comparability by raising the level of abstraction, but have a tendency to truncate the variation of human rights protection across different countries. In other words, their use of a simple limited scale may group together certain countries that actually show a great difference in their protection of human rights.

While these scales present a general picture of the human rights situation and are useful for drawing comparative inferences, they necessarily sacrifice the kind of specificity for pursuing direct legal action against perpetrators. Finally, survey data, especially those used across different political contexts are prone to cultural biases, where the meaning of standardised questions on rights protection are differently understood in different countries.

In this way, the debate about the universality of human rights affects the method of measuring rights through surveys, since it is not obvious that human rights are understood to mean the same thing across the world. It is important therefore that those measuring human rights in practice recognise the limits of their data.

GOVERNMENT POLICIES AND OUTCOMES

In addition to rights in principle and rights in practice, it is possible to provide more indirect measures of human rights using aggregate statistics on the outcomes of government policies. In her contribution to a 2001 conference on human rights impact assessment, Parr makes the useful distinction between human rights conduct and developmental outcomes that may have a bearing on human rights. She stresses the fact that certain dimensions of conduct and outcomes are simply not prone to quantifiable measurement.

In the language of this present thesis, her distinction fits well with the difference between rights in practice and government policy. In contrast, however, this object argues that practices and outcomes are more readily quantifiable than Parr assumes. The discussion in the preceding section demonstrated that human rights scholars have long been measuring rights in practice, albeit with a greater emphasis on civil and political rights. Qualitative information on the degree to which certain categories of rights have been violated is either summarised quantitatively (events data), translated into comparable quantitative ordinal scales (standards-based data), or acquired through individual level data collection techniques (survey-based data).

Traditionally, development studies and development economics have often relied on quantitative indicators of the outcomes of government policies, including gross domestic product, gross domestic product per capita, income inequality, expenditure on health, education, and welfare, among many others. Indeed, the UNDP's human development index (HDI) combines per capita income with literacy rates (knowledge), and life expectancy at birth (longevity).

While not providing a direct measure of rights protection *per se*, such measures can elucidate the degree to which governments support activities that have an impact on human rights. It is also possible to combine the HDI with standards-based measures of human rights to get a better picture of the interaction between human development and human rights. A scatter plot between the HDI and a 'factor score' created through principal component extraction from the two versions of the Political Terror Scale, the two Freedom House scales, and the torture measure. The assumption behind using factor analysis is that each of the five measures is measuring common human rights phenomena.

7

Standards in Social Work Practice Meeting Human Rights

BACKGROUND

A FRAMEWORK FOR STANDARDS IN SOCIAL WORK

The ongoing development of Standards in Social Work Practice takes place in the context of Social Work as a profession committed to the promotion and realisation of Human Rights. The International Federation of Social Workers recognises that Social Work originates variously from humanitarian, religious and democratic ideals and philosophies; and that it has universal application to meet human needs arising from personal-societal interactions, and to develop human potential. Professional social workers are dedicated to service for the welfare and self-fulfilment of human beings; to the development and disciplined use of scientific knowledge regarding human behaviour and society; to the development of resources to meet individual, group, national and international needs and aspirations; to the enhancement and improvement of the quality of life of people; and to the achievement of social justice.

IFSW is divided in five geographical regions:

- Africa
- Asia and Pacific
- Europe
- Latin America and Caribbean and
- North America.

Each region elects representatives to the IFSW Global Human Rights Network and Permanent Committee on Ethical Issues. The International Federation of Social Workers European Region has 40 member associations in 35 countries, with a total of 165,600 Social Workers-the membership is representative as it covers all corners of Europe.

IFSW Europe co-operates with other organisations in Europe. It has a long standing tradition of working closely together with the "European Association of Schools of Social Work" and the "European Region of the

International Council of Social Welfare". This cooperation is now brought into a formal frame called the European Network for Social Action, including three other member organisations in the social field. Co-operation with other European organisations includes the European Fundamental Rights Agency, the European Social Platform and European Federation of Public Service Unions.

SOCIAL WORK IS A HUMAN RIGHTS PROFESSION

The International Definition of Social Work states: 'Principles of Human Rights and social justice are fundamental to Social Work'. The 2004 ethics document is based on the definition and lists Human Rights treaties 'particularly relevant to Social Work practice and action'.

Among the most important are:

- The European Convention on Human Rights
- The International Covenant on Civil and Political Rights;
- The International Covenant on Economic, Social and Cultural Rights;
- The International Convention on the Elimination of All Forms of Racial Discrimination;
- The Convention on the Elimination of All Forms of Discrimination against Women;
- The Convention on the Rights of the Child;
- The Convention on the Rights of Persons with Disabilities;
- The Charter of Fundamental Rights of the European Union

The IFSW's Policy on Human Rights states amongst other things, that 'the Social Work profession accepts its share of responsibility for working to oppose and eliminate all violations of Human Rights. This IFSW International Policy states: 'Social Work has, from its conception, been a Human Rights profession, having as its basic tenet the intrinsic value of every human being and as one of its main aims the promotion of equitable social structures, which can offer people security and development while upholding their dignity'.

The Manual for Schools of Social Work and the Social Work Profession by the United Nations Centre for Human Rights and the International Federation of Social Workers and the International Association of Schools of Social Work was developed in acknowledgement of the centrality of Social Workers as professionals in the protection and realisation of Human Rights. Further to this Manual, The IFSW and IASSW have in 2010 created a Human Rights website as a global resource for social service workers.

The Manual states: 'More than many professions, Social Work practitioners are conscious that their concerns are closely linked to respect for Human Rights. They accept the premise that Human Rights and fundamental freedoms are indivisible, and that the full realization of civil and political rights is impossible without enjoyment of economic, social and cultural rights'. 'Human Rights are inseparable from Social Work theory, values and ethics, and practice ... Advocacy of such rights must therefore be an integral part of Social Work, even if in countries living under authoritarian regimes such advocacy can have serious consequences for Social Work professionals'. In 2002, IFSW has also published Social Work and the Rights of the Child, a professional training manual on the UN Convention.

SOCIAL WORK PRACTICE MEETING HUMAN RIGHTS

The Global Standards in the Social Work profession identify the core purposes of Social Work in the global context.

These clearly show how Social Workers promote the realisation of Human Rights by:

- Facilitating the inclusion of marginalised, socially excluded, dispossessed, vulnerable and at-risk groups of people;
- A ddressing and challenging barriers, inequalities and injustices that exist in society;
- Forming short and longer-term working relationships with and mobilising individuals, families, groups, organisations and communities to enhance their wellbeing and their problem-solving capacities;
- A ssisting and educating people to obtain services and resources in their communities;
- Formulating and implementing policies and programmes that enhance people's wellbeing, promoting development and Human Rights and collective social harmony and social stability, insofar as such stability does not violate Human Rights;
- E ncouraging people to engage in advocacy with regard to pertinent local, national, regional and/or international concerns;
- A cting with and/or for people to advocate the formulation and targeted implementation of policies that are consistent with the ethical principles of the profession;
- A cting with and/or for people to advocate changes in those policies and structural conditions that maintain people in marginalised, dispossessed and vulnerable positions, and those that infringe the collective social harmony and stability of various ethnic groups, insofar as such stability does not violate Human Rights;
- Working towards the protection of people who are not in a position to do so themselves, for example children and youth in need of care and persons experiencing mental illness or mental retardation, within the parameters of accepted and ethically sound legislation;
- E ngaging in social and political action to impact social policy and economic development, and to effect change by critiquing and eliminating inequalities;
- E nhancing stable, harmonious and mutually respectful societies that do not violate people's Human Rights;

- Promoting respect for traditions, cultures, ideologies, beliefs and religions amongst different ethnic groups and societies, insofar as these do not conflict with the fundamental Human Rights of people.
- Planning, organising, administering and manage programmes and organisations dedicated to any of the purposes delineated above.

A Europe-wide study on the role of Social Work in promoting Social Cohesion conducted by IFSW Europe e.V. found that Social Workers promote Social Cohesion by:

- D elivering services and being a positive presence for the entire community;
- O ffering empowerment and protection to individuals and the community through a rights-based approach;
- Working with vulnerable groups;
- Responding to the changing national and international contexts in professional and practical ways;
- U sing their expertise, knowledge and experience to critically assess and analyse social cohesion at a holistic level;
- Skilfully maintaining the balance in their key position between the individual and society, between service provision and service development, between social care and social control, between interpersonal and national politics and more;
- A ctively promoting economic and social justice that can sometimes be at considerable personal risk or political oppression.

THE BASIS FOR A COMMON FRAMEWORK OF STANDARDS IN SOCIAL WORK PRACTICE

This document, is intended to consolidate the basic parameters within which Social Work in Europe operates into a common framework for Social Work in Europe. This framework is considered a key step in contributing towards the ongoing development of Standards for Social Work Practice in Europe. As a number of authors have pointed out, action orientation is a great strength in Social Work that can make a real difference in peoples lives and in the context of their situations. Social Workers take action; they engage in securing human rights for individuals and communities. The global Social Work human rights agenda, as witnessed by this project, shows no signs of diminishing. However this work holds the fundamental realisation that Social Work does not exist in a vacuum. Social Workers exercise this responsibility in practice with individuals, groups and communities, in their roles as agency or organisational representatives and as citizens of a nation and the world'.

The contested nature of social work can be seen when one realises that the concept of social work has been shared between those who believe it is an activity that seeks to change the social structures that oppress certain individuals or groups of people and those who believe social work must assist individuals to adapt to their life conditions if those people are unwilling or unable to adapt to social norms and standards of behaviour.

This concept spans the dichotomy between:

- Structure and Action and
- Conflict and Order.

The dichotomy is characterised by Dominelli as the divide between those social workers who argue for 'liberation' and those who argue for the 'status quo'. This position is true across Europe and must be considered when addressing the issue of human rights and social work. The International Federation of Social Workers, Europe asserts the fact that the organizational contexts of Social Work cannot be ignored for the influence they bear on the profession's activities.

The 'Global Standards for Social Work Education and Training' and a new 'Ethical Document' are key reference policy documents jointly worked out discussed and finally agreed by both the International Federation of Social Workers and the International Association of Schools of Social Work in 2004. Social Work is a key profession in balancing service user needs and rights and contextual tensions.

In character with such a role this framework seeks:

- To inform services users about what they should expect of Social Work;
- Acknowledge the tensions between service user needs and rights, professionalism, management, political, economic and societal factors;
- To inform about the contribution, role and tasks of Social Work towards the wellbeing of the community within the broad European policy context;
- To support and maintain a good standard and quality of Social Work practice, education, training and regulation across Europe which inevitably depends on the relationship between the Social Worker and service user and the value base of the Social Work profession;
- To inform organisational settings on how to maintain good standards in Social Work raise practice so that organisational structures provide the environment and tools towards meeting service user rights and needs;
- To ensure that Social Workers in Europe abide by and in turn are not put in a position which conflicts with their professional code of ethics;
- To promote the status of Social Workers and enable scarce professional resources to be better used;
- To promote the links between Social Work and Human Rights.

DEFINITION, ROLES AND PROFESSIONAL TITLE

"The Social Work profession promotes social change, problem solving in human relationships and the empowerment and liberation of people to enhance well-being. Utilising theories of human behaviour and social systems, Social Work intervenes at the points where people interact with their environments. Principles of Human Rights and social justice are fundamental to Social Work." Social Work interventions range from primarily person-focused psychosocial processes involvement in social policy, planning and development.

These carry various job titles that may include the following:

- Clinical Social Work;
- Social pedagogical work;
- Counselling;
- Family treatment and therapy as well as;
- Group work;
- Efforts to help people obtain services and resources in the community;
- Agency administration;
- Community work and organisation and
- Engaging in social and political action to impact social policy and economic development.

Social Workers are change agents in society and in the lives of the individuals, families and communities they serve.

- Emerging clearly from the European debate is that Professional Social Work:
- Is focused on problem solving and change addressing the barriers, inequities and injustices that exist in society;
- Responds to crises and emergencies as well as to everyday personal and social problems;
- Works in partnership with services users;
- Has an important role in the implementation of social strategies, negotiation and interdisciplinary practice;
- Promotes prevention, integration and cohesion;
- Is a dynamic profession with a definition that is alive and renews itself according to the needs of people and society.

Social Work works reflectively, critically and creatively from existing identities in order to change the way that social differences are constructed. The realisation of Human Rights requires the respect for the rights of all those concerned and requires professional skill for creating a space for dialogue, the creation of meaning and correct interpretation. Social Work is unique in that it seeks to achieve social improvement, that is, positive social change, through interpersonal work while also seeking to work with the personal consequences of social change Payne, 2006.

CODES AND ETHICAL THINKING

The purpose of the work of IFSW and IASSW on ethics is to promote ethical debate and reflection in the member organisations, among the providers of Social Work in member countries, as well as in the schools of Social Work and among Social Work students.

- It is the responsibility of the national organisations in membership of IFSW and IASSW to develop and regularly update their own codes of ethics or ethical guidelines, to be consistent with the IFSW/ IASSW statement/s;
- All Social Workers and service users should have the possibility to refer to a body with the legally recognised remit of safeguarding of professional ethics and providing redress;
- It is the responsibility of Social Workers to raise breaches in Ethics and Human Rights;
- It is also the responsibility of national organisations to inform Social Workers and schools of Social Work about these codes or guidelines;
- Social Workers should act in accordance with the ethical code or guidelines current in their country. These will generally include more detailed guidance in ethical practice specific to the national context;
- The significance of the concept of complexity thinking in Social Work is that standards and codes of practice should not seek to oversimplify the complexity of the situations that Social Workers and their clients face;
- Ethical codes need to be set in a regulatory structure and should focus more on ethical dilemmas;
- Codes of Ethics should be accompanied by a code for employers of Social Workers.

THE KNOWLEDGE-BASE FOR PRACTICE

"The Global Standards for Education and Training of the Social Work Profession" jointly adopted by the International Federation of Social Workers and the International Association of the Schools of Social Work in 2004 is the basis for standards in social wok education internationally.

These standards elaborate guidelines for:

- The Social Work school's core purpose or mission statement
- Programme objectives and outcomes
- Programme curricula, including fieldwork
- Core curricula

The Social Work profession draws on theories of human development and behaviour and social systems to analyse complex situations and to facilitate individual, organisational, social and cultural changes. In response to these challenges and their consequences, Social Workers must be aware about users' needs in looking for sustainable answers. This means Human Rights realisation;

respecting each person; asserting the basic values and principles of Social Work of Human Rights and Social Justice, as stated in "Ethics in Social Work, Statement of Principles".

Social Workers must therefore be aware about the following perspectives:

- Humanist and sustainable perspective (focus on the dignity and needs of human beings in present and future generations and to their ecological life conditions);
- Democratic perspective (looking for adequate development conditions–economic, social, cultural-facilitating users participation at social and civil level in society);
- Political and economic perspective (promoting the subsidiary principle, equality of opportunities and political/social/cultural rights);
- Educational perspective (to be aware about their scientific knowledge, professional skills, and research competences that as student has reached from his/her academic education or as professional at life-long learning individual process.

These Foundations includes:

- "Praxis" a theoretical reflection that develops into action;
- "Morality" or "ethical sensibility" means to know the values and manage moral or ethical dilemmas;
- "Passion" a strong desire to change oppressed situations;
- "Ideology" an understanding of Human Rights not as an individual issue but as a collective issue;
- "History" a contextualized understanding of Human Rights over the time;
- "Structural disadvantage" to understand the failure of realization of Human Rights due to structural oppression or disadvantage;
- "Holism" to see Human Rights over western civilization, rejecting a restricted linear thinking accompanied by a critical understanding of "Postmodernism and post-structuralism" and its challenges and implications to Social Work intervention.

"Empowerment" as a second major theme is the capacity of Social Workers to enable people to define their rights and to act in order to have them realised.

- "Dialogical Praxis" a " dialogue" linking the personal and political;
- A process of "conscientisation" in the view of Paulo Freire;
- "Participatory democracy" another dimension of "Empowerment" that means to create specific conditions to all people for the maximum participation. "Feminism" or better, sensitivity in view to justice in gender-relationships and "Anti-Colonialist" practice as a way to fight against oppressive or dominate strategies of groups, individuals or states";

- Non violence" another dimension of "empowerment" that is adopted according to the Social Work principles;
- "Needs" because citizens must be "allowed" to express their needs. As a central component of Human Rights based Social Work needs are identified through professionals in partnership with people;
- "Research "methodologies that must be addressed towards empowerment and Human Rights and cannot therefore be neutral, positivist, value free research, but rather research with clearly articulated value positions";

"Contextual/universal issues"-"Confronting such universal/context dualism is a major challenge for Human Rights-based Social Work".

Dualisms are referred to as:

- "The personal and political";
- "Private and public";
- "Cultural relativism";
- "Macro and micro practice";
- "The global and the local".

QUALIFICATION

he most common and minimum education level for Social Workers in all of the participant countries is currently the undergraduate Bachelor Degree level. The structure and remit of competences and role of Social Work to be more clearly defined and appraisable:

- As the exigency for the profile of Social Workers becomes more and more felt, preparing the students to know themselves as persons, citizens and future members of a specific professional body (the questions of professional identity, according each, culture, historical and political context and region) becomes even more important;
- It is equally important to prepare students concerning the "market" exigencies (and services objectives) as well as meeting service users' needs and Human Rights (following historical and cultural Social Work paradigms, according to new challenges);

The balance between theoretical proficiency and practice experience:

- This balance is very pertinent to the professional development of the practitioner. It is important for students to be able to relate both practice to theory to develop their practice experience as well as relate theory to practice to develop their critical thinking towards theory;

The role of practitioners in the formation of students:

- This method results in a positive experience of mutual learning for both students and practitioners involving the experience of professionals teaching the students; the student's questions challenging reflection and continuous learning by the professionals.

Interdisciplinary practice; bringing the contribution of other disciplines' knowledge into operation in line with the objectives of Social Work:

- It is important to provide students with an open view about academic and professional knowledge sharing. This also goes for knowledge shared between students, practitioners and experts from different fields of knowledge. It is important for Social Workers to know the fundamental theories of other social sciences and be aware (be critical) about underlying philosophical contradictions concerning Social Work values and principles and must consequently learn to manage these.

THE INTEGRATION AND OPERATIONALISATION OF KNOWLEDGE

- This topic was identified as one of the most important objectives of all educational processes of Social Workers' formation: students must be able to apply, in the context of their academic practices: theoretical knowledge; methodologies; skills and ethical behaviour.
- This aspect requires the teachers to possess specific competences in order to integrate pedagogical methodologies that focus on essential subjects selected according to the students' experiences and personal options as future professionals.

Attention was drawn to the fact that in several curricula and in particular those following the Bologna Process, the courses had a tendency to become shorter and with less time assigned to reflective learning praxis. In view of the considerations and in view of the new emerging social model of society, the International Federation of Social Workers, Europe recommends that to support students' education as future Social Workers, Schools should move towards:

- Guaranteeing a Bachelor of (as a minimum qualification) 6 semesters (1st level) with a University credit and the availability of a Master degree of 4 semesters (2nd level);
- Introducing in the curricula disciplines on topics such as (optional disciplines or not) gender subject; sexual minorities; multiculturalism, environment/sustainability; incertitude and risk; terrorism/counterterrorism;
- Supporting the students with tutorial attendance by teachers that must possess the specific relevant competences;
- Using specific methodologies where the learning process can be guided (steps development) by the student and not only by the teacher (a learning process rather than a teaching process).

Another issue of key significance is that of further education. That means a life-long learning opportunity and challenge to develop one's skills.

ACCOUNTABILITY AND ORGANISATIONAL CONTEXTS TO ENABLE GOOD STANDARDS OF PRACTICE

All Social Workers and service users should have the possibility to refer to a body with the legally recognised remit of safeguarding of professional standards. Social Work is practised in a variety of settings including State services, Health Care, Specialist agencies, Independent practices, Voluntary and not-for-profit bodies, User-led organizations, Private sector companies and Private practice.

Many Social Work roles help implement European and National policies. Among others they are essential in enabling local government, schools, healthcare and justice services to carry out their roles. In safeguarding human, social and economic rights, governments and organisations that employ Social Workers have a responsibility for ensuring resources are sufficient to meet needs and maintain standards of good practice. These guidelines are being proposed in the context that the main organizational problems faced by Social Workers are found to be:

- Ethical issues
- Stress and Burnout
- Lack of Workload and caseload management
- Fragmentation of care

Social Worker's responsibilities:

- It is the responsibility of the Social Worker to exercise their professional duties towards their service users in accordance with the relevant national and international codes of practice (local codes, legislation, IFSW statements).
- The Social Worker has a duty to keep their knowledge and skills up to date and they must follow practice based on best evidence and current knowledge.
- The Social Worker is accountable for their work, and they must not delegate work unless they are confident that the person(s) to whom the work is delegated is competent to carry out the work in an appropriately safe and competent manner. They must not accept delegated work themselves unless they are confident they can undertake it in a safe and skilled manner.
- At the International Level Social Workers are accountable to the International Federation of Social Workers by means of:
  - The Guidelines and statements of International Federation of Social Workers and Global and Regional level;
  - Professional membership;
  - The Definition of Social Work;
  - The Joint Statement on Ethics;
  - The Global Standards for Education and Training in Social Work;
  - Regional Standards and Guidelines;
- At the National level, various models of accountability have been identified, however the following are considered of basic importance for the good and accountable practice of Social Work:

- National Social Work Codes of Ethics;
- National Standards of Social Work Education;
- Frameworks for professional accountability–*e.g.* regulatory entities, professional boards, professional councils, by self regulation and/or state legislation involving service user perspectives;
- Organisational policies and procedures regarding Social Work in an organisational setting;
- Standards of Social Work practice and services;

Employer responsibilities:

- The employer must ensure that they have the appropriate professional Social Work management and leadership in place to ensure that Social Work values of Human Rights and social justice are upheld throughout the agency and Social Work services;
- Ensure that people engaged as Social Workers must hold the necessary recognised qualifications and must be legally recognised to practice as Social Workers;
- The employer is responsible for ensuring that they comply with legislation and relevant codes of practice, and that they do not ask their employees to breach these; Have policies and procedures in place to enable Social Workers to meet the Standards and Guidelines set out by the International Federation of Social Workers and the International Association of the Schools of Social Work as well as those in the National Legislation/regulatory frameworks;
- It is the responsibility of the employer to create the right working conditions and structures that support the Social Worker to deliver safe, effective and accountable practice;
- The employer must meet their legal obligation to protect the occupational safety and health of all workers-a significant aspect of which relates to the identification, prevention and management of work-related stress;
- Having clear policies and procedures for minimising the risk of violence and managing violent incidents and supporting Social Workers who experience trauma or violence in their work;
- Have and regularly review written policies on: confidentiality; equal opportunities; risk;
- To support good practice, the employer must provide good quality induction (orientation) to new entrants and those moving jobs, good supervision, realistic workloads, access to continuous learning and professional development, enabling a suitable working environment;
- Provide professional remuneration to Social Workers that is comparable to that of other professions;
- Having systems in place to enable Social Workers to report inadequate resources or operational difficulties which might impede

the delivery of safe and effective working with service users and address these issues to the relevant authorities;
- Making service users aware of relevant policies, standards and codes of Social Work practice;

AN ORGANISATIONAL FRAMEWORK SUPPORTING GOOD PRACTICE

A framework for supporting good practice should be largely focused on practices of induction, supervision, workload management and continuing professional development. Such a framework has as its principle objective better outcomes for service users by helping the worker to deliver the best service they can at all times. In order to achieve this objective, along with ensuring safe practice, the Social Worker and the employer must be willing to engage jointly in these processes. The framework is based on the premise that both the employer and the Social Worker have responsibilities for supporting good practice.

- A well planned and executed induction, supervision, workload management and continuing professional development (CPD) framework:
- Provides a system of structured support for good practice, and enables the Social Worker to meet their responsibilities;
- Helps to address and combat the problem of work-related stress;
- Supports the recruitment and retention of staff by fostering the commitment of the employer/agency, and the employee, to their joint enterprise of providing a Social Work service. Hence, both the employer and the Social Worker benefit.

The following core values and principles should underpin the framework for induction, supervision, workload management and CPD (Adapted from Green and Myers, 2008):

- All staff working in Social Work settings, irrespective of their role, have the right to effective induction to their job role, high quality supervision, manageable caseloads and continuing professional development opportunities;
- Supervision must ensure the effective management of practice, develop and support staff and promote their engagement with the organisation;
- A review of workloads and caseloads must be an important part of the supervision process;
- The quality of induction, supervision and CPD and the workload have a direct bearing on the quality of service delivery and outcomes for service users;
- Social Workers and social care staff bear a responsibility for their own work and, to this end, should prepare for and make a positive

contribution to the supervisory process, and their own professional development;
- Induction, supervision, workload management and CPD must promote anti-discriminatory practice;
- All practice must be consistent with local and International Federation of Social Workers codes and statements referring to Social Work practice.

Induction (Orientation):
- On arriving at an agency for the first time as a new employee, a Social Worker, whether he/she is newly qualified or with long experience, should have a structured introduction to that agency to ensure that the worker is familiarised with the agency's methods of working and the context in which the work takes place.
- For newly qualified Social Workers, a period of more intensive planned support should be offered following arrival.
- Similarly, Social Workers moving across borders to practice in another legislative and cultural context need a more extensive induction programme to ensure that they are competent to practice in that country (Skills for Care, 2007).
- As a minimum, the agency should have policies or guidelines that set out the content of an induction programme and the method by which it is offered.
- The content of the formal induction process should include:
  - History and philosophy of the Social Work team/service
  - The aims and objectives of the team/service
  - Key staff within the team/service and the agency
  - The organisational and environmental contexts in which the team/service operates.
  - Key staff in partner agencies and services provided
  - Workload, including caseload and working methods (for example, use of computerised information systems)
  - All policies and procedures followed by the Social Work team/ service
  - A clear understanding of Human Rights legislation and the requirements of such legislation as it is set out in each country.
- IFSW Europe e.V Member organisations can support Social Workers by:
  - Engaging in the development of codes of practice for appropriate preparation and induction programmes for Social Workers entering the profession, or moving to new roles, including Social Workers who have obtained their qualifications outside the country;
  - Advocating with employers to ensure that they have written policies and procedures for providing induction to Social

Workers, including internationally qualified workers, to prepare for new or changing roles and responsibilities;
  - The policies and procedures, and induction programmes should cover all levels of staff, including managers, temporary and agency staff, students and volunteers on placement, and those moving jobs within the agency;
  - Advocating for the support of induction processes within statutory professional registration frameworks, where these are in place.

Supervision:

- Supervision is a vital component of support for Social Workers for the reasons. The tension must be managed between the use of supervision for the purpose's of accountability on the one hand and professional development on the other. Supervision is a tool to allow the Social Worker to reflect on his/her use of their professional knowledge and skills alongside the need to ensure that the service user is receiving an appropriate service.
- In this regard, supervision should also be used to examine the wider context of Social Work and service delivery and the role of Social Work and agency in this. Supervision should be used to develop the worker's critical thinking about issues such as anti-discriminatory practice and anti-oppressive practice to help evaluate how well these practices are upheld.
- Supervision, then, serves to:
  - Meet the worker's support and developmental needs
  - Help the worker exercise good professional judgement, and iv. meet the needs of the agency in offering a service.
- Agencies should have written standards regarding supervision. These could include the following:
  - Supervision takes place regularly (frequency to be stated)
  - Supervision is arranged and conducted in such a way as to permit proper reflection and discussion.
  - There is a written supervision agreement
  - Supervision is planned and purposeful activity
  - Supervision sessions are recorded promptly, competently and stores confidentially
  - Supervisors and supervisees are trained to carry out their role
  - Supervisor ensure that that the management and administrative functions are met (accountability)
  - Each supervision session considers the employee's/Social Worker's workload, and adjustments are made accordingly
  - An objective and transparent means is applied to measure workloads example by using set tools and criteria

  - Supervisor ensures that the CPD function is met
  - Supervisor ensure that the support function is met
  - Supervisor ensures that the engagement function is met (two way commitment and engagement with the agency)
  - Supervision promotes a commitment to Human Rights and diversity in all aspects of work.
  - Managers assure the quality of supervision (Adapted from Green and Myers (2008).
- IFSW Europe e.V Member organisations can support Social Workers by:
  - Engaging in the development of codes of practice for supervision, in partnership with employers and other stakeholders.
  - Advocating with employers to ensure that they have written policies and procedures for providing supervision to enable Social Workers and social care staff to practice safely and achieve positive outcomes for service users.
  - Supervision policies and procedures should cover all levels of staff, including managers, temporary and agency staff, and students and volunteers on placement.
  - Advocating for the support of supervision within statutory professional registration frameworks.

Workload management:

- High workloads can lead to poor service quality for the user and stress and burnout for the worker. Three factors are identified as creating a current need to manage workload effectively and transparently. High workload levels:
  - Have been connected with negative impacts on practice and outcomes;
  - Have been associated with increased stress in a profession that already suffers higher than average levels, and
  - Carry implications for the workforce in terms of the interaction between stress, burnout and turnover.
- Implications for implementing workload management systems are drawn from a number of workload measurement and management studies. Three issues are identified.
  - First, workload management systems need to be informed by good quality, up-to-date workload measurement.
  - Second, involving practitioners and other stakeholders in the whole process will be the key to its success.
  - Finally, changing patterns of demand and different models of practice carry implications for workload management systems, suggesting the importance of their regular review.

- Agencies should have written standards regarding workload management. These should include measures to meet the following purposes:
  - To offer guidance on what a reasonable caseload for a Social Worker should be in line with contemporary and researched best practice;
  - To enable managers to identify and prevent overload of the individual Social Worker or teams and to inform workforce planning;
  - To provide an avenue whereby Social Workers can have clear expectations about the acceptable workload which they can carry;
  - To inform case allocation by Social Work managers;
  - To establish a coherent system of priorities for individual Social Workers, the Social Work team, the family and individual/child care programmes;
  - To contribute to supervision process in terms of discussion about organisational, professional and personal objectives;
  - To provide an overall measurement of the workload;
  - To enhance the quality of service provided to service users; and
  - To highlight unmet need.
- Caseload and workload management tools should be based on the following principles:
  - A recognition that individual Social Worker's capabilities will vary depending on experience, skills, and knowledge;
  - Personal circumstances will also influence an individual Social Worker's capacity at times and must be given consideration by the manager when assigning points *e.g.* assessed year/induction phase.
  - Caseload weighting is not just a question of numbers. It has to be part of a framework to assist effective monitoring, evaluation, supervision, support and accountability.
- This Framework recommends the consideration of indicators although not prescriptively for the implementation of good practices for workload and caseload management tool.
- These include, however not exclusively indicators based on:
  - The distribution of working time
  - The number of clients
  - Risk
  - Complexity
  - T ravel
- The following are considered reliable examples of how the indicators may be used:

  - Normal working time is typically divided between direct and indirect client work with 70% of working time devoted to direct client work which includes preparation for a certain client or client group, planning, decisionmaking, documentation, reporting, cooperation, consultation etc.
  - While at least 30% of working time is devoted to indirect client work including cooperation, development, advocacy, continuing education, work counselling, familiarisation, mentoring and training, consultation etc.
- Social Work Caseloads should therefore typically range between 10-30 clients per Social Worker allowing a minimum of 4-12 hours work devoted to direct client work for each client per month.
  - The heavier and more intense the working process, the more demanding the service needs of the clients and their objectives, the more urgent their rehabilitation needs and their condition, and the more limited the available consultation or other support services, the closer to the minimum the maximum number of clients should be.
  - The demands that legislation poses on the working process, *e.g.* the social guarantee with its time limits or the obligatory service plan, should be taken into account in staff dimensioning.
  - Risk factors also need to be taken into account. These may include, but not only the following examples:
    a. Vulnerability
    b. Lack of information
    c. Likelihood of significant harm
    d. Lack of access to support services
  - Complexity may include the following examples:
    a. Multiple problems
    b. Child protection issues
    c. Legal status and other issues
    d. Care Placement
    e. Multi-agency involvement
    f. Travel issue may include the following examples:
    g. Siblings placed in different placements
    h. High level of contact
    i. Placement outside Trust area
    j. Location of court
- IFSW Europe e.V Member organisations can support Social Workers by:
  - Engaging in the development of policies and processes for appropriate workload management systems.

- Advocating with employers to ensure that they have policies and processes in place to measure and monitor Social Workers' workloads in a transparent and an equitable way.

CONTINUOUS PROFESSIONAL DEVELOPMENT (CPD)

- Continuous professional development provides for the ongoing development of the Social Worker's knowledge and skills base and increase on their competence in the changing context of Social Work practice.
- The aim is to continuously improve the quality of outcomes for people who use Social Work services by supporting the people who are delivering these services to be the best they can be.
- CPD includes the activities that develop professional knowledge, skills and competencies for Social Work practice in relation to work with individuals, families, groups, organisations and communities. It also includes knowledge and skills required for areas such as policy development, management, research, education and the promotion of the Social Work profession. Therefore, it should include the following:
  - Post-qualifying training;
  - Participation in conferences/seminars and skills development programmes;
  - Reading professional journals;
  - Providing practice placements for Social Work students;
  - Providing and receiving professional supervision;
  - Academic study;
  - Writing and presenting professional thesiss;
  - Participation in research activities;
  - Active membership of professional associations/other relevant bodies or committees;
  - Participation in the education of Social Workers and other health/social care professionals;
- IFSW-E Member organisations can support Social Workers by:
  - Engaging in the development of standards for culturally appropriate CPD.
  - Developing mechanisms for the provision of CPD and access to such CPD programmes.
  - Advocating with employers to provide opportunities and adequate resources for CPD.
  - Advocating for the support of CPD within statutory professional registration frameworks.

Work Related Stress and Burnout:

- Among the main Health and Safety hazards for Social Workers are stress, burnout and vicarious traumatisation.
- The issue of the stress has been identified at a general level in 2004 by the European Social Partners: European Employers and Workers who agreed on a document called "Framework agreement on work related stress" whose aims are to identify, prevent and manage the problem of work-related stress.
- The European Directive 89/391 states: 'the introduction of measures to encourage improvements in the safety and health of workers at work'.
- 'Under framework directive 89/391, all employers have a legal obligation to protect the occupational safety and health of workers. This duty also applies to problems of work-related stress in so far as they entail a risk to health and safety. All workers have a general duty to comply with protective measures determined by the employer. Addressing problems of work-related stress may be carried out within an overall process of risk assessment, through a separate stress policy and/or by specific measures targeted at identified stress factors.'
- To prevent, eliminate, or reduce work-related stress, the Agreement proposes some measures such as:
  - Management and communication measures such as clarifying the company's objectives and the role of individual workers, ensuring adequate management support for individuals and teams, matching responsibility and control over work, improving work organisation and processes, working conditions and environment,
  - Training managers and workers to raise awareness and understanding of stress, its possible causes and how to deal with it, and/or to adapt to change,
  - Provision of information to and consultation with workers and/or their representatives in accordance with EU and national legislation, collective agreements and practices.

CONCLUSION

This document, is intended to consolidate the basic parameters within which Social Work in Europe operates into a common framework for Social Work in Europe. This framework is considered a key step in contributing towards the ongoing development of Standards for Social Work Practice in Europe. More awareness needs to be raised regarding the activities of Social Work as human rights practice and of ways to build on individual case solutions to influence policy change. This projects also aims to contribute to raising this awareness and securing further the profile of the profession and the conditions required by Social Workers across Europe to continue to fulfil this mission.

As Social Work looks to the future, the profession has an opportunity to assert its human rights focus more clearly. The strong compatibility of the profession's mission and values with human rights suggests a natural linkage. Human rights provide the profession with a clear direction for a presence at the international level, while also bridging local and national issues with global concerns.

8

Human Rights Violations in Welfare Legislation

INTRODUCTION

OVERVIEW: WELFARE REFORM

The passage of the Personal Responsibility and Work Opportunity Reconciliation Act of 1996 (PRWORA), dismantled the former Aid to Families with Dependent Children (AFDC) and established Temporary Assistance for Needy Families (TANF). Under AFDC, families received federal cash assistance indefinitely, without threat of time limits or fear of arbitrary termination. Welfare reform in 1996 established a new system of time-limited and state-run benefits in the form of TANF block grants. Structurally, PRWORA devolved much of the federal government's responsibility to the states, which in turn, devolve implementation to individual counties or cities.

States currently receive federal block grants and despite federal guidelines, have almost full discretion to spend this money as they see fit. Although this move towards decentralization has allowed states more spending flexibility, devolution has also resulted in a lack of accountability within the welfare system. Further, regulations vary from state to state, making policy and service evaluation, as well as overall accountability, extremely difficult. In addition to structural changes, welfare reform established incentives for both marriage promotion and work, underscoring these within the established purpose of TANF. Mandates therefore, include encouraging the creation of two-parent households, as well as making recipients work for their benefits. The implementation of these mandates, left to the discretion of individual caseworkers, has led to a lack of accountability and ultimately, to a number of potential human rights violations.

Although current welfare legislation was drafted to reduce dependency on government assistance, poverty reduction has never been an implicit goal of federal TANF policy. Instead, the federal government drafted and implemented TANF with the clear goal of simply moving recipients off the welfare rolls and into work. Rather than developing policy that creates a better standard of living for both adults and children living in poverty, current law places a strict priority on "work first" as a solution to ending "dependency". With this heavy focus on moving recipients into work, any employment becomes adequate, with virtually no consideration for the presence of vital characteristics, such as job mobility or the opportunity to acquire job skills. Further, these policies do little to recognize education as a long-term solution to poverty. Those activities that are considered work have been narrowly defined, such as limited vocational training and exclude many postsecondary education opportunities.

States are permitted to exempt only thirty per cent of their caseloads into education or job training placements, forcing the large majority of recipients into mandatory work placements. With so few receiving adequate training or education, acquiring a job that pays a livable wage has proven to be extremely difficult and ultimately has resulted in many leaving the caseloads without leaving poverty.

For those who are able to pursue education, both federal and New York State laws limit participation to one year and in turn, participants are unlikely to obtain sufficient job skills or a higher degree. Despite studies finding that roughly 64% of single welfare mothers lack a high school diploma, TANF simply does not allow for adequate educational opportunities and instead, mandates families to jobs that rarely provide livable wages or adequate job security. These employment conditions hinder self-sufficiency and essentially fail to raise income levels above the poverty line. In addition, TANF recipients face a federal five-year lifetime time limit, restricting the amount of time that they can receive benefits. Ultimately though, states can shorten time limits to fewer than five years and can also extend time limits, but must use state funds to do so. Under these work-first conditions, recipients face multiple challenges and barriers to finding sustainable employment, while faced with the fear of reaching their time limit.

Much of the current discussion hailing welfare reform as a success has focused on the drastic decreases nationally in welfare rolls. But despite heavy caseload reduction, welfare reform has done little to promote poverty reduction, increase long-term employment, or develop a higher standard of living for recipients and their children. Instead, it has caused increased depravation of many fundamental human rights, such as the right to food, health, and housing. These conditions are not luxuries, but rather, basic human rights linked to the right to education, the right to employment, and the right to an adequate standard of living. As a member of the United Nations, the U.S. has an obligation to fulfill these rights, which are outlined in numerous international documents, particularly the Universal Declaration of Human Rights. With the expiration of TANF approaching in September 2002, poverty reduction must become an explicit and primary goal of new legislation and any amendments to PRWORA. Ultimately, caseload reduction can no longer be the primary measure of welfare reform's "success". Reauthorization must instead, target poverty reduction and securing the rights of those most economically and socially disadvantaged.

This policy brief will present the fundamental rights that current welfare policies and practices violate. The United States often fails to adhere to many of its global obligations and has neglected to ratify numerous international documents, concerning economic, social, and cultural rights, as well as the rights of the child. Regardless, the U.S. is not immune to human rights violations. In fact, the U.S. compiles annual Country Reports on Human Rights. Practices, using the Universal Declaration of Human Rights (UDHR) as its standard. These reports refer to the rights outlined in the UDHR and document human rights violations within each UN member state. Outlined within the Universal Declaration, are a number of economic and social rights, including the right to employment, education, and an adequate standard of living. Using this document as a standard for all other nations, the United States government must consider itself equally obligated to fulfill these economic and social rights. In this same manner, this brief will specifically examine potential domestic violations of economic, social, and cultural rights, with a particular emphasis on race and gender.

WHY A HUMAN RIGHTS APPROACH TO WELFARE REFORM AND POVERTY

Championed by the United States in 1948, the Universal Declaration of Human Rights guarantees the right to live free from poverty. Recognized by the international community, this document establishes the right to an adequate standard of living. In addition to the UDHR, the United Nations has reinforced the right to live free from poverty in numerous subsequent international treaties and declarations, including those

addressing both racial and gender discrimination, as well as economic, social, and cultural rights. In addition, the right to an adequate standard of living if further enforced through the Convention on the Rights of the Child. But regardless of the recognition that every human being is ensured this right, the United States has failed to take adequate action to guarantee its realization. Despite lower rates of absolute poverty in the U.S. relative to many developing nations, the government must not consider itself exempt from addressing domestic poverty, particularly when considering its role as a world economic superpower. Considering the vast resources available within the United States, poverty rates remain unacceptably high, particularly for women, children, and minorities. Both poverty and poor educational outcomes have consistently affected women and people of colour disproportionately in the United States. When considering that "more than 90% of welfare recipient household heads are women"' the correlation between poverty and gender become strikingly clear. In New York, TANF caseloads illustrate a strong correlation between poverty and race, where 41.3% of recipients are Black, while only 19.1% are

White. Nationally, the disproportionate representation of people of colour on welfare is equally evident.

Additionally, single female-headed households with children are more likely to live in poverty than any other household structure. Children therefore, are also at high risk for living in poverty and a 2001 study found the relative child poverty rate in the United States to be 20%. The inability of the U.S. to reduce its child poverty rate is inexcusable, particularly when considering that other developed nations, such as Norway and Sweden, have relative child poverty rates of only 3.9% and 2.6%, respectively. Further examination of poverty in the U.S. reveals that among those living in poverty, 57% are women and 40% are children under the age of eighteen, thereby comprising virtually the entire population living in poverty. Race and gender therefore, are clearly related to poverty in the nation ultimately has a legal responsibility to address these violations.

While human rights violations are often perceived as international concerns, many potential violations exist within domestic borders, particularly for vulnerable populations. The international community has accepted economic and social human rights, yet the U.S. government has failed to recognize formally the equal importance of these rights to civil and political rights. Essentially, a human rights approach to welfare reform and poverty reduction would integrate the economic and social rights that are widely accepted throughout the world into domestic legislation. This framework therefore, would bring the United States closer to meeting its international obligation. The terms of these rights call for more government accountability and sufficient civil society participation, as well as clear policies that address erasing poverty for the most vulnerable populations. In addition, a human rights approach redefines public assistance as a right, rather than a system of charity. Acknowledging the international community's higher standard of government responsibility therefore, provides greater leverage for those living in poverty to meet their basic human needs.

THE RIGHT TO AN ADEQUATE STANDARD OF LIVING

WHY POVERTY REDUCTION?

Virtually all human rights are correlated with the right to uphold an adequate standard of living. The realization of education, employment, and health rights, for example, is strongly connected to the ability to maintain adequate living standards. Similarly, without guaranteed housing or a livable wage, governments cannot assure its citizens basic living standards. However, within international law, "adequate" remains vaguely defined and may connote different definitions according to the population at hand. Based on available resources within a country, adequate mobilization of resources as well as the realization of an adequate standard of living may vary. Given the vast domestic resources available however, the United States has an obligation as an economic superpower to provide an adequate standard of living that includes at a minimum, the ability for all residents to live free from poverty. Upholding economic and social human rights is ultimately essential to movement out of poverty and is in turn, fundamental to poverty eradication in the United States.

Considering that women and people of colour are more likely to earn lower wages, as well as face employment discrimination, their disproportionate representation among those living in poverty is not surprising. Within New York City, poverty trends are strikingly clear according to race. These Black and Hispanic families have significantly higher chances of living in poverty as well as much lower chances of earning higher incomes than White families in New York City. To reduce poverty and ultimately increase the standard of living, legislation must recognize the uneven representation of different racial and ethnic groups among those living in poverty. Although the benefits of decreasing poverty are manifold, economic security is not a guaranteed Constitutional right, let alone a goal of TANF legislation. For systemic and economic reasons, access to health care, shelter, food, and clothing is more limited for those living in poverty. By reducing poverty therefore, those with low incomes are presented with greater social and economic opportunities. To reduce poverty however, livable wages and the level of education necessary to obtain them are fundamental. In effect, obtaining employment does nothing to increase independence if workers cannot remain independent. The right to an adequate standard of living therefore, must include not only the ability to live free from poverty, but also the ability to remain out of poverty.

INTERNATIONAL LAW

Multiple international documents and treaties outline various human rights in an attempt to increase the standard of living in countries worldwide, primarily through US funding. The United States is therefore, willing to support a higher standard of living internationally, yet does not recognize its domestic obligation to fulfill this right. Documents that strengthen women's rights, eliminate racial discrimination, and support the rights of the child all seek to provide a higher standard of living for vulnerable groups. In this sense, the majority of international law holds nations responsible for providing an adequate standard of living to its residents, with particular attention to its most vulnerable populations. As a Millennium development goal, eradication of extreme poverty and hunger is currently of foremost importance to the current goals of the United Nations. In addition, numerous international documents articulate and guarantee the right to an adequate standard of living.

- Universal Declaration of Human Rights, Article 25 (1):
- "Everyone has the right to a standard of living adequate for the health and well-being of himself and of his family, including food, clothing, housing and medical care and necessary social service, and the right to security in the event of unemployment, sickness, disability, widowhood, old age, or other lack of livelihood in circumstances beyond his control."
- *Article* 25 (2): "Motherhood and childhood are entitled to special care and assistance. All children, whether born in or out of wedlock, shall enjoy the same social protection."
- *Convention on the Rights of the Child, Article* 27 (1): "States Parties recognize the right of every child to a standard of living adequate for the child's physical, mental, moral and social development."
- *Article* 27 (3): "States Parties...shall take appropriate measures to assist parents and others responsible for the child to implement this right and shall in case of need provide material assistance and support programmes, particularly with regard to nutrition, clothing and housing."
- *International Covenant on Economic, Social and Cultural Rights, Article* 11 (1): "States Parties... recognize the right of everyone to an adequate standard of living for himself and his family...The States Parties will take appropriate steps to ensure the realization of this right".
- *Article* 12 (1): "States Parties...recognize the right of everyone to the enjoyment of the highest attainable standard of physical and mental health"

These international documents define the general conditions that contribute to an adequate standard of living, including housing, clothing, food, as well as physical and mental health. Limiting one's ability to maintain these conditions is clearly considered a human rights violation under international law. The Economic and Social Council of the General Assembly therefore, recognizes the need to adapt "a rights-based approach to poverty" to eradicate poverty and guarantee all a basic standard of living.

FEDERAL AND STATE OBLIGATION

While the United States guarantees its residents numerous civil and political rights, the federal government has regularly ignored economic and social rights. Various federal and state documents establish residents' rights, but do not establish a right to live free from poverty, let alone an obligation to reduce poverty. Within the United States Constitution however, are conditions that reflect a guaranteed minimum standard of living. The Preamble describes the Constitution and its Amendments as a means of promoting the general Welfare, thereby establishing a governmental obligation to provide minimum living standards. Without directly addressing economic or social rights within the Constitution and international treaties however, the Federal government does not specifically define adequate living standards, but only refers to civil and political rights. Ultimately, while the United States does recognize its Constitutional obligation to provide an adequate standard of living, it does not act upon this responsibility and fails to articulate this obligation into law.

The New York State Constitution also guarantees numerous civil and political rights, but does not specifically guarantee economic or social rights. It does however, include Article XVII, which refers to the Social Welfare and establishes an obligation to the State to provide for the "aid, care and support of the needy". Although weak in language, the State Constitution defines these acts as "public concerns", holding New York responsible for providing for the general welfare. The State also assumes the obligation to promote and protect the health of its residents, as well as establish systems to protect its vulnerable populations. While these protections do not necessarily include economic rights or the right to live free from poverty, they do establish conditions necessary for minimum living standards in the state. Both national and state bodies therefore, recognize the need to protect residents and provide for their general welfare, but fail to articulate these obligations into law.

TANF LEGISLATION VIOLATES THE RIGHT TO AN ADEQUATE STANDARD OF LIVING

Through policies such as the Family Cap, sanctions, and time limits, TANF legislation fails to guarantee recipients an adequate standard of living. States have the option to implement a "family cap", which denies additional benefits to families that have additional children while receiving public assistance. This policy, while not legal in New York, targets the reproductive habits of low-income women. Congresswoman Patsy Mink views the Family Cap as "a direct attack on the childbearing rights of poor women" and therefore, as a discriminatory policy based on economic status. Denying low-income children assistance further discriminates against the children in these families, based on their parents' behaviours and their economic status. Children who are excluded from receiving benefits in poor Family Cap policies however, bar children from benefiting from these programmes, further pushing them into poverty and hunger.

The Convention on the Rights of the Child specifically guarantees the right to an adequate standard of living, including sufficient social protection to children, yet the Family Cap explicitly denies them these rights.households fail to receive protections guaranteed by international law, specifically the right for every child to an adequate standard of living. Further, the Convention on the Rights of the Child holds governments responsible for implementing this right by providing children and their parents with "material assistance and support programmes", specifically concerning food, clothing, and shelter.

Federal legislation also restricts recipients from receiving public assistance past a five-year lifetime time limit, even if they remain in poverty. Imposing a time limit and denying benefits after a specified time allows governments to reduce resources available to recipients, regardless of their poverty status. Essentially, time limits reject the progressive realization of the right to an adequate standard of living and enable governments to terminate recipients' fulfillment of their economic rights. In addition, time limits establish that recipients are entitled to an adequate standard of living for a restricted period of time. Welfare reform in 1996 eliminated the previous entitlement to an adequate living standard and time limit policies further jeopardize this right. Should recipients be unable to achieve economic independence before five years, their right to social protection is essentially, terminated.

Included in this arbitrary limit is the assumption that public assistance is a means out of poverty and that poverty is temporary. Without an adequate system of supports, such as educational opportunities and fulfillment of employment rights, the opportunity to move out of poverty remains small. Poverty reduction and the fulfillment of one's right to an adequate standard of living therefore, rest heavily in systemic policy changes. Time limits that punish recipients for having low-incomes therefore, ignore the violations of economic rights in both Federal and State policies and in turn, do little reduce poverty.

THE RIGHT TO EDUCATION

WHY ACCESS TO EDUCATION IS IMPORTANT

Education is regularly tied to achieving a basic level of self-sufficiency and economic independence within a society. Strongly connected to the ability to maintain a minimum standard of living, "education is the primary vehicle by which economically and socially marginalized adults and children can lift themselves out of poverty" In this sense, the United Nations Committee on Economic, Social, and Cultural Rights regards the right to education as essential to the ability to participate fully in a community. To obtain employment and economic independence therefore, adults must have access to a standard level of education that correlates with the general population. A high school degree is therefore, rarely sufficient to compete in the United States' job market, particularly when considering that Census data show that low wages that correlate with low levels of education.

A woman who receives minimum wage and no income supports "must work 60 to 70 hours weekly for 50 weeks a year to come just above the poverty threshold." With higher levels of education though, obtaining higher paying work and maintaining economic stability both become more feasible. Improved ability to obtain higher paying work is particularly important for women, considering that "approximately 70% of working women in the United States earn less than $20,000 a year, and nearly 40% earn less than $10,000."

Further, in the United States, the average adult has a minimum of a high school degree and the average job requires at least this level of education.

Competition in the surrounding job market therefore, requires a minimum level of educational attainment. In the United States, where 88 per cent of those between the ages of 25 and 29 have at least a high school degree, attaining this level of education is imperative to anyone searching employment. In addition, according to the New York State Department of Labour, "75% of New York City's major employers require college degrees or training beyond high school for entry level jobs." Inability to participate in schooling limits one's capacity to compete for and obtain sustainable work. Particularly in the U.S. therefore, access to education is fundamental to one's stability and realization of economic human rights.

INTERNATIONAL LAW

While all states mandate school attendance until at least age sixteen, equal access to an adequate and quality education, particularly higher levels of education, does not exist. The United States protects against discrimination in educational programmes based on race, national origin, sex, disability, and age. Despite these protections, unequal access based not only on these conditions, but also on economic, racial, and gender disparities continues to exist.

Women are disproportionately affected by low levels of education compared to men with the same level of education. The average yearly wage for males between the ages of 25 and 29 who have a high school degree and are working full-time is $22,358, while women in the same category earn only $16,266. While women earn less than men on average, Black, non-Hispanic women in this same category earn only $15,019, illustrating that disparities clearly exist according to gender and race. To address these disparities and the prevalence of unequal access to education, international law guarantees the right to education in numerous documents. Among these documents are: the Universal Declaration of Human Rights (UDHR), the International Covenant on Economic, Social, and Cultural Rights (ICESCR), and the International Convention on the Elimination of All Forms of Racial Discrimination (ICERD).

- *Universal Declaration of Human Rights (UDHR), Article* 26: "Everyone has the right to education. Education shall be free, at least in the elementary and fundamental stages. Elementary education shall be compulsory. Technical and professional education shall be made generally available and higher education shall be equally accessible to all on the basis of merit."
- *International Covenant on Economic, Social, and Cultural Rights (ICESCR), Article* 13 (1): "The States Parties to the present Covenant recognize the right of everyone to education...They further agree

that education shall enable all persons to participate effectively in a free society."

- *Article* 13 (2): "The States Parties to the present Covenant recognize that, with a view to achieving the full realization of this right: Primary education shall be compulsory and available free to all...Higher education shall be made equally accessible to all...by every appropriate means."
- *International Convention on the Elimination of All Forms of Racial Discrimination (ICERD), Article* 5: "States Parties...guarantee the right of everyone, without distinction as to race, colour, or national or ethnic origin, to equality before the law, notably in the enjoyment of the following rights...Economic, social and cultural rights, in particular: (v) The right to education and training".

The right to education is further articulated in numerous documents published by the United Nations Educational, Scientific and Cultural Organization (UNESCO), which sponsored the World Education Forum in April, 2000. Declaring that "all children, young people and adults have the human right to benefit from an education that will meet their basic learning needs", UNESCO presents education as a fundamental human right. In addition, the Committee on Economic, Social, and Cultural Rights articulates this right in its General Comment 13 on the Right to Education.

FEDERAL AND STATE OBLIGATION

Neglecting to ratify the ICESCR, the United States fails to recognize directly the right to education, despite its obligation under ICERD and UDHR. Regardless of its failure to comply with international law, various U.S. policies have established the importance of education. In his most recent budget proposal for example, President George W. Bush supports continued federal funding for vocational and adult education, indicating a federal obligation to make educational programmes accessible regardless of age.

Similarly, New York State recognizes the need to promote education and provide accessibility to its residents. Both the State Constitution and the New York State Board of Regents recognize the government's role in providing adequate education. Essentially, Article XI of the State Constitution mandates that the state legislature "provide for the maintenance and support of a system of free common schools", thereby establishing the need for available schooling. The Board of Regents, which is part of the New York State Education Department, extends its focus to include not only childhood education, but also "secondary and continuing education; higher education; cultural education; and services for individuals with disabilities".

These documents and departments reflect a desire, as well as an obligation on both the federal and the state level to fulfill the right to education. Regardless of the established responsibility for government to provide adequate educational availability, both federal and state welfare policies fail to do so. Despite the United States' free public school system, discriminatory funding often disproportionately affects low-income and minority students, particularly in New York City. Further, specific policies within TANF legislation deny participation in programmes beyond primary education and essentially, violate the human right to education.

TANF LEGISLATION VIOLATES THE RIGHT TO EDUCATION

Specific TANF policies limit recipients' access to education and deny their right to participate in educational programmes and activities, including higher education and vocational training. Although federal legislation establishes that education and job training activities fulfill TANF's work requirement, only a limited amount of recipients can qualify. To assure that the vast majority of recipients perform employment-related activities, federal legislation limits education and training opportunities to "not more than 20 per cent of individuals in all families". This arbitrary restriction on who is eligible to fulfill their work requirement in such activities denies recipients equal access to education. Instead, this policy essentially legalizes unequal accessibility and availability, thereby disregarding the educational rights guaranteed by numerous international human rights documents.

In addition to a percentage limitation, federal legislation places a time limit on education and vocational training activities. Not only does TANF allow only a very small portion of those receiving welfare to count these activities as work, but also denies participation in training beyond one year. Because "85% of recipients report one or more multiple barriers that mitigate against employment", one year of training simply is not sufficient to prepare most for stable employment. An arbitrary time limit on educational participation therefore, is discriminatory and only limits recipients' ability to realise economic self-sufficiency. By limiting participation in training, TANF not only reduces access, but also limits one's capacity to participate in society, both of which are violations of educational human rights.

Clearly, TANF recipients are not receiving the skills needed to move off the welfare rolls and out of poverty. In addition to females earning lower wages than men in the United States in general, the average mother who leaves welfare for full-time, low-wage work, experiences "at least a 33% gap between her expected earnings and her necessary expenses." To understand why women are unable to obtain livable wages, TANF must address workers' need for higher levels of education to compete within the job market. Most jobs, particularly those that offer livable wages, require postsecondary education and TANF must be better equip recipients to compete for this work. High school alone simply is not enough to provide sufficient access to most jobs and move recipients towards economic self-sufficiency. Among African-American women for example, the poverty rate for those with one year of postsecondary education, as opposed to those with only a high school degree drops to 21% from 51%. Numerous studies have further supported the economic benefits of receiving even one year of education or training beyond high school. Without the ability to participate in higher educational activities therefore, few will obtain the skills needed to maintain stable and livable employment and in turn, move out of poverty.

THE RIGHT TO EMPLOYMENT

WHY EMPLOYMENT IS IMPORTANT

Outlined within the Personal Responsibility and Work Opportunity Reconciliation Act of 1996 are four specific purposes of welfare reform; the most important being the goal to reduce government dependence by promoting both job preparation and work. While the other three purposes include providing that children can be cared for at home or in the home of relatives, preventing out-of-wedlock births, and encouraging the formation of two-parent families, work goals have been the most heavily implemented. Through this legislation therefore, the United States government acknowledges employment as essential to self-sufficiency. Despite this focus on employment, federal TANF legislation fails to define or support sustainable employment, thereby forcing many into "work" that does little to "end the dependence of needy parents on government benefits". Work alone does not guarantee a path out of poverty, particularly when considering that "60% of poor families with children include at least one person who works outside the home". Under work-first policies, "work" is considered paramount to all other activities, including education, care giving, and obtaining other benefits such as Food Stamps and Medicaid. Within federal legislation, the heavy focus on work is coupled with participation rate requirements, which have increased since 1996.

The work participation rate requirements have increased in both federal and New York State law from 25 per cent of state caseloads in 1997 to 50 per cent of state caseloads in 2002 and after. Similarly, the federal number of required weekly hours has increased from 20 hours per week in 1997 to 30 hours per week in 2000 and after. New York State law mandates the same hours of participation as federal law, despite each state's ability to increase or decrease these required rates. While employment regulations exempt some special populations, such as those in domestic violence situations or with very young children, both federal and state policies overwhelmingly focus on moving recipients into work activities, regardless of recipients' needs, such as basic literacy activities. These forced work activities establish arbitrary requirements and represent a fundamental violation of the right to work.

For employment to reduce one's dependence on public assistance, it must provide benefits such as livable wages, health care, and practical job skills.

Among welfare recipients, these benefits are extremely difficult to obtain, given the low level of stable employment available, as well as the chance of facing employment discrimination. Because women and people of colour are disproportionately represented among TANF caseloads, attention to the experiences that they are more likely to face in the job market becomes essential when considering TANF work requirements. Both groups face higher chances of working at low wages, as well as facing employment discrimination. Among minimum-wage workers, two thirds are women, illustrating unbalanced access to higher paying wages according to gender. Further, people of colour receiving TANF tend to earn lower wages than white recipients and one study on welfare leavers found that among "whites on welfare, 40.1% left the rolls because they earned enough money to become independent, compared to 27.4% of minorities.

" The same trend holds true when accounting for educational differences among races. Studies on Job Readiness programmes indicate that among those participating, "67% of white participants without a high school diploma obtained employment, compared with 53% of black participants." Despite the strong focus within TANF legislation on promoting work, wide gaps according to race become obvious when addressing the ability to obtain employment and access to livable wages. While employment is fundamental to leaving poverty, adequate and stable employment must become equally accessible, regardless of race or gender.

INTERNATIONAL LAW

Clearly, equal access to sustainable employment is limited for the most vulnerable groups. Among TANF recipients who obtain subsidized employment, most overwhelmingly find low-wage work and jobs that provide little to no job skills. In 1998, only 8% of welfare recipients' new jobs paid wages that were able to lift them above the poverty line. Ninety-two per cent of recipients' new jobs therefore, did not pay enough to achieve self-sufficiency and in turn, reduce government "dependency". While international law guarantees equal access to employment, as well as adequate pay for work activities, the United States has yet to address these disparities in domestic legislation. Various employment rights are outlined in a number of international documents, including UDHR, ICERD, ICESCR, and the Millennium Declaration.

- *Universal Declaration of Human Rights (UDHR), Article* 23 (1): "Everyone has the right to work, to free choice of employment, to just and favourable conditions of work and to protection against unemployment."
- *Article* 23 (3): "Everyone who works has the right to just and favourable remuneration ensuring for himself and his family an existence worthy of human dignity, and supplemented, if necessary, by other means of social protection."

- *Article* 23 (4): "Everyone has the right to form and to join trade unions for the protection of his interests."
- *International Convention on the Elimination of All Forms of Racial Discrimination (ICERD) Article* 5: "States Parties undertake to prohibit and to eliminate racial discrimination in all its forms and to guarantee the right of everyone, without distinction as to race, colour, or national or ethnic origin, to equality before the law, notably in the enjoyment of...Economic, social, and cultural rights, in particular: (e) The rights to work, to free choice of employment..."
- International Covenant on Economic, Social and Cultural Rights (ICESCR),
- *Article* 6: "the right of everyone to the opportunity to gain his living by work which he freely chooses or accepts...The full realization of this right shall include technical and vocational guidance and training programmes...and full and productive employment".
- *Article* 7: "The States Parties to the present Covenant recognize the right of everyone to...a decent living for themselves and their families...safe and healthy working conditions...Equal opportunity for everyone to be promoted in his employment to an appropriate higher level...and reasonable limitation of working hours and periodic holidays with pay, as well as remuneration for public holidays."
- *Millennium Declaration (MD), III* (20): "We also resolve...To develop and implement strategies that give young people everywhere a real chance to find decent and productive work."

The right to employment is further articulated through a number of documents published by the International Labour Organization (ILO), as well as the Economic and Social Council. In its report on the Employment Policy Convention, the ILO underscores the need for "freedom of choice of employment" as a means of raising the standard of living and continues to recognize economic, social, and cultural rights as fundamental to this outcome. Similarly, the Economic and Social Council emphasizes the need for quality jobs, which include provisions such as "adequate remuneration and social protection and decent working conditions." Ultimately, employment alone is not considered sufficient to reduce poverty, but must be coupled with conditions such as adequate wages and equal access.

Federal and State Obligation

Similar to the right to education, the United States does not recognize directly the employment rights outlined within numerous United Nations documents, despite its obligation under international law. While the U.S. government is reluctant to adhere to the conditions of these documents, various government officials and policies clearly recognize the importance of work. Federal TANF legislation pinpoints job preparation and work as solutions to government "dependence" and lack of economic self-sufficiency. Employment therefore, is recognized as fundamental to moving recipients not only off welfare rolls, but also out of poverty. Similarly, the federal Workforce Investment Partnership Act of 1998 recognizes that workers require academic and employability skills to participate in the labour market successfully. While this law connects basic skills to "successful employment", PRWORA fails to form the same connections. As a result, federal and state TANF policies overwhelmingly promote work, but without the fundamental work supports necessary for stable employment.

Through the application of work-first policies, any form of work becomes acceptable for welfare recipients and virtually all emphasis on job skills and education disappears. When looking at those participating in work requirements in New York State, the focus on work-first, rather than on skill building becomes exceedingly clear. While both federal and New York State policies allow 30% of recipients to participate in these activities, New York clearly does not meet this authorized level and in turn, fails to attribute much significance to education or job training. The success of welfare reform is therefore, often measured not only by how many leave the caseloads, but also how many recipients participate in work activities. Tommy Thompson, Secretary of the U.S. Department of Health and Human Services (HHS), "welfare reform means finding poor people jobs". But, if these jobs are to reduce government "dependency", then HHS and New York City's Human Resources Administration (HRA) must mandate work that provides true opportunities both to leave and remain out of poverty.

TANF LEGISLATION VIOLATES THE RIGHT TO EMPLOYMENT

Because work placements are mandated to TANF recipients, federal legislation violates the right to choose one's own form of employment. Outlined in both the Universal Declaration and ICERD, "free choice of employment" is fundamental to employment rights. In New York, recipients and caseworkers are supposed to develop an employability plan to determine recipients' work activities. Although the process involves both worker and recipient, "the district does not necessarily need client agreement with the finished plan", thereby giving local governments ultimate authority in determining work placements. Because employability plans often ignore both recipients' needs and skills, this process provides recipients essentially with no input towards their work placement.

In addition, TANF recipients can be lawfully sanctioned and lose their benefits for refusing to accept their assigned work activity. This process therefore, violates recipients' rights to choose and to accept the work that they perform, both of which are guaranteed employment rights. While the International Labour Organization asserts that the right to choose one's own employment is fundamental to raising the standard of living, this process clearly hinders recipients' ability to achieve a higher standard of living and represents a clear violation of the basic employment rights guaranteed by international law. To realise the right to employment fully, work must also include "favourable remuneration", as guaranteed by multiple international documents. Workfare programmes, however, require welfare recipients to work in unsubsidized employment in return for their benefits. Such programmes not only fail to move recipients towards economic self-sufficiency, but also deny recipients wages for the work they perform. New York City's Work Experience Programme (WEP) in particular, reflects this violation of the right to receive pay for work performed. In all unsubsidized employment activities, recipients must participate in their placements to "work off" their monthly benefits.

In New York City, after accounting for recipients' "cash, food stamps and shelter allowances", WEP workers cost the City only $1.80 per hour' drastically the minimum wage of $5.15 per hour. The City therefore, forces WEP workers to perform activities that pay well below standard wages, which is a direct violation of the right to adequate pay for work. Failing to provide adequate wages, unsubsidized employment does little to help recipients establish "a decent living for themselves and their families" and directly violates the employment right to adequate remuneration for work performed.

In addition to working without receiving adequate pay, workfare workers are not protected by many of the provisions that protect workers in the United States. Because the state does not recognize WEP workers as "employees", protections such as the Fair Labour Standards Act (FLSA) and the right to unionize do not apply.

The Department of Labour, recipients "must be compensated at the applicable minimum wage" if they are considered "employees" as defined by the FLSA. Because the Act's definition is vague, New York has been able to deny WEP workers "employee" status and in turn, denies multiple employment rights, including the right to unionize. Despite being denied "employee" status, WEP workers perform the same work as hired employees, but at much lower costs to the City. Since WEP workers are not considered employees, the Occupational Safety and Health Act does not apply to WEP worksites or work conditions. In addition to safety and health protections, the City also denies WEP workers protection from sexual harassment. In a recent federal lawsuit against the City of New York, a federal district court found that female WEP workers are not entitled to "the same workplace protections as most city employees" regarding sexual harassment, simply because the City does not consider them employees. Failure to grant workfare workers employee status therefore, allows state and local governments not only to place recipients in unsafe working conditions, but also to force them to remain in these conditions.

This process is in direct violation of numerous aspects of the right to employment and permits governments to exploit workers based solely on their low-income status. This lack of protection coupled with the inability to unionize, results in the City's failure to guarantee the "safe and healthy working conditions" mandated in international law.

Welfare recipients therefore, are denied multiple protections that are guaranteed to other workers based on discriminatory measures. The inability to choose employment freely, receive adequate pay, form and join unions, and remain protected under safe working conditions, all represent violations of the right to employment.

CONCLUSION

Prior to Welfare Reform in 1996, public assistance was considered an entitlement, guaranteeing those with low incomes a minimum standard of living indefinitely. Public assistance assured that those living in poverty would receive government support in the form of social protection. Under the previous system therefore, the United States recognized its obligation to provide for the general welfare, particularly for marginalized groups such as people of colour, women, and children.

Welfare reform however, created a system of time limits, which deny an adequate standard of living to those with low incomes after a designated time. This policy therefore, allows governments to exclude a very specific population of people from enjoying minimum living standards based on arbitrary limits. Further, these limits do not account for the greater systemic and policy failures in TANF legislation that prevent recipients from moving off public assistance independently.

Included in these systemic and policy failures are the multiple violations of both educational and employment rights. The challenges of moving out of poverty result not from lack of personal motivation, but from multiple environmental and societal barriers, such as discrimination and unequal access to work supports.

To increase recipients' movement towards economic self-sufficiency, TANF legislation must first fulfill the right to education. When considering that nearly 50% of all recipients in New York State lack a high school degree, the Federal and New York 30% limits on educational participation clearly do not acknowledge the educational needs of TANF recipients. If recipients are expected to obtain jobs that move them off welfare after five years, as well as remain off public assistance, then their education rights must include at a minimum, the ability to obtain a high school degree. Only through the realization of this right will recipients obtain and maintain work that allows them to leave TANF and become economically independent.

In conjunction with the right to education, legislation must fulfill the right to employment if recipients are to leave poverty. While work experience can benefit recipients, current TANF work placements rarely provide the job skills or educational opportunities that recipients require. Requirements that mandate recipients to perform unpaid community service, for example, do not provide wages necessary to become economically independent. Further, this type of work is a direct violation of workers' right to fair pay for work performed. Despite employment being a key condition for economic independence, TANF violates basic employment rights, leaving most recipients without the sufficient work experience necessary to move off public assistance. Legislation therefore, must acknowledge poverty reduction as an essential role of public assistance and in turn, must recognize that economic human rights violations contribute to recipients' inability to become economically self-sufficient. With recognition of economic rights however, recipients will face fewer barriers to achieving economic independence.

9

Human Rights and the Global Economic Crisis

Coming at the confluence of the financial, fuel and food crises, the global economic crisis is devastating lives and livelihoods across the world. And it is rapidly turning into a human rights crisis. One year on from the near-collapse of the international financial system, this briefing explores the human rights dimensions of the crisis, its causes and consequences, and worldwide responses. From an economic perspective, the harmful impacts of the crisis on human lives and dignity tend to be seen as tragic but inevitable consequences of unpredictable and uncontrollable market forces. A human rights perspective challenges this complacency; these devastating consequences are not inevitable, nor should they be acceptable. The causes of the crisis can be clearly located in human decisions and concrete actions of governments and powerful economic actors, and should not be seen as the result of forces outside of human control. A human rights approach demands accountability for these human decisions. It requires that negative effects be avoided or mitigated and it empowers people affected to demand respect for their human rights.

WHAT IS HAPPENING AND WHY

Far from being an unpredictable event, the financial crisis was predicted by a number of organizations, including the Bank for International Settlements which warned in June 2007 that "years of loose monetary policy have fuelled a giant global credit bubble, leaving us vulnerable to another 1930s slump". The financial crisis began as the "sub-prime crisis" in the United States in August 2007 and then erupted into a global credit crisis in September 2008. It was caused by the combination of loose monetary policy, deregulation, excessive risk-taking by banks, and the explosion of credit/debt between 2002-2007.

The "sub-prime crisis" was the result of the unsustainable and predatory lending of mortgage brokers to people whose salaries were too low to pay off the loans. Instead of keeping these high-risk loans on their books, banks and brokers invented new ways of packaging and selling them to other banks and investors. At the same time, many banks and investors took out insurance against the default of these new assets from companies such as U.S. insurer American International Group. This contributed to an explosion in credit derivatives, which investor Warren Buffet called "financial weapons of mass destruction" because of the huge threat they posed to the stability of the financial system. Such warnings were ignored, however, because of the opportunities for vast, short-term profits.

But these profits were unsustainable: as soon as house prices started to fall and borrowers started to default on high-risk loans, the system collapsed. The value of "toxic assets" was wiped out, insurance failed as AIG collapsed, and the credit markets froze, bringing down a series of banks–including major U.S. investment bank Lehman Brothers on September 15, 2008. Banking regulators, who had stepped back from strong regulation because of an increasingly strong belief in the infallibility and efficiency of markets, had to step in to rescue the banking system and prevent systemic collapse. In a rapid and unprecedented response, trillions of dollars were spent bailing out bankrupt banks.

However, the prevention of systemic financial meltdown did not prevent the global economic downturn. As problems of the financial sector spilled over into the real economy, economic crisis emerged not only in developed economies, but across the world. In developed economies, the credit crunch triggered a collapse of consumer demand which quickly translated into rising unemployment, in turn further affecting consumer demand, particularly given unprecedented levels of household debt. But the crisis also spread to developing countries, transmitted first through an abrupt decline in trade finance and then through a precipitous drop in demand for the exports of developing countries, many of whose economies have become disproportionately dependent on an export-driven model of growth promoted by the international financial institutions.

Exacerbated by a decline in migrant workers' remittances, aid and private capital flows, this has created massive unemployment, pushing millions more people into poverty around the world. While trillions of dollars were made available for bailing out the banking sector, this has not been matched by funds to support those who are suffering most from the crisis. As ODI notes, so far there has been a "minimal social protection response to this crisis".

THE CONSEQUENCES OF THE CRISIS–IMPACTS ON THE REALIZATION OF HUMAN RIGHTS

As the financial crisis has spilled over into the real economy, it has had, as we shall see, devastating effects on lives and livelihoods across the world, especially on the poorest people in the poorest countries, with women and children, migrants and minorities bearing the brunt. The economic crisis threatens the full range of human rights. It threatens not only economic, social and cultural rights, including the right to an adequate standard of living and the rights to health, housing, food and education, but also civil and political rights.

It is still too early to tell the full extent of the damage caused by the crisis, but poor and low-income families across the world are being hardest hit. The World Bank is estimating that up to 90 million more men, women and children may be pushed into poverty, in addition to the estimated 160 to 200 million people who fell into poverty as a result of the food crisis between 2005 and 2008. Greater poverty, and the hunger that it brings, will threaten the right to life and health of many of these people, especially children. Every year during this crisis, as many as 400,000 more children will die before they reach their fifth birthday simply because their families cannot afford food or basic medical care for preventable diseases, according to one estimate. And the impacts will be hardest in the poorest countries: "While people in developed countries are feeling the impacts on their standards of living, their jobs and their homes, people in developing countries are bearing the brunt of the crisis, with few safety-nets to protect them from severe poverty and deprivation, and without the fiscal capacity and space to soften the blow".

World hunger will reach an historic high in 2009 with more than one billion people going hungry every day. This means that one in six people will be too poor to eat adequately. The food crisis that occurred as a result of the rapid rise in food prices in 2008 is far from over, as food prices remain high in 40 developing countries and the loss of jobs and remittances produce further food insecurity. Chronic malnutrition will affect children's physical and intellectual development for the rest of their lives. This also has consequences for other rights: in Zambia, an increased number of girls and young women are reportedly being forced to turn to sex work out of economic desperation, while in Kenya, teachers in Nairobi have reported an increase in student pregnancies as girls exchange sex for food.

Bankruptcies and economic retrenchments mean that the increase in global unemployment as a direct result of the economic crisis is likely to reach 38 million by the end of 2009. The right to decent work is under threat as companies radically reduce costs, ramping down wages and allowing working conditions to become more hazardous. At the same time, the housing crisis has left many people without homes or shelters. The sub-prime mortgage crisis has left many people facing foreclosure, some of them victims of fraud and abusive practices by mortgage brokers. In developing countries, the number of people living in slums will rise, and millions more slum dwellers will face lack of access to clean water and sanitation, and increased insecurity of tenure. The crisis has also had a direct impact on children's right to education, as children are pulled out of work to help support their families, though children who leave school early will never catch up. Meanwhile, as millions of people fall into desperate circumstances as a result of a global crisis not of their own making, the provision of social safety nets is limited and shrinking, depriving people of their right to social security. As taxes, exports, foreign investment and other sources of revenue decline, government budgets are falling, and spending on social programmes is likely to be slashed first.

This means that governments will be cutting back on social services and social safety nets just at the time they are most needed to guarantee minimum levels of economic and social rights essential for survival and human dignity, including the rights to health, food, housing and education. The economic crisis is also having disproportionate impacts on the rights of specific groups of people, particularly the poorest and most marginalized, who are the most vulnerable because they already suffer from discrimination and abuses of power. The protection of the rights of migrants is weak, but becoming worse as fear and anxiety caused by the economic crisis have generated a wave of xenophobia. In Malaysia for example, a rise in xenophobic attitudes is reflected in greater discrimination in the workplace against migrants and the unlawful termination of employment without payment of wages.

There are increasing reports of severe abuses of migrants, including in Russia, Greece and several Eastern European countries. Even though working conditions are worsening around the world, few migrant workers have the resources to return home and their families are suffering as remittances dramatically decline. The rights of women are also particularly at risk, as unemployment and social unrest can translate into greater violence against women. Female workers, who tend to be concentrated in the informal economy with lower wages and less employment protection, are losing their jobs and incomes. Especially in developing countries, women predominate in many export industries that have been hardest hit by the economic crisis. Whenever women lose their financial independence, they are more likely to face sexual violence in the home or be pushed into sexual exploitation or other slave-type labour through trafficking. Oxfam cites one female union leader in Thailand: "Factories are closing everywhere–and now the women are being approached by sex traffickers asking if they want to go and work in the West". Human trafficking is expected to escalate as the economic crisis fuels poverty and unemployment.

The full impact of the crisis on civil and political rights around the world is not yet clear, but there is already evidence that these rights are at risk. Social protests were brutally repressed in many countries during the 2008 food and fuel crises. In February 2008, up to 100 protesters were shot and killed in Cameroon by armed forces and more than 1,600 were imprisoned, after protests against the rising costs of basic food became violent. Concerns are rising that social frustration is also being exacerbated in many countries, as people feel a loss of control over their lives and cannot understand or challenge the reasoning behind policy responses. Failures to respect the right to information and the right to participation in government policy decisions around the crisis abound.

THE CAUSES OF THE CRISIS–IMPLICATIONS FOR IMPLEMENTATION OF HUMAN RIGHTS OBLIGATIONS

The economic crisis is a human rights concern not only because of the serious consequences on human rights, but also because of the underlying structural causes of the crisis which relate directly to failures to fulfill human rights. Under human rights law, governments are responsible for creating the conditions in which their citizens can exercise the full range of their human rights, including economic and social rights. Human rights set out the basic minimum standards against which the actions of governments can be judged.

Over the last three decades, however, a package of economic policies was promoted globally which effectively enabled governments to abdicate many of their responsibilities towards their citizens, particularly those related to the fulfillment of economic and social rights, by leaving the fulfillment of these responsibilities up to the "market." The underlying causes of the crisis lie in what has been termed "market fundamentalism" the belief that unfettered pursuit of self-interest though self-regulating markets would ensure economic prosperity for all the most efficient allocation of resources.

In this view, the market was prioritized over the state as driver and guarantor of human development. Any form of government action was seen as interference with the working of the market mechanism, and discouraged on the assumption that this would reduce, rather than increase aggregate social welfare. These beliefs, which dominated international economic policymaking throughout the 1980s and 1990s, supported the promotion of a policy package of liberalization, deregulation and privatization of the "Washington consensus" by international financial institutions including the International Monetary Fund and World Bank. This meant effectively "rolling back the state" in the belief that this would benefit global economic growth and, by extension, all of the world's people. But the financial crisis has clearly demonstrated that the unfettered pursuit of self-interest in the financial markets has done little more than encourage greed and the pursuit of unsustainable short-term profit.

As UNCTAD has argued, "Market fundamentalist laissez-faire of the last 20 years has dramatically failed the test". Vast wealth has been generated, but much of this has depended on the illusory profits of the financial markets and the creation of financial products with no economic or social utility. Little of that wealth has trickled down to the majority of people. While aggregate economic growth has boomed, disaggregating its impacts shows the rise in inequality, the widening gap between rich and poor, and the concentration of wealth in the midst of widespread persistence of hunger, poverty and desperation. Without an effective government role in redistribution, markets have failed to guarantee basic human needs or the conditions in which everyone can secure an adequate standard of living consistent with human dignity. The rolling back of social safety nets, particularly in developing countries, has left people even more vulnerable to the effects of economic crises. Without government regulation, markets have become more prone to crises. In the Outcome Document of the UN's June 2009 conference on the crisis, governments recognized that the crisis was caused by "regulatory failures, compounded by over-reliance on market self-regulation, overall lack of transparency, financial integrity and irresponsible behaviour...".

It is ironic that irresponsible banks, which have long campaigned against government regulation or intervention in markets, have been the first to demand government help to rescue them from bankruptcy. Trillions of dollars in banking bailouts have effectively transferred losses onto taxpayers, amounting to a massive transfer of wealth from ordinary people to the wealthy. This has been popularly referred to as "privatizing profits and socializing losses" or "socialism for the rich, capitalism for the poor". At the same time, it is ironic that governments who have long claimed that they have insufficient resources for social programmes, have suddenly made available trillions of dollars to save the international financial system. As Shalil Shetty, director of the UN Campaign to achieve the Millennium Development Goals, has pointed out:

- "The massive bailouts we have seen for the financial industry have shown us that the real issue we face in addressing this global crisis is not the availability of money, but the availability of political will. The amount of money needed annually to achieve the Millennium Development Goals is a miniscule fraction of the estimated $5 trillion of public money mobilized for the bank bailouts."

The rapid and unprecedented response to the crisis in developed countries has also highlighted for developing countries the unfairness and hypocrisy in how economic policies have been implemented and imposed. As Nobel prize-winning economist Joseph Stiglitz has pointed out:

- "During the East Asia crisis, just a decade ago, America and the I.M.F. demanded that the affected countries cut their deficits by cutting back expenditures–even if, as in Thailand, this contributed to a resurgence of the AIDS epidemic, or even if, as in Indonesia, this meant curtailing food subsidies for the starving. America and the I.M.F. forced countries to raise interest rates, in some cases to more than 50 per cent. They lectured Indonesia about being tough on its banks–and demanded that the government not bail them out. What a terrible precedent this would set, they said, and what a terrible intervention in the ... mechanisms of the free market."

But now even the prophets of free markets are repenting. Markets left to themselves have not maximized social welfare. Even the oft-lauded Alan Greenspan, former president of the Federal Reserve admitted that he placed too much faith in the ability of markets to self-regulate. Billionaire investor, George Soros, has argued that governments must regulate to correct for the excesses of selfinterest that markets encourage. Long a critic of market fundamentalism, Joseph Stiglitz has argued that "...what is required for success is a regime where the roles of market and government are in balance, and where a strong state administers effective regulation. They [States] will realise that the power of special interests must be curbed". Former IMF economist, Simon Johnson has also argued that special interests, particularly those of the powerful financial elite, must be curbed, otherwise they will capture and skew the government's actions to benefit themselves:

- "...elite business interests—financiers, in the case of the U.S.—played a central role in creating the crisis, making ever-larger gambles, with the implicit backing of the government, until the inevitable collapse. More alarming, they are now using their influence to prevent precisely the sorts of reforms that are needed, and fast, to pull the economy out of its nosedive. The government seems helpless, or unwilling, to act against them."

From a human rights perspective, governments must act in the public interest, not in the interests of the powerful, and their actions must be judged against the standards set in human rights law. Governments have a binding obligation to ensure that all their economic and social policies are consistent with standards of human rights law. At the same time, the role of the state is to act as the guarantor of human rights of its citizens, including economic and social rights. These responsibilities cannot be left only up to the market. Rather the state must play an active role in harnessing the operations of the market economy towards the realization of human rights. According to a former UN Special Rapporteur on the right to education, "the raison d'etre of economic and social rights is to act as correctives to the free market". This does not mean that a human rights framework is anti-market.

In contrast, a human rights framework recognizes the emancipatory potential of markets to break down feudal relations of power and unsettle traditional forms of discrimination, including gender discrimination. From a human rights perspective, however, governments must step in when markets fail to create conditions in which all people, including the poorest and most marginalized, can exercise the full range of their human rights. Human rights set out various types of obligations of governments.

These include the duty to take positive measures to fulfill human rights, as well as the duty to respect human rights and to protect people against abuses of human rights by corporate or other private actors. Some human rights obligations are immediate, including the duty of non-discrimination and the duties to refrain from harming or abusing human rights. Other human rights obligations, given the context of limited resources, may be achieved progressively over time but governments have to prove that they are taking positive steps, using the maximum of available resources and making constant progress in the realization of these rights.

Human rights advocates, like many human development economists, cite evidence that "private enterprises and market forces cannot be relied upon to produce outcomes that satisfy the immediate obligations for non-discrimination and equality and minimum core standards. To achieve this, private enterprise and market forces need to be carefully regulated by the state and complemented by a substantial and well-functioning public sector." Redressing the balance between the state and the market is therefore an essential part of constructing a sustainable long-term response to the crisis. This will require replacing the ideal of the "minimal state" with the ideal of a "rights-fulfilling state" that acts in accordance with the standards set out in human rights law.

CHOICES OF POLICY RESPONSES TO THE CRISIS–ADOPTING A HUMAN RIGHTS APPROACH

Despite the human rights dimensions of the crisis, the language of human rights is still largely absent from the diagnoses or prescriptions proposed by national governments or the international community. Responses to the crisis have so far neglected or ignored human rights. There has been little analysis of either the causes or the consequences of the global economic crisis in human rights terms. International meetings have recognized the human dimensions of the crisis, but not the need for human-rights-based responses.

This must change. There is an urgent need to identify immediate responses that address the devastating human rights consequences of the crisis, and to identify longer-term measures that address the structural causes of the crisis that impinge on governments' capacities to meet their human rights obligations. This should start with governments' recognition of the legally binding human rights obligations enshrined in the Universal Declaration of Human Rights and the core international human rights treaties, including the International Covenant on Economic, Social and Cultural Rights. While international human rights law does not prescribe a specific economic system, nor provide a set of detailed and specific prescriptions on how to re-orient financial, economic and social policy, it does set clear priorities and clear boundaries.

IMMEDIATE RESPONSES TO ADDRESS THE CONSEQUENCES OF THE CRISIS

In the immediate term, the first responsibility of governments must be to prevent and alleviate the devastating impacts of the crisis on human lives. It is unacceptable that 400,000 children under the age of five should die because of this crisis. Or that millions should starve or become malnourished for lack of sufficient food, or be forced to sleep in the streets because they have lost their homes or shelter. Or that people should lose their lives in protests against precipitous rises in food prices.

Refraining From Violating Civil and Political Rights

Governments must refrain from violating civil and political rights, including the rights to freedom of expression, freedom of association and rights to information. Rather than using disproportionate force against protesters, social protest should be defused by permitting democratic debate and enabling active and meaningful citizen participation in the design and monitoring of policy responses.

Prioritizing a Basic Minimum of Effective Economic and Social Rights for all

Governments have an immediate obligation to ensure the "minimum essential levels" of social and economic rights which are essential to the survival and a life with dignity. Meeting this obligation must trump all other policy considerations. This means immediately instituting social protection programmes to relieve poverty, hunger and homelessness. It also means ring-fencing government budgets to ensure that there is no retrogression in the provision of essential goods and services. It also means ensuring that economic stimulus packages and counter-cyclical economic policies should be focused on limiting the worst human consequences of the crisis, and priority in distribution of resources must be given to the most vulnerable and marginalized.

Protecting the Most Vulnerable and Ensuring Non-Discrimination

Governments have an immediate obligation of non-discrimination which must be applied to all policies and programmes. This prohibits responses to the crisis that benefit wealthier groups over traditionally marginalized groups or peoples. It also means taking into account, and compensating for the disproportionate effects of the crisis on different groups, in order to ensure substantive, as well as formal, equality. It also requires that governments take special measures to protect the rights of women, migrants, minorities and other groups that are being particularly threatened in this crisis.

Respecting Human Rights Principles in Policy Processes as well as Outcomes

The human rights principles of participation, transparency, accountability and redress, must also be integrated into policy responses. A human rights approach requires a focus not only with the consequences of policies and programmes, but also on the processes by which those policies are adopted. This means that, in the crisis response, programmes must be designed, implemented and evaluated in a manner that ensures transparency, full participation and institutes mechanisms for accountability and redress.

LONG-TERM RESPONSES TO ADDRESS THE CAUSES OF THE CRISIS

The global economic crisis is a threat to human rights, but also an opportunity to rethink the role of the state in complying with human rights obligations, particularly those related to economic and social rights. It provides an opportunity to rethink governance and accountability both at the national and global level. "This systemic collapse calls for a new framework for national governments–both domestically and increasingly at the international level–in which people and the environment, not banks or business, are at the center of economic policy-making,".

The eruption of the financial and economic crisis has demonstrated that markets may be necessary, but are not sufficient to guaranteeing the conditions for the realization of rights. An essential starting point for redressing the imbalance between the state and the market, is to recognize and reaffirm that governments have duties to respect, protect and fulfill human rights, as well as obligations to meet the human rights principles of non-discrimination, participation, transparency and accountability. The implications of these standards and principles for longer-term responses to the crisis at the national level are outlined here.

The Duty to Respect Human Rights

The duty to respect is essentially a duty to "do no harm." This means that governments must prevent, avoid or mitigate any negative impacts of government policies and programmes, paying particular attention to the poorest and most marginalized groups, whose rights are most likely to be violated. Many of the economic measures implemented over the last three decades in the policy package of liberalization, deregulation and privatization have had harsh impacts on the poorest. This is often not evident from aggregate economic data. Redressing the balance will mean that the state cannot leave the distribution of benefits and harms only up to the market, but must take an active role to identify who is likely to be harmed and to minimize those harms. This is necessary not only to be able to introduce safeguards and compensatory measures, but also to guard against policies and programmes that benefit only special interests.

The Duty to Protect Human Rights

The duty to protect is essentially a duty to regulate, and it requires the provision of remedies in the case of abuses by non-state actors. This means that governments must regulate the activities of corporations and other non-state actors and hold those actors to account and seek redress in cases of abuses of human rights. The trend of de-regulation has undermined governments' capacities to regulate. This is particularly clear in the case of financial markets and the shift towards "self-regulation" of the financial industry. Many of the rules governing financial markets, which that had been put in place after the financial abuses of the 1920s and the original Great Depression, were rolled back. Yet had these rules remained in place, much of the damage caused by this financial crisis may have been avoided. Redressing the balance will require recognizing that the state must play an important role in regulation, control and oversight of the financial industry to guard against excessive risk-taking, speculation and greed and to protect citizens and consumers against abuses of their rights.

The Duty to Fulfill Human Rights

The duty to fulfill is a essentially a duty to take positive action, by putting in place measures and policies to guarantee rights, including the minimum essential levels of each right necessary to guarantee human survival and a life of human dignity. This means providing emergency programmes in times of crisis, but it also means maintaining a social safety-net to guarantee a basic social minimum at all times. The trend to "roll back the state" has reduced the redistributive role of the state, leaving ever fewer resources for social programmes that guarantee a basic minimum and reduce inequality. Redressing the balance will require recognition that the state needs to step in when the market does not provide for the poorest, as market prices for food, housing, health, and education move beyond their reach.

Integrating Human Rights Principles with National Economic Policymaking

Human rights principles require establishing processes for policymaking that are participatory, transparent and institute mechanisms for accountability and redress. Rather than being subject to forms of democratic deliberation, decision-making on economic policies has become increasingly left to technocratic experts. Redressing the balance will require recognizing that it is not only outcomes, but also the processes that are important. The rapid escalation of the financial crisis into a global economic crisis also demonstrated that the liberalization of trade and markets has brought an unprecedented degree of integration and interdependence amongst economies and countries. While the economic crisis was generated in the countries of the global north, its impacts have dispropo-rtionately affected the countries and peoples of the global south, which are more vulnerable to economic shocks and have fewer resources to respond. A new system of global governance is necessary which is just and fair and capable of addressing the concerns of all countries and all peoples. This will require reforming the rules that govern global economic policymaking, recognizing the relations of power between governments and rebalancing the forces that have undermined government capacities to meet their obligations to respect, protect and fulfill human rights.

REFORM OF INTERNATIONAL FINANCIAL INSTITUTIONS

The one-size-fits-all policy package of the "Washington Consensus" has been widely promoted by the World Bank and the IMF, and often coercively imposed on developing countries through conditions on loans and grants. Reform of the financial institutions should include ensuring that they operate in accordance with the UN Charter, the UN Universal Declaration on Human Rights, the ICESCR and other international treaties and ensure that the policies that they propose or impose do not undermine the capacities of governments to respect, protect and fulfill their human rights obligations.

At the same time, when acting within the World Bank, the IMF, and or other ad hoc meetings of the G-20, governments should guarantee their policies are consistent with and conducive to the realization of human rights. Reform of the governance of the World Bank and IMF should result is greater inclusion of less powerful states, on the basis of basis of "a fair and equitable representation of developing countries, in order to increase the credibility and accountability of these institutions". Both institutions should also refrain from setting conditions that limit the policy and fiscal space of developing countries to take counter-cyclical economic stimulus policies in the context of urgent crisis responses.

REFORM OF GLOBAL ECONOMIC GOVERNANCE ARCHITECTURE AND REGULATORY FRAMEWORKS

The economic and financial crisis is a global crisis that requires global solutions. It is a crisis generated in the global north, yet having disproportionate impacts on the global south. Decision-making on global policy responses and new regulatory frameworks cannot, therefore, remain in powerful, selfselected decision-making forums such as the G8 or the G20, but should be carried out in multilateral forums such as the United Nations where 192 countries are represented.

As Joseph Stiglitz wrote in his comments on the June General Assembly UN conference, "If globalization is to work for everyone, decisions about how to manage it must be made in a democratic and inclusive manner—with the participation of both the perpetrators and the victims of the mistakes.". Reform should include the adoption of a new UN-based coordination mechanism, such as Global Economic Coordination Council proposed by the UN Commission of Experts on Reforms of the International Monetary and Financial System. Decision-making on economic policies and responses to the crisis at the global level should also meet the human rights principles of non-discrimination, participation, transparency and accountability.

FULFILLING THE DUTY OF INTERNATIONAL ASSISTANCE

The primary responsibility for meeting human rights lies with national governments. But, under the UN Charter and human rights treaties, governments also bear a legal obligation of international cooperation and assistance in the realization of economic, social and cultural rights. As well as positive responsibilities to assist other states in the fulfillment of these rights, governments have duties to respect and protect rights trans-nationally. They must ensure that their trade and investment policies do not negatively impact human rights beyond their borders. In relation to their positive duties, the commitments of donor countries to assist developing countries in meeting the Millennium Development Goals must be honoured. Without external financing, there is little scope for developing countries to put in place the kind of fiscal stimulus packages that developed countries have been able to implement and are needed if developing countries are to meet their basic human rights and development commitments. Among other things, this means that northern governments must not reduce their aid budgets, but rather heed the calls to assist developing countries in the fulfillment of their core human rights obligations. At the UN Human Rights Council Special Session in February 2009, states committed themselves to respond to the consequences of the crisis from a human rights perspective, ensuring that there was a safety net whenever possible, and refraining from reducing their Monterrey commitments to international aid, though so far few states have honoured this commitment.

ACTION ON THESE HUMAN RIGHTS RESPONSES IS NEEDED NOW

Despite the human rights causes and consequences of the crisis, governments have been loathe to recognize their obligations in their responses to the crisis. Indeed, "human rights principles have been studiously avoided in the international declarations and commitments made by states since the crisis". At the UN General Assembly's conference on the crisis in June 2009, governments did recognize and rhetorically commit to addressing the human costs of the crisis but fell short of reaffirming their human rights obligations. This signals a profound lack of political will, not only to take the immediate responses required by the human rights framework, but also to undertake the larger process of replacing the ideal of the "minimal state" with the ideal of a "rights-fulfilling state". Ordinary people, and civil society, including human rights organizations have, however, found a voice to demand and push for urgent change in different forums around the world. The framework of human rights may not provide the specific, detailed prescription for that change, but it does provide a language for making those claims and it starkly sets out the basic responsibilities of governments. The human rights framework roundly challenges the pervasive complacency in the face of the terrible consequences of the crisis. It locates the causes of the crisis, not in unpredictable, uncontrollable market forces, but in the human decisions, actions and inactions that produced the crisis. Recognizing this opens a path for accountability and offers the potential for profound change.

10

World Trends in Social Welfare and Human Rights

The most important international trend for all peoples of the world, that affects both social welfare and human rights, is, of course, globalisation. The world is shrinking, and a new level of global inter-connectedness is made possible by new technologies. But so far, this new global experience has been dominated by the economy.

Globalisation, as we have come to understand it, is almost exclusively an economic, market-driven phenomenon. It is about the rights of people and corporations to invest where they choose, to make profits wherever they can, and to move capital rapidly from one part of the world to another in the interests of profit maximisation. In doing so, globalisation has ignored most other aspects of human existence, and in emphasising only the economic it therefore represents a particularly one-dimensional form of the global experience. It is true that we are also seeing a globalisation of culture; increasingly the people of the world are encouraged to eat the same food, wear the same clothes, watch the same television, listen to the same music, play the same games, and so on, often to the detriment of cultural diversity and the preservation of indigenous and minority cultural traditions. But it needs to be remembered that this cultural globalisation is really in the interests of the dominant economic globalisation; it is concerned with creating global markets, because it is much easier to market products globally if people can be persuaded to consume the same things, regardless of culture.

One of the most interesting aspects of globalisation has been the counter trend of localisation. In many parts of the world, people at the local level are turning away from the global economy, perceiving that it does not meet their needs, and are setting up local community-based alternatives. One example is with banks; the large traditional banks have become players in the global market, and have as a result often ignored the needs of local people; branches that played a vital role in local communities have been deemed to be not sufficiently profitable, and so have been closed, often with devastating results at the local level.

The reaction has often been to establish community banks, local co-operatives, local trading schemes, and similar forms of local community-based economic activity; such initiatives are now well established in many different countries, and in diverse cultural contexts. This local activity is an important trend, and it has produced both positive and negative outcomes. As well as the positive programmes of local initiative and the increasing emphasis on community development that we now see in many nations, there are also the worrying developments of citizen militia and vigilante groups, the politics of exclusion, scapegoating and racism.

Localisation is, therefore, neither good nor bad, just as globalisation is neither good nor bad; both can have enormous potential for human development, and both also have the potential for increasing exploitation and oppression. But localisation is important, because it demonstrates that a purely economic form of globalisation is not inevitable, nor, in the views of many people, is it necessarily all that its advocates have promised. We believe that we have to accept the inevitability of some kind of globalisation and also some kind of localisation, and that the task is now to seek to influence each to take account of the values of social justice and human rights.

One of the important consequences of the twin trends of globalisation and localisation has been the erosion of the power of the nation state. Commentators differ as to the extent to which the nation state is eroded, but there seems little doubt that with the power of global markets, national governments do not have the degree of autonomy that they once had, and that government policy is circumscribed by what 'the markets' will accept. The capacity of the state to address the social needs created by inequality is therefore limited, in part because it is increasingly difficult for nation states to tax the global economy effectively. We are seeing a steady erosion of public services in many countries of the world, both rich and poor, as health, education, housing and income maintenance are increasingly required to rely on the vagaries of the market rather than the generosity of the state.

The sociologist Manuel Castells has described the emergence of the 'network society'. He sees the development of networks of power, where powerful forces in different parts of the world are linked by communications technology. These networks are temporary and changing, but they nonetheless increasingly represent the location of economic power. Our relative advantage or disadvantage is determined by how closely connected we are to these networks. The networks link powerful interests across borders, and for this reason national boundaries are becoming less important as the lines of division of power and wealth; in all countries there are power elites that are linked to the networks of power, and also in all countries there are those who are excluded from the networks, and who are therefore powerless and disadvantaged. Thus we are seeing, in many countries of the world, a widening gap between the rich and the poor. It is still the case, of course, that some nations are richer and more advantaged than others, but these rich nations also contain people, communities, and in some cases whole regions, that are in poverty and have little chance to benefit from the economic miracles promised by globalisation. This combination of globalisation and the network society poses new challenges for social welfare. We would like briefly to touch on eight of these, and then later in the thesis to consider the implications for the idea of human rights. The first challenge is how to serve the marginal communities created by the network society, those people that are simply unnecessary for the operation of global markets. The German writers Martin and Schumann have suggested that this is as much as 80% of the world's population.

These are the communities that are by-passed by the global economy, and it has now become clear that while globalisation can have positive effects for many people, these benefits are not evenly distributed, and there are people who lose from globalisation: the urban poor, village communities, those living in areas where major industry has collapsed, those made redundant by the mobility of capital, those who are forced to take casual and unpredictable employment, migrant workers, refugees, and so on. The second challenge is to link the global and the local. People's lives are affected by global forces; those who are in need are often in that position precisely because of globalisation.

Yet their lives and their perceived needs remain stubbornly local. It is difficult to provide local resources for the meeting of human need when those resources are controlled and rationed not by local forces, but by global forces. Linking the local and the global, in creative ways, is the key to the future effectiveness of human services, and this has been a major focus of the thinking of those concerned with community development; community development will have little significant impact unless the communities involved are able to network effectively and to impact global issues as well as local needs.

The third challenge is the reliance placed on market mechanisms for the solutions of problems. Markets are very good for achieving some things: economic growth, technological innovation and prosperity. But they are not so good at achieving social equity, as the history of large-scale markets clearly demonstrates. Indeed, many social workers spend their time working with the people who are the victims of the market, those who have been unable to compete effectively in the market place and whose lives have been negatively affected by market forces. It is therefore something of a contradiction to seek to solve these problems through the very mechanisms that caused the problems in the first place, as is advocated by the supporters of market mechanisms to achieve social policy ends. The relationship of welfare services to the market is problematic; some argue that we should be providing a critique of market mechanisms and seeking to establish an alternative for the delivery of human services, while others argue that the dominance of the market requires that welfare workers be entrepreneurial, and seek the support of the market for the meeting of human need. Probably both strategies are necessary; there is certainly a need for sustainable alternatives, but at the same time it is important to meet immediate needs by working as best one can with the existing system.

The fourth challenge for social welfare is the breakdown of traditional family and community structures, which have traditionally provided social support, but which at a time of increasing mobility, individualism and personal consumption can no longer be expected to do so. The crisis in aged care in some Asian nations is a good example; with the changes to traditional family structures and values, many people are now seeking institutional care for their elderly relatives, who would once have been cared for at home. This is just one example of changes to the family that represent a major issue for policy makers in the coming decades, when still further changes in family structure seem likely.

The fifth challenge, closely related to the fourth, is that of changing demographics. High birth rates in the middle period of the twentieth century, coupled with improved health services and medical care, have resulted in an ageing population in many of the world's developed and developing nations. This has presented policy-makers with a serious problem of how the rapidly increasing older generation can be adequately supported financially, and in terms of services, by a smaller proportion of the population of working age. In Africa, however, where health services are still inadequate and where the HIV/AIDS pandemic has caused such devastation, the demographics are reversed, with large numbers of children requiring care. Such demographic changes shatter many of the assumptions on which social security and poverty-alleviation policies are based, and if indeed the world is heading towards increasing instability and possible ecological crisis, such shifts in demographic structure seem likely to continue.

The changing nature of work is the sixth challenge. In developed countries, as in developing countries, the casualisation of the work force has led to the end of the predictable, established career. Most people, in the course of their working lives, will face career changes and periods of unemployment, and the workplace has become a more unstable and uncertain place. The global economy is able to move capital investment in a matter of seconds, to make the most of market opportunities, and labour is not so mobile, so gets left behind. Large-scale unemployment, especially in those regions not connected to the global network society, is the inevitable result, and even those in work do not generally have the security that they once enjoyed.

Even though the movement of people can no longer keep pace with the movement of capital, there is nevertheless more personal mobility than ever before in history, and this represents the seventh policy challenge. People move within and between countries with increasing frequency, for a variety of reasons: economic, political and personal. This has resulted in large populations of migrant workers, increasing numbers of refugees and asylum seekers, illegal immigrants, transient populations, and a professional workforce that has become increasingly internationalised. The traditional forms of social welfare are inadequate and inappropriate for such a population, as they are based on assumptions about national citizenship and stability of settlement that simply no longer hold. This is forcing a major re-evaluation of the idea of citizenship, and the emergence of new understandings of global citizenship, which as suggested, discuss more a little later.

The final challenge that we wish to mention is that posed by cultural diversity, and in particular by the recognition of the needs and rights of Indigenous People. While on the one hand cultural globalisation is increasing, the rise in mobility has resulted in most of the nations of the world now being multicultural. The rights and needs of cultural, ethnic, racial and language minorities have come into sharper focus, and can no longer be ignored by assumptions of cultural uniformity. In particular this is true of Indigenous People; many of the world's nations have indigenous populations, most of which have been dispossessed and oppressed in ways that shame our humanity. Conventional welfare policy regimes have proved to be quite inadequate in addressing the issues raised by the presence of such populations.

These, then, are some of the challenges facing social welfare policy in the contemporary world. Taken together, they create a climate of instability and uncertainty for policy makers in all countries. We do not have time today to discuss them in detail, let alone to suggest solutions, as each is highly problematic. However they form the backdrop to a discussion of human rights, which will occupy the remainder of the thesis.

In an era of globalisation, human rights become critically important. One of the lessons we have learned from the policies of the past has been that economic development and citizenship rights must proceed hand in hand. Economic development that does not take account of citizenship rights leads to inequality, social division, and the few profiting at the expense of the many. And human rights in the absence of economic development are of only limited value; indeed, many have argued that to benefit from economic development is itself a human right which should not be denied to anyone. It is only when economic development takes place in a context of the rights of the citizen being maintained that social equity and progress can result. Thus the nations that have successfully achieved economic development and stability have done so while at the same time ensuring that the rights of citizens are respected. In retrospect, one of the mistakes of the communist regimes was their attempts to develop economic prosperity for the whole society without due concern for the rights of individuals, families and communities, and this unbalanced approach led, in the end, to failure. We are now living an increasingly global economy, and this means that the idea of global citizenship rights must be taken seriously. With increasing mobility, most countries of the world now have large numbers of residents, legal or illegal, who are not citizens of that country. While we define rights in terms of national citizenship, as guaranteed in constitutions, bills of rights, etc, such people have no rights, as they are not citizens. This enables refugees and asylum seekers, for example, to be denied human rights that are given to the citizens of the country concerned, hence in a number of countries–and we are ashamed to say that this includes our own country, Australia–asylum seekers are subject to human rights abuse which would not be tolerated for ordinary citizens of that country. In an era of the global economy, and of the breaking down of national borders, some acceptance of global citizenship rights becomes essential. And global citizenship rights are, simply, human rights: the rights we can all claim, not on the basis of our national identity, but on the basis of our common humanity.

They are the rights we should be affirming and respecting for all the people of the world. At present, the term 'global citizen' or 'citizen of the world' is used by the advantaged, those who are able to move freely from country to country, who can invest and make profits wherever they wish, who are welcomed in any country they choose to visit, and who can change nationality almost at will for their personal benefit. Such rights are not given to the poor; when they seek to move, they are labelled 'refugees', 'illegal immigrants' or 'migrant workers', and are likely to be detained, abused and sent home. True global citizenship suggests that we need to establish the set of rights that all people can claim on the basis simply of their humanity, and those, of course, are human rights.

It is interesting to note that the protesters against globalisation frame many of their protests in terms of the impact of globalisation on human rights. They claim, and there is strong evidence to support them, that the present form of exclusively economic globalisation is violating people's human rights, creating poverty and disadvantage, and resulting in mass exploitation. This argument is not really an argument against globalisation as such, or against the world becoming ever more interconnected; to make such as argument is to fly in the face of the inevitable. Indeed, as human rights are, by their very nature, a global discourse, the protesters are themselves using a global argument. What the protesters are saying is a simple message: that economic development cannot proceed without a parallel attention to human rights and social development. It is therefore hardly surprising that, in this period of globalisation, there is an increasing interest in human rights.

To engage with an idea of human rights that will adequately meet the needs of people in a diverse but globalising world, it is necessary to expand our understanding of human rights, beyond the rather narrow definitions that have been accepted by many media commentators. The popular perception of the meaning of the term 'human rights' has been largely confined to civil and political rights, sometimes referred to as the 'first generation' of human rights: the right to vote, freedom of speech, freedom of expression, freedom of assembly, the right not to be imprisoned without fair trial, the right of access to the law, the right to be protected from torture, the right to join a trade union, the right to minimum labour standards, and so on. These rights are, of course, important. But they are only one aspect of human rights, and the idea of human rights, as understood both in the literature and in international treaties, is much broader than this.

The so-called 'second generation' of human rights incorporates economic, social and cultural rights: the right to work, the right to adequate health services, the right to housing, the right to education, the right to economic security, the right to freedom of cultural expression, and so on. These are often not associated, in media reports, with 'human rights'; for example a country with inadequate health services or a poor education system would not be described as a country with a 'poor human rights record'.

Yet such human rights are just as important as the first generation of civil and political rights, and indeed they go together; there is not much point in allowing people the right of freedom of written expression of they do not know how to read or write, freedom of association is of little use for people who are too ill to participate because of inadequate health care, and freedom of speech is greatly enhanced if the people who are exercising that right have a good education and so can express informed rather than uninformed opinion. In addition, there is increasing recognition now being given to so-called 'third generation' human rights, or collective rights. These are the rights we can only achieve collectively rather than individually, and they include such things as the right to economic development, the right to political stability and the range of environmental rights, such as the right to breathe clean air, to drink clean water, to eat toxic-free food, and so on. Such rights are also critically important, and belong alongside the other two sets of human rights.

There is not much point in having good education or health services, and adequate legal protection for the right of free speech, if people cannot drink clean water, are breathing polluted air, and are unable to participate in the benefits of economic development. All three generations of human rights are, therefore, important. However there has been a tendency for people who talk about human rights to concentrate only on the first generation, or civil and political rights. These are sometimes referred to as 'negative rights', because they require the state, or some other body, to protect them and to prevent human rights abuse.

The other two, however, are sometimes referred to as 'positive' human rights; the state must not only protect them through adequate legal processes and constitutional safeguards, but it must also provide for those rights to be realised, through adequate health, education, housing, social security and environmental programmes, and through appropriate intervention in, and management of, the economy. This is one reason for the unpopularity of second and third generation understandings of human rights; they are more expensive, because they require active state intervention in the economy and state-funded or supported provision of human services; at a time when conventional economic wisdom prescribes reduced government spending and lack of intervention, they often cannot be afforded by governments. There are other possible reasons for the current concentration on civil and political rights. One is that these are the rights that are readily safeguarded through legal mechanisms, for example through the courts and through legislation. At a time when we commonly seek legal mechanisms to resolve problems, and where lawyers have reached a position of power and privilege, it is not surprising that those rights that lend themselves most readily to legal interpretation are those that have become dominant. But a more significant reason for the domination of first generation civil and political rights lies with their association with Western liberalism. These rights were emphasised in the western Enlightenment tradition, and grew out of the individualist notions of that era.

Indeed calling them 'first generation' only emphasises the dominance of western thought in recent human rights discourse; they are called 'first' simply because they were the first to emerge in modern western thought, and have thus been privileged in the last two hundred years when intellectual discourse has been dominated by the western liberal tradition. This however represents a very limited understanding of human rights. Human rights are not an exclusively western concept; there are human rights traditions in all major religions and cultures, though they are expressed in different ways. And ideas of human rights stretch back many centuries before the western 'Enlightenment'. Those who see human rights as purely western, and having their origins in eighteenth century liberalism, are making an essentially racist assumption and are denying the other important human rights traditions in human history. Embracing a broader approach that includes all three socalled 'generations' is an important way to move beyond such a sterile position.

It values other human rights traditions, including the more collective understandings that have been so important in many of the cultures and traditions of the Asian region. This broader approach to human rights, now evident in some, though not all, of the human rights literature, thus enables some of the issues of cultural diversity in human rights to be addressed and debated. As suggested, return to this topic later, but for the moment the important point is to see the incorporation of economic social and cultural rights, and collective rights, as a major development in reconceptualising human rights in a globalising world.

Another important development in recent thinking about human rights has been the increasing emphasis given to inter-generational rights. This suggests not only that we have an obligation to redress human rights violations that exist in the present, but also that we have an obligation to consider human rights violations in the past and the future. One important example of human rights abuse to previous generations which is of concern to the present is the issue of wrongs done to Indigenous Peoples. In countries such as Australia, Canada, New Zealand and the USA there are increasing demands that there be recognition and also compensation for past human rights abuses such as dispossession, cruelty, discrimination and the forced removal of children from their families.

The claims that Nazi war gold stored in Swiss banks should be returned to Holocaust survivors and their descendents is another example. This idea that a generation has an obligation not only to redress human rights violations in the present, but also to redress the wrongs of previous generations, is relatively recent, and is an important extension of human rights thinking. Similarly, there is a perceived obligation to future generations, particularly in regard to environmental rights. The policies and practices of the present are causing pollution, environmental degradation and climate change on such a scale that we are betraying future generations who will inherit a poisoned, polluted and devastated world.

This can be seen as a human rights violation, committed against those who are yet unborn, as our actions are violating their third generation collective rights. This is, for many people, a new way of thinking about human rights responsibilities and human rights abuse, and this development is very important. Human rights are a powerful discourse, and to represent current policies and practices of ecological devastation as human rights violations can add a sense of urgency and moral imperative to one of the most fundamental problems facing the human race in this century.

Another important extension of the idea of human rights, beyond the narrow conventional civil and political framing, is the extension of human rights from the public sphere to the domestic sphere. Civil and political rights are essentially about the right to participate freely in public civil society: the right to vote, the right to speak freely, the right to free association, and so on. These rights protect the people who choose to be involved in such civil and political action. But for many people, human rights and human rights abuse are more personal and private.

Women's experience of human rights abuse, for example, is largely in the private domain: rape, domestic violence, and subjugation within the family. The same applies to the rights of children, the rights of older people, and the rights of people with disabilities. None of these groups will have their human rights protected if it is only human rights in the public sphere that are considered, and the women's movement has criticised traditional formulations of human rights, exclusively in the public domain, as being concerned largely with the human rights of men, and ignoring the human rights of women. This is an important criticism, and it requires different responses from governments.

The extension of the idea of human rights to the private sphere as well as the public sphere is therefore a major issue for policy makers, and for those concerned with working towards the protection and realisation of human rights. In the contemporary world, we need understandings of human rights that reach across the public/private divide, and that see both the public and the private as essential contexts for human rights work.

Human rights do not exist in an objective sense. They cannot be discovered or measured. Rather, human rights are defined and redefined, in different historical and cultural contexts. Human rights are what we understand to be necessary for us to achieve our full humanity, and this understanding is not fixed. Human rights, therefore, will change over time, as human values change, and as people reach new understandings of what being fully human really means. They will also be understood differently in different cultural contexts, and just because human rights are universal does not mean that human rights will be defined or realised in the same way in all cultures. The universal right to housing, for example, does not mean that everybody has to live in the same sort of dwelling; indeed, housing that is appropriate in one culture and climate will be quite inappropriate in another.

Similarly, the right to education does not mean that all children should go to the same sort of school, or learn the same things in the same way. Universality of human rights does not mean uniformity; in fact it is only in a world that affirms and values diversity that everyone's human rights can truly be met. Often it is through statements of need that we place universal human rights in their cultural context; there may be a universal right to education, but this can translate to very different educational needs in different communities and different societies. Human rights, although by definition universal, are pluralist in their realisation.

If we understand human rights as being defined or constructed through on-going debate and dialogue about what it means to be human, we need to ask ourselves who is controlling and contributing to that debate. A major criticism in the past is that it was largely western voices who had controlled the debate, and had shaped the definition of human rights. This led some people to argue that human rights was a western concept and thus to advocate that the very idea of human rights ought to be abandoned. This argument is based on faulty logic: just because the west has dominated the debate on human rights does not mean that we should abandon the concept.

The west has dominated many things in the last century–human rights are only one among many–and if we were to give up everything that the west has come to dominate we would have very little left. The western domination of food production and consumption, for example, does not mean that we have to give up eating. The task rather is to liberate ideas of human rights from their western domination and instead to reconstruct them in a spirit of genuine cross-cultural dialogue, and this is now happening. The literature on human rights now contains substantial writing from authors from Asia, Africa, Latin America and Indigenous Communities, who are making major contributions to the reconstruction of human rights across cultural boundaries, and this is a welcome and important development in human rights thinking.

There is, however, another question that needs to be asked about the human rights debate. It is no longer the exclusive domain of western voices, but it is still very much the domain of the powerful and the privileged. Those who write and talk about human rights, and those who seek to define human rights, are typically lawyers, academics, politicians, diplomats, journalists, and a handful of privileged activists from human rights NGOs. These people no longer come from exclusively western backgrounds, but it is still a narrow and privileged section of the population.

If human rights are about people in dialogue about what it means to be fully human, it is not enough to confine the debate to the privileged few, and we need to be looking to ways to ensure that the voices of the marginalised, the poor, the disadvantaged, and the many victims of human rights abuse, are also heard in the debate. Indeed, it is itself a human rights abuse to deny such people a say in the debate about what constitutes human rights that belong to the entire human family.

The various human rights conventions, including the Universal Declaration of Human Rights, were drafted and discussed only by a very few people, from the most privileged part of society. As such, they are hardly representative of the voice of humanity. Human rights are so fundamental, that this represents a major problem, and a major contradiction, in the current human rights debate. That debate, at present, is a discourse of the powerful about the powerless, and it therefore itself represents a violation of human rights. We believe that this is one of the greatest challenges facing those of us who are concerned with human rights. The problem of western domination of the human rights discourse is being addressed, but the problem of the exclusive and undemocratic nature of the human rights debate itself has barely been recognised. It is important that we find ways to involve a far greater number of people, from all strata of society, in the debate about human rights, what they are, and how they should be both protected and realised. This will involve public education, and the incorporation of ideas of human rights into processes of community development and deliberative democracy. In the meantime, a debate about human rights that remains the exclusive domain of the privileged few is a contradiction, and a betrayal of the people in whose interests we claim to be acting.

Rights imply duties or obligations, and one of the most difficult challenges for policy makers has been to strike the right balance between the two. To emphasise rights at the expense of obligations is to encourage irresponsibility and a selfish approach to rights that does not recognise that we live in communities and have obligations to our fellow citizens. On the other hand, to emphasise obligations at the expense of rights is to invite oppression and coercion, and to deny the importance of individual and family autonomy and self-determination. Both rights and obligations are important, and we would like to identify briefly three important obligations implied by human rights.

The first is the obligation on the part of the state to ensure that human rights are met and protected. First generation rights require strong and independent legal systems, with full access to, and equality before, the law. These need to be backed with strong legislation guaranteeing fundamental rights and freedoms for all citizens. Second generation rights require governments to ensure that there is adequate provision of health services, education, housing and income security for all the population, to ensure that there is enough paid work, and so on. And third generation rights require an active economic policy, community development, and strong policies of environmental protection. Human rights, in other words, require a strong state, or a strong non-government sector that is resourced to provide these public functions.

The second set of obligations attached to human rights is the obligation of the citizen to respect the human rights of other citizens. A society that respects human rights cannot be a society of only self-seeking individuals with no respect for other citizens. Rather, a society that respects human rights is a society where people acknowledge and celebrate their mutual interdependence, and where we understand our responsibilities to others as well as to our own self-advancement.

This underlines the importance of community, and the necessity of strong communities if human rights are really to be recognised and respected. The third set of obligations is the obligation on citizens to exercise their rights. There is no point in having a society where there is freedom of speech, for example, if very few people choose to exercise that right; if that were to happen, the right becomes eroded. Similarly the right to education only really makes sense if people are prepared to exercise that right and to educate themselves to the maximum level possible in order that they may better contribute to society.

The rights which many of us take for granted–such as the right to vote, the right of free speech and the right to join a trade union–were not easily won. Many people struggled and suffered in order that we can have those rights, and hence we have an obligation to exercise those rights in an active and constructive way. A society that respects human rights is therefore an active, vibrant, participatory society, where people value their human rights and exercise them vigorously. For this reason, those who believe in the importance of human rights need to be working towards increasing the level of participation in society as a whole, and helping people to realise that their citizenship obligations extend beyond the role of tax payer and passive consumer.

We can see, therefore, that a commitment to human rights, if understood in the broadest sense, requires a great deal more than simply supporting bills of rights, international treaties and conventions, and ensuring that legal structures and processes are strong and independent. These are important, but they are only part of the whole human rights picture. A commitment to human rights requires that we also are concerned with community development, with promoting an active, participatory society, with developing strong public services, and with balancing independence with interdependence. For these reasons, human rights and social welfare are intimately connected. Social welfare is, at heart, a matter of human rights, and those concerned with social welfare are, in a real sense, human rights workers. Similarly, human rights is about social welfare; it is about making sure that the welfare of all human beings is adequately safeguarded and adequately realised.

There is one more thing to be said about human rights. Human rights are a powerful ideal. They are not just about academic analysis, research and the provision of legal and social services. They are also a vision of our common humanity. They are something to be passionate about, and they can be a real driving force towards creating a better world. The anti-globalisation demonstrators realise that; they know that showing how globalisation adversely affects human rights has an immediate appeal to the people of the world, who believe that human rights are important, and worth fighting for. The idea of human rights represents one of the most powerful human ideals of the present day; this creates many possibilities for creative action, and for that reason alone human rights are worth our attention. They have the potential to unite the human race and bring about a society based on peace, justice and mutual respect; this might sound like an impossible dream, in a world racked with war and conflict; but can we afford any less?

11

Human Rights and Social Accountability

INTRODUCTION

There is an emerging consensus within the international development and academic communities that development means much more than just the growth of the Gross National Product. Amartya Sen has called for an understanding of development as "a process of expanding the real freedoms that people enjoy" in which both "substantive" freedoms like food, life and health and "instrumental" freedoms like free speech, transparency and protective security are equally important. The United Nations Development Programme has articulated a vision of "sustainable human development" defined as "expanding the choices for all people in society" and including the principles of Empowerment, Co-operation, Equity, Sustainability and Security.

The World Bank's mission of "fighting poverty and improving the living standards of people in the developing world" demonstrates its commitment to understanding development as a multi-faceted and complex process. The United Kingdom Department for International Development also explicitly claims that it is an "investor in the people" whose mission is to "promote sustainable development and eliminate world poverty." A "rights based approach to development" promises to offer solid ground on which to base these efforts at restructuring the theory and practice of development. DFID defines this approach as "empowering people to take their own decisions, rather than being the passive objects of choices made on their behalf". The Office of the High Commissioner for Human Rights understands it as an approach that "links poverty reduction to questions of obligation, rather than welfare or charity". The World Bank has not explicitly endorsed a human rights approach to development.

Nevertheless, in documents such as Development and Human Rights: The Role of the World Bank, published in celebration of the 50th anniversary of the Universal Declaration of Human Rights, it has made statements that reveal its general support for the approach. "Creating the conditions for the attainment of human rights is a central and irreducible goal of development.

By placing the dignity of every human being—especially the poorest—at the very foundation of its approach to development, the Bank helps people in every part of the world build lives of purpose and hope". In recent years, the World Bank has begun to support a diversity of "social accountability" initiatives.

Such initiatives range from citizen report cards in the Philippines, Albania and Uganda and community scorecards in the Gambia and Malawi, to access to justice programs in Indonesia and the development of a "system of social accountability" in Peru. One may well look at such projects as building the basic lessons of a rights based approach into the World Bank's lending practices. As a recent World Bank document claims, "social accountability is a right" which is grounded in "a new manifestation of citizenship based on the right to hold governments accountable by expanding people's responsibility". How exactly are social accountability initiatives linked to human rights?

In what ways are social accountability and a rights based approach complementary and when and where might they come into conflict? How is social accountability linked to the broader international human rights agenda? The second part of the paper presents an overview of both rights based approaches to development and social accountability and explores the possibilities for articulating the two approaches. The third part then presents four specific cases of social accountability initiatives which have served as models for or are directly supported by the World Bank: the Bangalore Citizen Report Cards implemented by the Public Affairs Centre in India, the Malawi Community Scorecard implemented by CARE, the Justice for the Poor programme supported by the World Bank in Indonesia, and the construction of a "System of Social Accountability" in Peru also supported by the World Bank and other development partners. In this third part the central issue is to explore how these projects are grounded in and constitute a step towards fulfilling a rights based approach to development. Finally, the paper ends with some concluding remarks on how social accountability initiatives can be more closely linked to a human rights approach in the future.

RIGHTS BASED APPROACHES AND SOCIAL ACCOUNTABILITY

This part provides a general introduction both to rights based approaches to development and to social accountability. In addition, it proposes a general framework for exploring the interrelation between these two approaches.

RIGHTS BASED APPROACHES TO DEVELOPMENT

The promotion and defence of human rights have become increasingly important values in the world today. The vast majority of countries have signed the International Covenants on Civil and Political Rights and Economic,

Social and Cultural Rights. In addition, the Universal Declaration of Human Rights holds sway over national practices and international relations.

Indeed, human rights talk is perhaps even more mainstreamed today than talk about democracy. It is difficult for a country to explicitly defend non-democratic politics, but it is almost impossible for it to affirmatively promote violations of human rights. People typically think of human rights as involving the defence of what are called civil and political rights, the so-called "first generation" of human rights. This involves rights such as those to life, liberty and security, protection against torture, and freedom of speech and assembly. Nevertheless, just as to the principal of the "indivisibility" of human rights, "whether of a civil, cultural, economic, political or social nature, they are all inherent to the dignity of every human person. Consequently, they all have equal status as rights, and cannot be ranked, a priori, in hierarchical order".

Therefore, "economic" and "social" rights like the right to work, social security, education and health are just as fundamental as civil and political rights. Upon signing the principle international covenants, states are thereby obliged to defend and promote all of the fundamental human rights of their citizens. There are always issues of resource scarcity and "justiceability" which complicate this task. This is especially the case in the area of "second generation" rights. Nevertheless, governments who sign these agreements have placed upon themselves the duty to do all that they can to guarantee a minimum floor of livelihood for the population. The "progressive realization" of rights is sometimes the only possibility.

It is not always possible to fulfill all rights all of the time. Sometimes tough choices need to be made in order to guarantee overall forward progress. Nevertheless, there is a self-obligation to move towards the fulfillment of all rights in the medium to long term. In addition to self-obligation, the international human rights agenda usually implies international pressure and sanction through conditionality or other means. If a country or an international organization has a "human rights policy" this is normally interpreted to mean that it is willing to consider this also as the basis of its foreign policy or development assistance.

This agenda is essentially judgmental. If a country is evaluated as having failed to defend the basic human rights of its inhabitants it is marginalized from the international scene. The World Bank has been hesitant to adopt such a stance since it appears to violate Article IV, Section 10 of its Articles of Agreement which state that "the Bank and its officers shall not interfere in the political affairs of any member; nor shall they be influenced in their decisions by the political character of the member or members concerned." Conditionality based on the human rights record of a country has therefore been interpreted to be equivalent to meddling in "political" affairs.

Nevertheless, the World Bank has found other ways to talk about human rights. On occasion of the fiftieth anniversary of the Universal Declaration of

Human Rights the World Bank clearly stated its commitment to promoting human rights. In this document, the World Bank enumerates how it "contributes directly to the fulfillment of many rights articulated in the Universal Declaration. Through its support of primary education, health care and nutrition, sanitation, housing, and the environment, the World Bank has helped hundreds of millions of people attain crucial economic and social rights".

The document also mentions how the World Bank contributes in a "less direct, but perhaps equally significant" manner to the strengthening of human rights. "By helping to fight corruption, improve transparency and accountability in governance, strengthen judicial systems, and modernize financial sectors, the World Bank contributes to building environments in which people are better able to pursue a broad range of human rights". The World Bank's effort to engage with the practice and discourse of human rights in this document and others is clearly a move in the right direction. This is a much more fruitful strategy than simply writing off human rights as a purely "political matter".

The World Bank here implicitly takes the contrasting position that the defence of human rights is a moral or ethical issue intimately linked to the process of economic development. Nevertheless, the perspective offered in this document is a long way from what has come to be considered a "rights based approach to development". This is because the World Bank here envisions human rights as purely an outcome, not a method of intervention. The World Bank, any action that leads to the fulfillment of basic necessities automatically also helps the realization of human rights precisely because it resolves basic necessities. This argument is circular and it folds economic development and human rights promotion into one. From this perspective, there is no value-added to incorporating human rights into economic development. RBA should therefore be distinguished both from the application of international pressure and conditionality and from perspectives like those of the World Bank's 1998 text on Development and Human Rights.

The central question for RBA is not so much whether a particular regime does or does not respect the rights of its citizens or what the final result of a development project is with regard to the rights of the population, but how we approach the task of development. Specifically, the core objective of RBA is to invert the power relationships between policy makers, service providers and the poor. Instead of envisioning development as a process by which governments, foundations or international agencies channel resources to "help" excluded groups overcome poverty and suffering, the human rights approach starts by acknowledging the entitlements of the poor. As a result, just as to this perspective "service providers" and "policy makers" are better conceptualized as "duty-bearers". It is their obligation, not their choice, to guarantee the human rights of the poor, the "rights-holders". The legal structures which make the claims of the "rights-holders" judicially defensible are not always in place. Although some countries have constitutional provisions which guarantee citizens right to employment, health care and education, many others simply do not. In addition, even in those countries which do have such legal guarantees, there are few examples in which normal citizens have actually successfully brought legal suits against the government for the failure to fulfill basic economic, social and cultural rights.

Regardless, from the perspective of RBA, development programs should be designed as if these structures were in place. This does not mean that development planners should always be watching their backs, wary of the next potential law suit. But it does mean that development should be conceptualized as something which originally belongs to the people, not to the government or to international agencies. In practice, this means that development projects should live up to the following five basic principles common to most understandings of RBA:

- First, the poor should be placed at the center of the design, control, oversight and evaluation of the development projects, programs or policies that affect them. Empowerment and active participation of the poor is one of the backbones of RBA. Indeed, just as to authors such as Clare Ferguson and J. Hausermann the right to participation should be seen as the foundational base of the rights approach since it is the prerequisite to claiming all of the rest of the human rights. The very act of demanding the fulfillment of one's rights requires an active subject who is in control of his or her life, a participant in his or her own process of development.
- Second, the institutions responsible for implementing development programs or policies should be fully accountable for their actions. As "duty bearers" they are obliged to behave responsibly, look out for the larger public interest and be open to public scrutiny. From this perspective, corruption, inefficiency and secrecy are more than just unfortunate practices. They are morally wrong and constitute an aggression against humanity.
- Third, non-discrimination, equality and inclusiveness should underlie the practice of development. Development should be understood as a "public good", similar to public parks or national defence, from which no one can be excluded and the benefits are shared among all. If development is seen to be the privilege of a few or projects are managed in an exclusive fashion favouring only those with "good connections" or from the "right" ethnic group we have departed from the RBA approach. This also means that participation should not be limited to "professional", "well behaved" NGOs. Grassroots and political organizations should also be included.

- Fourth, citizen participation and voices should be "scaled up" and linked with national and international policy processes and international rights frameworks. All too often participation occurs at the local community or neighbourhood level with regard to programme implementation, but citizens are not involved in the broader decisions that have an impact on the structure of national public policy. A human rights approach obliges development programs to constantly be on the look out for the links between the local, the national and the global, between service delivery, public policy and international relations.
- Fifth, RBA encourages the active linkage between development and law. This means at least two different but related things. On the one hand, the citizen participation, accountability and inclusiveness which ground the RBA approach should be institutionalized in law, not left to the good will of public servants or the presence of specific civil society leaders. On the other hand, development projects should use the language of rights explicitly and encourage citizens to pursue the legal defence of their rights at the national and international levels.

RBA therefore gives a very different taste to development. As Andrea Cornwall has argued, instead of talking about "beneficiaries with needs" or "consumers with choices" the human rights approach speaks of "citizens with rights". Citizens are active subjects in the political sphere, not objects of intervention by government programs or passive choosers in the marketplace. This of course does not mean that RBA cannot be applied when working with "consumers" or "beneficiaries".

To the contrary, these areas offer some of the most productive opportunities for applying this approach. For instance, the organization of consumers to evaluate the quality of the goods provided at a local store or the intervention of beneficiaries in the design of government social development programs are both good examples of the RBA approach. RBA draws on the "logic" of political citizenship but it can and should be applied to all areas of human life, including the market, society, and service delivery. In the end, RBA can be envisioned as the application of the basic principles of the Universal Declaration of Human Rights in the area of development. For instance, the Norwegian government has defined RBA as "a concept that integrates all human rights norms, standards and principles of international human rights systems, including the right to development, into the plans, policies and processes of development".

SOCIAL ACCOUNTABILITY

An accountable government is one that pro-actively informs about and justifies its plans of action, behaviour and results and is sanctioned accordingly. The core elements of accountability are therefore information, justification and sanction. A fully accountable government would approach these tasks in a pro-active manner and do so along all three temporal dimensions. Accountability is one of the most effective ways to combat corruption, clientelism and capture and thereby assure "good governance", but it is not the only strategy.

For instance, democracy, economic development and international pressure are other strategies that may be equally effective depending on the circumstances. Nevertheless, pro-accountability reform is an essential element of any good governance strategy. Accountability reform has traditionally been thought of as an essentially internal governmental affair. For instance, "Weberian reforms" like civil service reform and the improvement of internal auditing, evaluation and surveillance usually have little to do with civil society.

Indeed, the central idea behind such "old" public management reforms is to rationalize and isolate the bureaucracy. Alternative strategies like the creation of independent pro-accountability agencies also usually fail to incorporate society. Most independent agencies are isolated bastions of technocrats. Marketization strategies such as privatization or the implementation of private sector management techniques involve society in an indirect fashion as consumers but are also a far cry from stimulating civic engagement.

"Social accountability" is therefore a relatively new strategy which is distinct from Weberian reform, independent agencies and marketization. It can be defined as "an approach towards building accountability that relies on civic engagement, *i.e.* in which it is ordinary citizens and/or civil society organizations who participate directly or indirectly in exacting accountability".

There are a great variety of initiatives that fall under this category. Initiatives as different as participatory budgeting, administrative procedures acts, social audits and citizen report cards all involve citizens in the oversight and control of government and can therefore can be considered social accountability initiatives.

Specifically, there are six different distinctions which can be used to capture the variety of social accountability mechanisms: punishment vs. reward based mechanisms, rule following vs. performance based mechanisms, level of institutionalization, depth of involvement, inclusiveness of participation, and branches of government. In short, social accountability initiatives can be as diverse and multifaceted as society itself.

ELECTIVE AFFINITIES

RBA and social accountability initiatives are natural partners. RBA requires citizen participation and government accountability, precisely the central concerns of social accountability. Equality, non-discrimination and inclusion also should find a comfortable home in social accountability initiatives since these initiatives stimulate the participation of common people in the supervision and control of government. Social accountability also scales up participation. Instead of seeing citizens as simple "users" whose participation should be limited to deciding when and where X or Y service should be implemented, social accountability envisions them as "citizens" who can engage in and evaluate the entire planning and evaluation process from beginning to end. As Anne Marie Goetz and Rob Jenkins have argued, There is almost nowhere on earth that citizens or their associations have either been given access and information on, let alone a more substantive role in, formal auditing processes.

Indeed, even in the far less sensitive area of expenditure planning, there is just a handful of experimental cases world-wide encouraging citizen involvement. Citizen auditing strikes at the heart of practices that preserve the powers of bureaucrats and politicians: the secrecy in public accounts that can mask the use of public funds for personal advantage. Citizen participation in holding government to account breaks with the superficiality of much of "civic participation" discourse and practice. It is one thing to take into account the opinions of the poor or the citizenry in general when planning public policy.

It is quite another to allow the people to watch and evaluate the actions of government as they unfold. The latter is far more effective in stimulating good government and much more empowering for the citizens who participate. Social accountability also easily supports the legal defence of human rights. Once citizens are mobilized in supervising the government it is a small step for them to start demanding and designing new laws as well as using the existing laws to back up their claims against the state.

There is great potential for setting up positive feedback loops between social accountability and the law. In addition, the respect for human rights, in particular basic civil liberties, are a pre-condition for effective social accountability initiatives. There is, therefore, an "elective affinity" between RBA and social accountability initiatives. Each one has its own distinct identity, neither one is a subset of the other, and there is not a direct link of "causality" between the two. Social accountability does not automatically and mechanically lead to the adoption of RBA or vice versa. Nevertheless, there is a magnetic attraction between the two concepts/practices. Each one needs and significantly strengthens the other in both theory and practice.

There are different forms and degrees by which social accountability initiatives can fulfill the promise of rights based approaches to development. For instance, there is a tendency for social accountability initiatives to come up short on the last two elements of RBA, "scaling-up" and "legal recourse". In addition, there are sometimes problems with the issue of inclusiveness, as when social accountability initiatives are designed in a "top-down" fashion and only involve elite NGOs. In general, when social accountability initiatives break wiThexclusive localism and elitism, are designed in a bottom-up fashion and are legally institutionalized, or otherwise give rise to legal recourse, they can be said to be more fully grounded in a human rights approach.

STRENGTHENING SOCIAL ACCOUNTABILITY

The implementation of social accountability initiatives is an excellent way to implement the central principles of rights based approaches to development. All four cases examined represent serious efforts towards making citizens participants in their own development. The Bangalore Citizen Report Card significantly breaks with the inward looking nature of government bureaucracies, the Malawi Community Scorecard involves communities directly in improving public services, the Indonesian Justice for the Poor programme encourages community empowerment and mobilization in making the justice system work, and the emerging System of Social Accountability in Peru brings citizens to the table when deciding national policy.

Nevertheless, it is still possible to strengthen the human rights content of these and other social accountability initiatives. Three challenges appear to be the most important. First, exclusive localism continues to be a problem. With the exception of Peru, all of the cases are local level initiatives that don't clearly or directly engage with the national or international political spheres. For instance, in the Indonesia case although links are made to the national level debate on judicial reform and some mention is made of the forces that oppose reform, these seem to be more of an afterthought than a central motivating force for the initiative. In the "Idea Note" on the programme the authors claim that at the national level there are "entrenched interests opposing reform both outside and within the sector, and there is reluctance of the government to challenge such powerful stakeholders during the current phase of the transition" but there is no analysis of exactly what these interests are or of how they have tried to resist reform.

Instead of engaging with the complexities of national reform, the programme seems to turn its back on this issue with the statement that "the same national-level stakeholders who oppose national reform in some sense have a strong interest in local reforms since they wish to retain popular acquiescence or support for the current regime". The "stakeholders" are not mentioned by name and the problem of their resistance is entirely skirted by shifting to the local level. There are no doubt advantages with having the opposing forces on your side.

But there are also disadvantages. Won't their involvement at the local level militate against the possibility of the local reforms "moving the overall national governance agenda forward" as is apparently the intention of the initiative? The absence of a full discussion of who the opposing forces are and of the complexities of the scaling up process puts into doubt the extent to which the Justice for the Poor initiative will truly be able to confront and transform the power structure that maintains so many people without their most basic human rights in Indonesia. Second, "top down" design remains an important challenge. With the exception of Malawi, all of the cases have had difficulties with involving full grassroots participation.

For instance, in the case of Peru while there has been a great deal of success in the consolidation and expansion of the government run Integrated Financial Management System which provides information to the public about government budgets and spending, the citizen side of the equation has lagged behind. One example of this is that the World Bank's Implementation Completion Report for PSRL II reveals that the much touted System of Social Vigilance "has not progressed as intended". The blame for this is placed on the fact that the Defensoría del Pueblo, which was supposed to coordinate the initiative, "has been without a designated chief executive for almost 3 years and appears to have lost the dynamism needed to play its expected role as promoter of transparency and social control".

However, the Defensoría was not the only actor supposedly responsible for designing the SIVISO. The "Task Force" put together for the project was made up of the Defensoría along with the Ministry of Finance, the World Bank and civil society groups. In addition, the Defensoría does not consist only of its chief executive, but employs thousands of Peruvians committed to defending human rights. If the problem is three years old, why wasn't it dealt wiThearlier? Why weren't alternative partners identified who could push forward this community organization agenda? Overall, it appears that there has been a stronger commitment on the part of the government and the World Bank to strengthening the top-down and technical aspects of the accountability system than to engaging with the messier bottom-up elements of the system. Third, the existing social accountability initiatives still generally fail to link themselves up to the legal structure. With the exception of Indonesia, all of the cases ignore legal recourse as a central strategy and thereby fail to fully conceive of service providers as duty holders.

For instance, the Bangalore Report Card conceptualizes the problem with public services as one of incentives looks to convince or "nudge" public servants to change their ways. The obligation that service providers have to perform well is not emphasized either in the survey or in the dissemination of the information. In Malawi there is a similar problem. The LIFH programme does not explicitly understand service providers as duty-holders. Shah admits as much when she claims that "interestingly, the pilot process has led the partners towards a rights-based approach without actually discussing any 'rights' *per se*". This is especially worrisome given the fact that there already exists a charter of citizens' health rights in Malawi. Shah has argued that "maybe in the next 6-12 months these will be shared with the service users and providers in this project. This will be done only when the process has matured enough to handle new ideas from outside". Such a perspective seems to hold onto an artificial separation between what is "internal" and what is "external". If the right of citizens to adequate health care is not explicitly mentioned in the process it is difficult to imagine how one can speak of service-providers as duty-holders. The first step towards such a strategy is to inform the citizens of their rights and explicitly help them see public services as obligations which the government has towards them.

Overall, the Citizen Report Card methodology appears to be the social accountability initiative which is the farthest away from the fulfillment of the promise of the human rights perspective. The top-down nature of its organization and its firm commitment to conceptualizing the people as consumers greatly limits its ability to put human rights in action. This does not mean that report cards are ineffective or that they actively violate human rights. To the contrary, experience has shown that citizen scorecards are highly effective at improving government accountability and performance and that they can play an important role in complementing other initiatives which have strong human rights content.

The application of a full human rights perspective should not lead us to abandoning scorecards, or any of the other initiatives, but should encourage us to rethink their design and to go beyond them to implement other initiatives which more fully empower the people as citizens. The most positive case from a human rights perspective is the Justice for the Poor Programme in Indonesia. The program's solid commitment to engaging citizens in a long term fight for justice and in synthesizing preexisting practices with legal recourse demonstrates that it has its feet solidly planted in the human rights perspective. The Peruvian case is particularly interesting because of the national reach of the programme. The Malawi case is the only one that involves outside agencies directly in the messy process of community organizing and mobilization.

The World Bank has thus far not explicitly endorsed a rights based approach to development. Nevertheless, the recent initiative to support a "Community of Practice on Social Accountability" within the World Bank is a crucial step in the right direction and pushes the institution towards many of the central themes of the human rights approach. Any agency that is interested in allowing such social accountability initiatives to flourish should more wholeheartedly endorse a human rights perspective. In this way social accountability entrepreneurs would be able to tap into a great diversity of new practices and discourses which would greatly strengthen their initiatives.

CASE STUDIES

This part explores four case studies of social accountability initiatives which have served as models for or are directly supported by the international development community: the Bangalore Citizen Report Card implemented by the Public Affairs Centre in India, the Malawi Community Scorecard implemented by CARE, the Justice for the Poor programme run by the World Bank in Indonesia, and the construction of a "System of Social Accountability" in Peru also supported by the World Bank. For each case we give a brief summary of the initiative and then explore how it can be considered to be an example of RBA.

THE BANGALORE CITIZEN REPORT CARD

The use of citizen "report cards" is on the rise throughout the world. In recent years, report cards have been supported by the World Bank in Uganda, the Philippines and Peru. Beyond the World Bank, the methodology has been taken up by municipal residents in the Ukraine and numerous cities in India. The experience that began this flurry of innovation is the report card originally organized by Samuel Paul in Bangalore, India in 1994, and then repeated in 1999 and 2003 by the Public Affairs Centre. The original motivation for the report card in Bangalore was the deficient provision of public services in the city. This problem was widespread for most services. Transportation, telephone, electricity, water and waste disposal services were all profoundly unsatisfactory, especially in the poorest areas of the city. The hypothesis grounding the report card methodology is that the reason why the services are so poor is because government agencies are not enmeshed in an effective incentive structure. Many of the services are monopolies that are not exposed to the discipline of the market and all of them are run by an overloaded government that operates in the context of an outdated legal and regulatory system.

The report card methodology was therefore developed in order to expose government agencies to the "consumer feedback" they are lacking. As one report on the application of the methodology in the Philippines states, "The Filipino Report Card reflects a shift in thinking about Filipinos as clients rather than beneficiaries".

Samuel Paul puts the same point in a different manner:

- The 'take it or leave it' attitude one comes across—especially at the lower levels of the bureaucracy—is no doubt due to the fact that the government is the sole supplier of most services. This is in sharp contrast to the practice of seeking 'customer feedback' that is common in the business world, or at least among those who produce and sell goods in the competitive market place.

The guiding idea behind the methodology is to introduce market-type incentives to the functioning of government. Through the report card methodology, agencies can see how their performance changes from year to year as well as compare themselves to other agencies in a comparative, competitive dynamic similar to that imposed by the market. This occurs through the independent action of a civil society organization and the power of information. As one PAC staff member has written, "the long term significance of [the report card] process is its message to the staff of government agencies that citizens matter, their voice has to be heard and responded to, and that the process is neither temporary nor reversible".

Report cards have seven key phases:

- Identification of Scope, Actors and Purpose,
- Design of Questionnaires,
- Sampling,
- Execution of Survey,
- Data Analysis,
- Dissemination,
- Institutionalization.

Experience reveals that the three core elements which are most important for a successful initiative are:

- Technical expertise in the design, implementation and analysis of the report card,
- An active civil society that is willing and able to use the information provided in the report card to pressure the government for reform, and,
- Reform minded top public officials who are willing and able to use the information to implement changes in service provision.

In Bangalore the report card has played a crucial role in reenergizing public services. Specifically, nudged forward by the results of the report card, various agencies like the Bangalore Water Supply and Sewerage Board and the Bangalore Development Authority have initiated training programs to improve customer service skills of their staff. The Bangalore Municipal Corporation has established a new, more transparent and less corrupt property tax system. The Karnataka Electricity Board has installed a system that facilitates bill collection through the use of mobile counters. In addition, in the year 2000, shortly after the release of the second report card, the Chief Minister of the state government where Bangalore is the capital created the Bangalore Agenda Task Force. This was an innovative effort to improve public services through the participation of civil society. The BATF institutionalized citizen voice by inviting civil society leaders to sit on its board of directors and implementing its own report cards evaluating the quality of public services. This initiative can be credited with much of the improvement in services in Bangalore that has taken place over the past decade.

When the PAC repeated the report card in 2003 it discovered that there had been a radical transformation in the evaluations of public services. While overall satisfaction levels had ranged between 5% and 25% in 1994, and between 16% and 67% in 1999, by 2003 they had skyrocketed to between 64% and 96%. Even the lowest ranking of 64%, given by the poorest households to the police department, is extremely high given the sensitive area it deals with. In addition, scores of 94% for the Bangalore Electric Company and 96% to the Transit Corporation amid middle class households are absolutely phenomenal.

It is difficult to attribute these changes and new programs exclusively to the report card. For instance, the radical change in public services experienced since 1999 occurred when the new minister had a strong majority in the legislature. Nevertheless, it is clear that the implementation of the report card methodology has had a great deal to do with the improvement of the satisfaction scores registered between the three report cards. Samuel Paul has explained that there are three different ways in which the report card served as an important stimulant to change.

- First, it compensates for weak government selfmonitoring by providing information to agency heads about consumer satisfaction. This information is invaluable to reform minded public servants in so far as it allows them to best orient their efforts at agency re-engineering.
- Second, it creates a "glare effect" which pressures badly performing agencies to improve their performance and introduces competitive pressures into the management of all government agencies as heads constantly compare their performance to others.
- Third, report cards stimulate the organization and mobilization of society. The information gives civil society a solid basis on which to pressure for improved services and obliges government agencies to open themselves up more to the voice of clients. Viewed from a human rights perspective, the report card methodology clearly moves proaccountability reform in the right direction.

By forcing public servants to take into account the opinions of citizens the power relationship between bureaucrats and the people begins to shift. As we saw in the quote by Samuel Paul, report cards put the typical "take it or leave it" attitude of bureaucrats into question by demonstrating that they are not the only ones whose opinions or comfort matters. As citizens, the people have a right to express their opinions on the quality of the services the government provides and a right to know the general opinion of these services. The Bangalore Report card therefore strengthens the peoples' right to information and to freedom of expression.

As Paul has written elsewhere, The relevance of this tool for the poor cannot be overemphasized. It is difficult and costly for poor people to make their voice heard in powerful and large public agencies. Often their voice may not be correctly represented by their leaders or even mediating organizations. The survey methods used by report cards permit the poor to make their voice heard directly an with minimal bias. Report card findings can empower the poor by giving them information that they can use in their interactions with service providers. It is important to point out that report cards also have some important weaknesses when viewed from a human rights perspective. They do not put citizens directly in charge of their own development; they are designed by NGOs, often applied by market research firms and do not automatically give citizens access to any new government information about how public services are run. In and of themselves, the use of report cards does not necessarily link up to a human rights approach to development. Nevertheless, the use of citizen report cards can play a crucial role in the implementation of a human rights approach. When report cards are linked up to capacity building initiatives in civil society, widespread dissemination of information and hard nosed advocacy work, the human rights potential of report cards is multiplied a manifold.

When grassroots groups are involved from the very beginning of the process we are even closer to fulfilling the promise of the human rights approach to development. As Paul has written, "though a report card on public services can be conducted as a technical exercise, the dissemination and advocacy work to follow will benefit a great deal if concerned civil society institutions are involved in the process from the start". The original 1994 Report Card was much more of a "technical exercise" than the following ones.

In 1994 PAC held a press conference and spread the results widely through the media. But in 1999 and 2003, in addition to organizing a large press conference the Centre also presented the results directly to top public officials and organized a series of public meetings at which citizens and bureaucrats could discuss and anlayse the results as well as start to design strategies for change. In addition, in a follow-up report card applied specifically to users of Maternity Homes run by the Bangalore Municipal Corporation, PAC became directly involved in designing possible solutions to the problems uncovered by the survey.

As A. Ravindra writes, "a progression in the influence of the report card can be seen to move from limited impact to more impact to greater impact corresponding to the reactive, proactive and reformist roles of the PAC over a period of time".

COMMUNITY SCORECARDS IN MALAWI

The community scorecard methodology is inspired by the experience of the citizen report cards applied in Bangalore and elsewhere, but includes various new innovations. First, while citizen report cards are run by professional NGOs and consulting firms, community scorecards are developed and applied by the service users and service providers. Second, while citizen report cards are oriented principally towards providing and disseminating information on public opinion, the central objective of community score cards is to make decisions and develop action plans. The community scorecard methodology was first developed in communities surrounding the Chileka and Nthondo Health Centers in Malawi by CARE through its Local Initiatives for Health project in 2002. In Malawi there is a long history of deficient provision of health care services to the poor. The central objective of the project is to improve the provision of health services to the rural poor through the empowerment of the user community. Since 2002 the methodology has been expanded to many more health centers as well as "scaled up" to the district level. The model applied in Malawi includes four basic elements. First, facilitators organize community meetings with villages surrounding the specific health center to be evaluated. These meetings are organized and run in close coordination with village leaders and particularly with the members of the Local Health Committees which are made up of citizens concerned about the state of health care in the area.

The meetings in the first villages were facilitated by CARE staff with the idea of training community leaders to run them themselves. Later meetings were run by the trained community leaders with only occasional support from CARE staff. At these meetings the participants are asked to talk about their health problems, their access and use of health services and their opinions of the health center under evaluation. The facilitator then works to help the participants design a list of indicators that can be used to evaluate the health center. In the case of the Chikuzamutu and Ndevu clusters surrounding the Chileka health center the communities together generated a total of 22 indicators.

Finally, the participants are asked to rank the performance of the health center along each one of the indicators. In this case the communities used a 1-100 scale. Representatives from each village then get together at the "cluster" level of various villages and prepare a collective scorecard which takes into account the concerns of the community as a whole. Second, the staff at the health clinic goes through a similar process. They are asked to discuss the present situation at the clinic, develop a series of indicators and rank their performance along these indicators.

In the Malawi case the indicators and the evaluations of the clinic workers were very similar to the indicators and evaluations developed by the community members. Third, an "interface meeting" is organized where community members and clinic staff present their respective scorecards, compare the outcomes and try to work together to design solutions to the common problems identified.

In the Malawi case the action plans that arose from the interface meetings emphasized various ways in which service could be improved by changing the behaviour of the health center staff, providing information to service users, administrating resources better and increasing the amount of resources available to the health center. Fourth, the action plans need to be implemented and followed-up. In Malawi a second scorecard was implemented six months after the first one in order to see how much of the action plan had been fulfilled and to develop a new plan for the following six months. The central issues included in the second action plan and also indicates which of the elements of the first action plan had already been initiated or accomplished by the time of the second interface meeting.

There is evidence that there was significant improvement in the service of the health center between the two scorecard processes and that most of this improvement can be attributed to the implementation of the community scorecard. Almost all of the indicators received higher scores in the second scorecard and there was quite significant improvement particularly in the areas of "respect for patients", "listening to patients' problems", "honest and transparent staff", "giving priority to serious cases", "no discrimination in providing supplementary nutrition", and "no preferential treatment". From a human rights perspective the Community Scorecard methodology represents a significant improvement over the Citizen Report Card strategy.

Unlike the experience in Bangalore, the Malawi process was truly citizen run and "bottom-up". The community is involved from the beginning to the end of the process and is encouraged to directly participate in the design of solutions and the oversight of compliance. In addition, since the scorecards are designed and implemented by the service users themselves in an open community meeting there is much greater room for them to discuss issues beyond simply their "satisfaction" with a particular service. There is an opportunity for them to discuss the fundamental right itself, their health, and the reasons for why it is as it is and they are not limited exclusively to evaluating the performance of service providers. Indeed, CARE explicitly claims that the implementation of the community scorecard falls within a "rights based framework" which, for them, implies the principles of "access to information", "participation in decision making process", "accountability", "transparency", "equity", and "shared responsibility".

The strength of the community scorecards in terms of human rights is therefore the area of "bottomup participation". The scorecard methodology builds on previously existing community organizations by working with village leaders and with the members of the Local Health Committees.

It also encourages the expansion of participation, as evidenced by the differences between the proposals in the first and the second action plans. As Shah writes, "while the first scorecard, and the action plan, stressed the behaviour and attitude of the health centre staff...the second action plan seems to focus more on the quality of services provided by the health centre". She then continues on to argue that the participants "may be testing the process for what it can deliver...Once they gain some confidence in the process, and see some positive outcomes, they may attempt the more difficult and complex issues".

This is an extremely positive outcome indeed and is a clear indicator of community empowerment. In addition, over the past two years the LIFH project has developed a district level model and has even begun to explore possibilities for scaling up the methodology to the national level. At the district level, authorities have now started to involve the local health facilities in the annual planning and budget formulation process. In this way citizen participation and empowerment has begun to filter up to the broader level of policy making.

At present, "local level action plans now feed into the district level planning and monitoring process. Results from the local level scorecards have not only been discussed and used at the health facility level, but there have been opportunities for the different communities and service providers to meet and share experiences at various fora". This incremental expansion of the project is crucial in so far as it helps overcome the "localism" often present in participatory initiatives. The community scorecard initiative is an excellent example of a rights based approach to development in action. It breaks with many of the problems identified with citizen report cards and promises to lead to the very real empowerment of the users of public services. Indeed, there is no reason why such a strategy should be limited to small rural areas. Similar mechanisms can be used just as effectively in highly urbanized settings and at the district or national level. This scaling-up as well as the institutionalization that would necessarily go along with it represent the two principal challenges to the future consolidation of the community scorecards as an example to follow.

JUSTICE FOR THE POOR PROGRAMME IN INDONESIA

The Justice for the Poor programme represents a highly innovative effort to make justice work in the developing world. The Indonesian justice system has recently emerged from almost forty years of an "integralist State" under Sukarno's New Order government, where the lack of a true separation of powers severely undermined the autonomy and the strength of the judicial branch.

"The New Order government homogenized, co-opted and corroded many of the informal institutions through which people resolved disputes and defended their interests, putting in their place a powerful, centralized bureaucracy backed by a strong military". As in many places in the world both North and South, the Indonesian people have learned to distrust judges, prosecutors and the police. These figures are thought of as working either in their own personal interests or in the interests of the powerful, instead of justice or the public interest. As one village leader expressed in an interview with World Bank staff, "our legal system is like a spider's web; if it's a little insect that flies past it will be caught, but if it's a bird that comes along, it will just break the web".

The Indonesian government has recently showed some signs of interest in implementing national level reforms that look to professionalize and strengthen the judicial branch, captured in the Supreme Court's recently released "Blueprints for Legal Reform". Such reforms include changing the recruitment, selection, promotion and transfer policies for personnel who work in the justice system, including the police force, the prosecutor's offices and the courts. In addition, the government has talked about increasing salaries, expanding operational funds and improving decaying infrastructure.

Such technical solutions are crucial to strengthening the judicial system and making it more autonomous and effective. Nevertheless, the World Bank's Justice for the Poor initiative is based in the conviction that such reforms are not enough. The "demand side" for justice also needs to be strengthened. Individuals, communities and civil society at large need to be empowered both to use the judicial system to resolve their disputes and to oversee the judicial system to assure that it functions well.

In addition, the initiative looks beyond the formal judicial system to explore how "informal" justice institutions work. These other institutions are "informal" in so far as they are spaces where disputes are resolved outside of the law. Nevertheless, they are often quite structured and effective at reaching definitive solutions to problems. Examples include the local village governments, semi-official forums set up by development projects and the more traditional adat institutions.

The programme therefore takes a multi-dimensional perspective on the situation of access to justice in Indonesia. Its central purpose is "to develop a sub-national justice reform and dispute-resolution strategy to improve poor people's access to justice institutions and the likelihood of a just outcome from them". The focus is on "the social institutions that underlie a society of law" instead of on the technical aspects of judicial reform. The central conclusion of the program's first major study is that the mobilization of civil society is the most important factor that determines whether disputes are resolved in an effective fashion. This goes for both informal and formal dispute resolution mechanisms.

"The crux of the findings was that although power and institutional history still largely shaped how village communities handled disputes, how justice institutions responded and how cases were resolved, community mobilization and external interventions were able in some circumstances to break the institutional impasse and enable poor communities to defend their interests successfully". Power and empowerment are at the center of this study. Cases are only resolved successfully when power imbalances are explicitly challenged through the use of extra-institutional mobilization.

For instance, it is not enough to simply provide technical legal aid for communities or individuals looking to use the legal system. The most effective legal aid is that which is conceptualized as part of a "broader community advocacy effort". "Legal empowerment efforts should target concrete cases and use them as opportunities for integrated activities: providing legal assistance, mobilizing socially and fostering links to civil society institutions to monitor the legal system". In addition, the study points out that informal mechanisms are most effective when they are backed up by a strong legal system. We should not romanticize the effectiveness of informal, communitybased forms of dispute resolution. "Community leaders in all the cases that were resolved informally employed some threat of legal sanction, whether direct or indirect: the threat of legal sanction was used as a means to improve informal bargaining power". In other words, "informal negotiations take place in the 'shadow of the law'. In cases where the courts are strong, informal negotiation should be strong.

Where the courts are weak, informal negotiation will often be weak". In sum, this study successfully deconstructs the typical dichotomy between strong states and strong societies. Here we have a clear example of "state-society synergy" in action. State institutions like the justice system are most effective when civil society is mobilized and social institutions such as informal dispute mechanisms are most effective when the state can back them up with credible threats of justice. The study therefore concludes that one of the most effective strategies for reforming the justice system in Indonesia is through bottom up community empowerment.

"Formal legal improvements should focus not just on systemic improvements to the legal system, but on providing the information and facilitation that villagers need to access it, linking them with civil society groups and media, and helping them to monitor it. They should also be conceived as part of a broader effort at community empowerment". This of course does not mean that the national political debate is unimportant. As the World Bank itself points out, "the problems to be tackled through the Justice for the Poor programme are national institutions that operate at the local level, not local problems".

Nevertheless, "building up pressure from the bottom and a track record of using the legal system successfully is expected to move the overall national governance agenda forward". To advocate for justice reform does not necessarily imply taking up a rights based perspective. Indeed, most justice reform programs are designed in an entirely technical, top-down fashion. Although the results of such programs, if successful, almost inevitably imply an improvement in the defence of the rights of the population, this does not mean that the programs themselves are designed from a rights based perspective. Fortunately, the Justice for the Poor programme takes a rights based approach. First, "service providers" are clearly conceptualized as duty-bearers. This applies both to those who are responsible for running development projects and for those who work in the justice system. On the one hand, the initial study focuses on cases of corruption in World Bank funded programs.

Fourteen out of the seventeen cases explored are of this nature. This emphasis on corruption clearly arises out of a rights based approach which emphasizes that development funds are not the property of those who administer them, but of the public at large. The community is therefore within its rights to protest against malfeasance. Legal recourse is eagerly encouraged. On the other hand, the emphasis is on the duty of the justice system to respond to the public interest. The police, the prosecutors and the judges are not kindly asked to behave in an institutional and objective manner, but are required to do so through the pressure of civil society. Justice is clearly conceptualized as a right, not as a gift that comes down from high. Second, "bottom up" participation is given a high value. The emphasis on taking "informal" village institutions for dispute resolution seriously demonstrates a careful sensitivity to previously existing practices. "Villagers whose lives are so strongly bond by relationships of trust and reciprocity are thus reluctant to solve many kinds of disputes through litigation or criminal prosecution, which are by nature adversarial and deliver win/lose outcomes that are seen to be at odds with the demands of village life". In addition, proposals like the establishment of village tribunals or "conciliation councils" that would give formal recognition to local organic dispute resolution mechanisms also show a committed interest in building from the ground up. Finally, the recommendation that "one of the most effective ways for donors to ensure that their interventions are made relevant to villagers' interests is to use pre-existing projects at the local level as avenues for legal empowerment interventions" also shows a clear commitment to a bottom-up understanding of participation. The participation envisioned by the programme is also clearly expansive in nature.

The idea is not simply to get some cases resolved, but to mobilize society so that it is able to better resolve its own cases and pressure the judicial system to function better in the long run. For instance, the report argues that "the most successful case leaders were those who were able to build coalitions with civil society organizations to place scrutiny on the legal system while mobilizing a range of institutions—each with its own stake in seeing the cases resolved, such as the World Bank or local government—around the cases at hand". In general, power is at the center of the Justice for the Poor initiative. The programme looks to compensate for power imbalances both within the formal justice system and within the communities. "Shame" and social pressure are often not enough. Legal action and social mobilization are key elements in any pro-accountability initiative grounded in a human rights perspective since they are some of the few instruments that actually check the influence of powerful elites. The programme is presently only at the preparatory stage. Nevertheless, the approach being taken in the preparatory studies holds great promise for the future implementation of a full human rights approach to development.

PERU'S SOCIAL ACCOUNTABILITY SYSTEM

After the fall of the Fujimori government in September 2000 Peruvian society was thirsty for both greater accountability and expanded democracy.

The corruption scandals that brought down the president left the population with a profound distrust of government and Fujimori's heavy handed style of rule had limited the democratization of the Peruvian state. It was therefore natural for Paniagua's transition government, and Toledo's government afterwards, to emphasize accountability and citizen participation in their attempt to reconstruct government legitimacy. As the World Bank argues, "governance in Peru was long characterized by its lack of popular participation and transparency, either in the design or in the implementation of public programs.

By the end of the 1990s, however, transparency, participation and social control had become strongly asserted priorities of the country's citizens". One of the most important initiatives taken during the transition period in 2001 was the creation of Mesas de Concertación para la Lucha Contra la Pobreza. These "Round Tables for Attacking Poverty" brought together government officials with representatives of civil society to design social policies to combat poverty. The objective of the Mesas was to "institutionalize the participation of civil society in the design, decision-making and control of poverty-related programs". Half of the Executive Committee of the MCLCP consisted of civil society representatives and a central element of the Carta Social that emerged from the discussions was the active participation of civil society organizations in the planning and monitoring of local development programs. These Mesas built on the experience of the national Poverty Forum which had been held each year between 1998 and 2000 in which over 250 representatives from governments, donors, NGOs and the academia participated. Shortly afterwards, in 2002, building on the experience with the Mesas, national development goals were put together and then formalized in a National Agreement. This agreement involved seven national parties, the church, industry, business sector and labour unions committed to the agreement.

The National agreement includes four strategic areas:

- Institutionalization of democracy,
- Social equity and the fight against poverty,
- Competitiveness, and
- Anti-corruption.

Beginning in 2001, the government also launched an ambitious decentralization programme. It created regional administrations as a new level of government and began to transfer a significant amount of resources to these sub-national units. Simultaneously, it involved the regions in a participatory budget experiment which led to wide ranging public discussions about the priorities for public investment. As a result, 22 out of the 24 regions formulated "concerted plans" and participatory budgets for 2003. Indeed, "40 per cent of the regions completed participatory budgets with support from all of the public regional administrations, all mayors, and the principal civil society organizations".

Felicio and John-Abraham point out that future plans include:

- Training local and regional authorities to formulate concerted plans and participatory budgets,
- Constructing a legal framework to establish a stable institutional environment, and
- Updating plans and participatory budgets for the upcoming national budgets.

Other initiatives include the strengthening of community participation in the management of local health clinics through the expansion of the Comunidades Locales de Administración de Servicios de Salud. One of the benchmarks for the first stage of the Programmatic Social Reform Loan that the World Bank extended to Peru beginning in 2001 was the expansion of the proportion of the public primary clinics under the CLAS arrangement from 15 to 20%. In addition, under this loan a "Task Force" was created between the Ministry of Finance and the national Ombudsman to "recommend measures for building the capacity of beneficiaries/grass roots organizations to utilize proactively budget information that will be increasingly available to the general public".

Finally, the Ministry of Education has begun to open itself up more to public participation. On January 13, 2001 the ministry launched a new Comisión para un Acuerdo Nacional por la Educación which includes representatives from civil society, academia, the teachers' union and industry. These "bottom-up" initiatives have been joined with other equally important "top-down" initiatives to form an emerging "system of social accountability" in Peru. For instance, the ministry of finance has updated its "Integrated Financial Management System" to include budget information on all three levels of government and made its internet site much more user-friendly and easily accessible by civil society organizations.

Indeed, facilitating public access to this information was an important benchmark for the first stage of the World Bank loan and a "trigger" for the second stage of the loan. As the World Bank states, this "information and data will help beneficiaries, NGOs, civil society and others to exercise social control over social programs by allowing them to verify whether programs are actually spending resources in those areas where they claim to be, whether geographic targeting is appropriate, and whether there appears to be any politically-motivated use of social expenditures". Finally, the National Statistics and Information Institute was granted greater autonomy and strength and questions regarding public perceptions about government transparency have been included in the National Household Survey applied throughout the country.

Jointly with other donors the World Bank has supported the emergence of this system mainly through a Programmatic Social Reform Loan divided into three parts, initiated in 2001 and continuing through today, for which strengthening social accountability mechanisms has been a central element. The objective of the accountability aspect of the loan is the depoliticization of social spending, the elimination of corruption and the improvement of targeting of social programs. "Transparency regarding allocations, expenditures, and the on-the-ground operation of poverty alleviation programs is important to facilitate appropriate targeting, prevent any politicallymotivated use of expenditures, and eliminate corruption".

The other areas of the loan have focused on safeguarding critical social expenditures during a period of economic transition and crisis, improving the articulation and coordination of social policy, facilitating the access of the poor to social programs, and rationalizing of social expenditures. During the second period of the loan these diverse areas were reorganized into three "pillars" of social reform: the "dignity" pillar which shifts government spending towards the basic needs of the poor, the "equity" pillar which expands coverage of health and education programs, and the "institutionality" pillar whose central objective is to improve transparency and social control over resources. In sum, with this loan the World Bank seeks to apply a "partnership approach to policy formulation".

The World Bank explains that this is so important because "at this critical time in Peruvian history, the role of civil society organization in promoting constructive open debate and exercising social control over the use of scarce public resources becomes even more relevant. New voices and groups are beginning to emerge during this transition period in the country, such as groups led by young professionals, youth organizations, and local committees". People often mistakenly think that social accountability mechanisms are only practical or effective at the local level of communities or neighbourhoods. When we think of such mechanisms the first images that tend to come to mind are small, face to face community meetings in rural areas or, at the very largest, participatory budgeting at the level of city governments.

The Peru case is so important because it shows how social accountability can also be an effective strategy at the national level. The broad based nature of the initiative immediately moves it closer to a human rights perspective. For instance, one test for whether a project sees the people as citizens, beneficiaries or consumers, is to evaluate whether the participants are encouraged to look beyond localistic and immediate concerns. The Mesas de Concertación and the participatory process for the formulation of the 2003 national budget are national efforts which involved society at large in discussing the future of the country as a whole.

As a result, they necessarily tapped into the full capacities of the population as citizens, not only as beneficiaries or consumers. The fact that the concept of citizenship and rights as the basis of social policy is explicitly drawn into the Peruvian government's policy framework is also a positive sign. "The main objective of social policy is to generate conditions of equity where the population will have access to more opportunities that will allow them to reach an acceptable standard of living. This implies access to basic goods to satisfy their essential needs, wiTheffectiveness, efficiency and adequate quality, and with the ultimate purpose of raising their productive capacities and assets. This will allow a sustained promotion of economic growth and fostering of human and citizenship rights". The participatory mechanisms also have a healthy dose of "expansiveness".

Participation is not limited only to information provision and protest. The involvement in participatory budgetary processes and the design of a new community based mechanism for social control, the SIVISO, show that there has been a clear commitment to expanding citizen participation beyond just its "watch-dog" function of oversight and towards a more full involvement with decision making as well. For instance, the Peruvian government clearly states that "a fundamental component of the [social development] strategy will be promotion of the population's active participation, not only to exercise control over the direction of social expenditure, but also to involve them gradually in the process of local management of the resources related to the development of social policies and the decentralized provision of basic social services".

Overall, the Peru case is extremely important in so far as it challenges pro-accountability reformers to think about innovative ways to tap into the dynamism of civic engagement at the national level. It obliges us to think about truly expansive participation in which the population is understood as a "partner" to development, as full citizens with a say equal to that of government bureaucrats and politicians.

12

Human Rights and Social Development

THE RELEVANCE OF HUMAN RIGHTS TO THE COPENHAGEN DECLARATION ON SOCIAL DEVELOPMENT AND PROGRAMME OF ACTION

The Copenhagen Declaration on Social Development recognizes the urgent need to address profound social problems, especially poverty, unemployment and social exclusion, that affect every country and sets as the task of the governments to address both their underlying and structural causes and their distressing consequences in order to reduce uncertainty and insecurity in the life of people.. It adopts a broad view of social development, as meeting the material and spiritual needs of individuals, their families and the communities in which they live.

This can only be achieved through social and people-centred sustainable development.. As an aspect of sustainable development, there is a commitment to the protection of the environment. Social development is inextricably connected wiTheconomic development, for some of its primary goals the eradication of poverty, unemployment and social exclusion depend on it.

The Declaration identifies a number of factors that have prevented the goals of social development from being achieved: chronic hunger, malnutrition, illicit drug trade, organized crime, corruption, foreign occupation, armed conflicts, illicit arms trafficking, terrorism, intolerance, xenophobia and incitement to racial, ethnic, religious and other hatreds. Many of these factors are connected with the violation of human rights. It is therefore not surprising that the Declaration places considerable emphasis on human rights and democracy in order to achieve these goals.

Indeed more than any other international declaration, with the exception of the Declaration on the Right to Development the Declaration places human rights at the centre of development. It states, for example, that democracy and transparent and accountable governance and administration in all sectors of society are indispensable foundations for the realization of social and people-centred sustainable development.. At another point it refers to the acknowledgment that social and economic development cannot be secured in a sustainable way without the full participation of women and that equality and equity between women and men is a priority for the international community and as such must be at the centre of economic and social development. The Declaration places particular emphasis on the eradication of poverty, and this is perhaps its closest connection with human rights. Poverty is the greatest cause of the denial of human rights. It is obvious that poor people enjoy a disproportionately small measure of economic rights such as education, health and shelter. However, they are equally unable to exercise civil and political rights, which would require not only an understanding of the dynamics of society and access to public institutions, but also confidence in themselves.

They are for the most part unable to use the legal process to vindicate their human and legal rights. Nothing destroys confidence so much as poverty. Poverty also compels people into the violation of the rights of others, particularly of their own children and women. Child labour is essential to the survival of millions of families throughout the Third World and, increasingly, so is prostitution. Bonded labour is a direct result of poverty, and its exploitation by the well off. Poverty produces massive inequalities, and the subordination of some groups to others in circumstances that deny them their basic dignity. The first of the principles and goals enunciated in the Declaration, and a central theme of the Programme of Action, is a commitment to a political, economic, ethical and spiritual vision for social development that is based on human dignity, human rights, equality, respect, peace, democracy, mutual responsibility and cooperation, and full respect for the various religious and cultural backgrounds of people. More specifically, governments have agreed to promote democracy, human dignity, social justice and solidarity at the national, regional and international levels; ensure tolerance, non-violence, pluralism and non-discrimination, with full respect for diversity within and among nations.

They have undertaken to promote universal respect for, and observance and protection of, all human rights and fundamental freedoms for all, including the right to development, and to ensure that disadvantaged and vulnerable persons and groups are included in social development.. Particular mention is made of the right of self-determination of all peoples, in particular of peoples under colonial or other forms of alien domination or foreign occupation and support for indigenous people in their pursuit of economic and social development, with full respect for their identity, traditions, forms of social organization and cultural values.

Without trying to exhaust the references to human rights in the Declaration, the last paragraph of the first Commitment is worth quoting: As suggested, reaffirm and promote all human rights, which are universal, indivisible, interdependent and interrelated, including the right to development as a universal and inalienable right and an integral part of fundamental human development, and strive to ensure that they are respected, protected and observed.. Several points about these formulations are worth noting. First, the importance of the language of rights. Repeated references to them might indicate a broad international consensus on human rights and freedoms and attest to the moral and political force of the idea of human rights or at least of its rhetoric. In recent decades the idea of respect for human rights seems to have become a driving force in international and regional policies and conduct, as in the intervention of the United Nations in the restoration of rights and democracy in Bosnia and Herzegovina, Cambodia, East Timor, Haiti and Nicaragua; or in the more specific regional mediations and interventions by the]Organization for Security and Cooperation in Europe.

Extensive references to democracy and human rights in the Declaration are evidence of the desire, if perhaps not necessarily the feasibility, of using human rights as a framework for sustainable development and solving other ailments of humankind. All of this enthusiasm and commitment to human rights must be taken with some caution, for the international human rights movement has been distinguished more by rhetoric than practice. Human rights are understood differently in different places, and the apparent consensus on rights conceals profound differences on, and even conflicts over, values and goals.

Second, the frequent invocation of rights in the different contexts in the Declaration attests to the enlarged scope of the concept and content of human rights. Rights have travelled a long distance from their origins in the emerging liberal economic orders of Europe and the United States since the seventeenth century, when the focus was on civil and political rights as the means to restrict the power of the government and enhance that of economic entrepreneurs. Their philosophical foundations have broadened, fed by various political and intellectual traditions.

A large and diverse number of groups and interests have advanced their claims in the language of rights. The first additions to the classical liberal category of rights were economic, social and cultural rights. Since then specialized instruments have dealt with the claims and rights of vulnerable groups, such as women, children, refugees, migrants, indigenous peoples and people with disabilities. More broadly, but also ambiguously, there is the right to develop-ment, and notions of the preservation of the environment are being woven into the regime of rights. There is now a rich menu of rights, perhaps too rich as some complain, and the rights do not appear to be seamless. The regime of rights guarantees democracy and participation, and the accommodation of diversity. A fundamental assumption of contemporary human rights is social justice, and thus the alleviation of poverty, which is a primary concern of the Declaration. Social justice has also promoted the idea of equity as between men and women, between groups, and between generations. There is a considerable widening of the range of entitlements of citizens and others, transforming people from supplicants into citizens. The broadening of human rights has focused attention on the state not merely as facilitator but also as provider. The logic of social, economic and cultural rights is positive obligations of the state, necessitating an active role, to ensure basic needs of people, and thus their dignity.

It is not surprising that these developments in the concept and scope of human rights have produced controversy. Behind the seeming consensus on the formulations in the Declaration on rights and democracy lurk several disagreements. How far the apparent disagreements reflect genuine differences of values is hard to say, for there is considerable hypocrisy and posturing in the position of governments. Human rights have become one of the frameworks for international relations, and the debates about them have become highly politicized. Having said that, it is possible to identify differences in approaches to human rights, and to their contents. These differences have been a major obstacle to a genuine consensus and the feasibility of consistent and effective international action to promote and protect human rights. The challenge to human rights of the Declaration is to achieve coherence of rights, founded on common values and understandings as to their purpose.

There are considerable advantages in using the human rights framework for social develop-ment. Despite the controversies that have prevented unified action on human rights, they seem to attract broad international support and few governments publicly condemn their values. The language of rights has the capacity to evoke a response and to provide moral and legal justification for certain forms of action. The ideology of, and claims based on, human rights have become increasingly effective ways to pressure governments and the international community. The regime of rights provides a basis for international or regional action and justifies the imposition of sanctions and, in extreme cases, humanitarian intervention.

Human rights standards can also compensate for the weakness of international political institutions and machinery. In contradistinction to the growth of the idea and substance of rights in national systems where they followed the establishment of the apparatus of the state in the international system rights have developed with remarkable speed and are well ahead of the development of political institutions. However, that does not mean there is not sufficient authority or mechanism for their international enforcement.

The framework of rights is feasible because rights are now being defined in detailed terms and there are numerous decisions of courts and other tribunals that have elaborated the parameters of rights and their implications. They are no longer abstract formulations. Moreover, the regime of rights is now complex and multilayered, dealing with different kinds of claims and interests. It speaks to a variety of concerns, and provides doctrines as well as mechanisms for striking a balance between different claims. Rights are a way to mobilize and empower the disadvantaged, and in many parts of the world this is their principal function. The language of rights makes people conscious of both their oppression and the possibility of change. Rights have been extraordinarily effective as a basis of networking in and across states and have demonstrated the possibility of international solidarity, particularly for women and indigenous peoples. Many non-governmental organizations justify their existence by the need to promote rights and it is the regime of rights that has enabled them to perform their promotional and investigative role, which has generally proved more effective than internal state mechanisms for accountability. It would be fair to say that the human rights regime has sustained civil society in its confrontation with the state.

Even more fundamentally, the regime of rights is crucial because it speaks in the language of entitlements. Poverty is not just a matter of a deprived economic situation; it is defined and sustained, on the part of the poor, by a sense of helplessness and dependence, and by a lack of opportunities, self-confidence and self-respect. It is increasingly being recognized that poverty can only be eradicated if the poor are given a greater share in decisions about programmes of poverty alleviation and their implementation. The language of rights makes it clear that the poor are not the subject of charity or benevolence, but are entitled to a decent standard of living and that civil and political rights are the vehicles for their participation and empowerment.

The effectiveness of the rights regime is, however, diminished by the fact that not all of them have been integrated into the international economic or financial systems, which are market oriented and primarily protect the interests of capitalists. Many types of rights are not favoured by the capitalist system. Historically only those rights have been upheld that support the interests of the dominant classes thus civil and political rights were propounded by a bourgeoisie coming into power. Today's economic and social rights speak to the claims of the oppressed and the powerless, and the chances of their fulfilment are slim. Developments in human rights have been at the level of rhetoric and to some extent the establishment of institutions, but they have not led to the redistribution of resources or to building the economic base that favours economic justice. Although norms of the human rights regime represent a serious challenge to the international market system, and an alternative vision, the material forces of the international market system are more powerful than the moral claims and rhetoric of human rights.

One further point needs to be made to establish the context for a rights-oriented strategy: it concerns globalization.. The Declaration correctly identifies the contradictory nature of globalization, on one hand opening up possibilities of increased economic growth, and on the other foreclosing options central to the Copenhagen aspirations, such as those of income redistribution, alleviation of poverty, employment opportunities and equity. It states that the global transformations of the world economy are profoundly changing the parameters of social develop-ment in all countries. The challenge is how to manage these processes and threats so as to enhance their benefits and mitigate their negative effects upon people.

There are grave doubts as to whether this challenge can be met successfully. The inherent tendency of economic globalization is to diminish democracy and to privilege market-oriented rights, reducing the importance and feasibility of social and solidarity rights. It is impossible to discuss the salience of the human rights strategy for the Copenhagen social development envisioned in Copenhagen without taking on board the impact of globalization and the redistributions of power that it has produced.

THE HUMAN RIGHTS SYSTEM

In order to explore the potential of the human rights framework to achieve social development, it is necessary to briefly describe the human rights system. The essential components of the system are ideology, substantive rights, functions, beneficiaries, actors, institutions, procedures and the levels at which it operates. The human rights system is rich in texts, rhetoric and institutions, but it is lacking in material resources to make rights effective. States place interests such as national security or economy, and the cultivation of international relations. Popular consciousness of rights is often dulled by ethnic conflicts or the burden of traditional values and authority.

IDEOLOGY

Surprisingly, there is no great consensus on the ideology of rights. There is substantial agreement that the purpose of human rights is to protect human dignity, but there are different views on the source of that dignity. The principal difference lies between those who seek a religious basis for that dignity, and those who seek a secular basis. There is a widespread perception that the origins of the concept of human rights lie in Western, individualist or liberal philosophy and for that reason some in the East argue that it is alien to their own cultures.

Even in the West there is criticism of the individualistic bias of human rights. There are also historical and pragmatic explanations for rights the former consisting of an analysis of the growth of classes and their relationship to the state, and the latter justifying rights in terms of fairness, stability and peace. These differences bear on the acceptance and realization of rights, but perhaps their importance has diminished with the elaboration of rights under the auspices of the United Nations. It has been possible to reach broad agreement on the scope and substance of rights, and the key international instruments have been ratified by a large number of countries adhering to differing religions and cultural traditions. The ideology of human rights is one of the most powerful forces today largely at the level of rhetoric, but also as justification for action, particularly the collective interventions by the international community in oppressive states. The ideology of rights and the acceptance that the international community has the overriding responsibility for their protection has been invoked to justify limits on state sovereignty, a cornerstone of the international system.

LEVELS: INTERNATIONAL, REGIONAL AND NATIONAL

The national, regional and international levels constitute the global system of rights. Historically, the concept and practice of human rights developed in national systems. Before the establishment of the United Nations, a number of states provided for the protection of rights in their constitutions. The League of Nations and the International Labour Organization facilitated the internationalization of specific rights of workers and minorities, but it is only since the existence of the United Nations that there has been an exponential growth in international human rights law. The United Nations Charter committed its members to the promotion and protection of human rights. The United Nations marked its entry into this area in 1948 by adopting the Universal Declaration of Human Rights since then many conventions have been negotiated and ratified by member states.

The growth of conventions and institutions at the international level was paralleled by the establishment of the European Convention of Human Rights, providing the first instance of the protection of rights at the regional level. The Convention is enforced by the European Court of Human Rights. Since then, regional systems of human rights have been established for Africa and the Americas, though there are differences in the scope of rights and the method of enforcement.

Another regional system has developed in recent years under the auspices of the OSCE, in which Canada and the United States also participate so far the progress has been in developing norms and in the method of persuasion. There are many advantages in having regional systems: for instance, they take the load off the international system, and bring the pressure of friendly, neighbouring states to bear on offending states. Equally important, they represent the consensus of the states as to the standards of government behaviour acceptable in the region. Perhaps the absence of regional systems in Asia and Pacific-Australasia is due to the lack of this regional consensus. Consequently, regional systems are uneven, wiTheurope's being the best integrated and certainly the most effective.

The third level is the national. It is the most important level for giving legal effect to human rights norms, which is done by guarantees in the constitutions and laws, and by giving effect to international or regional treaties. It is also the most important level for the enforcement of rights; most violations of rights are dealt with, at least in the first instance, in national courts or other human rights institutions. It is at this level that the key struggle for human rights is conducted and the resistance to it waged. The different levels are being integrated through a regime of treaties that are effective at the national level but supervised at the regional or international level, and through the respect paid by national governments and judiciaries to elaborations of rights by regional or international tribunals. Nevertheless, there is a division of labour between these levels as regards the different functions of the human rights system, to which I now turn.

FUNCTIONS

One of the most important functions is developing a consensus on rights and interests to be protected. This is often done by interest groups women, minorities, migrants, corporations and so on. In recent years NGOs have played an important role in lobbying for the recognition of particular interests many norms on indigenous peoples, minorities and protection against torture owe their origin to the efforts of NGOs. Sometimes regional or international conferences have also performed this role.

Once there is a substantial consensus, the task of norm setting can be undertaken. This involves the elaboration of treaties or legislation and has historically been the role of national governments and legislatures. However, in recent years the international system has played a crucial role. The United Nations has provided the forum for negotiating treaties on human rights. By its nature, norm setting is the responsibility of official bodies, but NGOs have also played a significant role in developing treaties or legislation.

The promotion of respect for rights consists of various activities including information on and education about human rights, and support for the institutions that uphold them. This function is the responsibility of official and non-official bodies. In many countries official human rights commissions have a special responsibility for the propagation of rights. In more authoritarian states, the primary responsibility is discharged by NGOs and social groups, including trade unions.

Closely connected to the respect for rights is mobilization of groups on the basis of rights. Claims of rights have constituted forms of protest and challenges to authority. In so far as one function of rights is the empowerment of vulnerable groups, mobilization is crucial and, since the aim of mobilization is to organize social groups and challenge authorities, human rights defenders are often harassed or even oppressed. Human rights also provide the basis for networking, nationally and internationally. Indigenous peoples and women have been particularly successful in networking, which is almost always the preoccupation of non-official bodies.

Protecting rights is the primary responsibility of the state which together with other official bodies is generally bound to respect human rights and most legal actions are directed at the state's violations of rights. Protecting rights takes various forms, ensuring that:

- There is law and order in which people can enjoy their rights;
- The police and army are trained in human rights norms, and respect and uphold people's rights;

- Institutions in the front line of securing rights, like the judiciary and human rights commissions, are independent and adequately resourced; and
- There are effective sanctions against those who violate the rights of others.

The United Nations has played a limited role in protecting rights. The principal UN agency for this purpose formerly the United Nations Centre for Human Rights, now incorporated into the Office of the United Nations High Commissioner for Human Rights has had very limited resources, and had a low profile until the appointment of the current Human Rights Commissioner, Mary Robinson. Unlike other UN agencies, it had no field offices until recently it now has over 20, supervising the protection of rights and offering technical assistance. The task that receives most attention is enforcing rights, most typically through the judicial process. In recent years other institutions, such as ombudsmen, and human rights or equality commissions, have been established for the protection of human rights. These institutions tend to follow less adversarial procedures than courts, and offer mediation and reconciliation. Access to these bodies is also easier, cheaper and more informal than it is to courts, and they tend to be multifunctional, with information and education being a primary responsibility. However, courts remain the final arbiters of violations, and the ultimate authorities for the interpretations of human rights provisions. Therefore the interpretation of judges and legal practitioners, who have a key role in access to the courts, and a well functioning legal system are indispensable for an effective system of enforcement of rights.

The primary institutions for the enforcement of rights are national, but in countries that are part of a regional system of human rights, regional commissions or courts can play an important, supplementary role. The role of the European Court of Human Rights is crucial in that it makes the final interpretations of the European Convention, which are binding on national governments and courts. The international system plays little role in the enforcement of rights. The first steps in international enforcement have been taken with the establishment of tribunals for war crimes in Rwanda and the former Yugoslavia, and with the imminent establishment of the permanent international tribunal as agreed in Rome three years ago.

The international system has an important, or, more accurately, a potentially important, role in the supervision of the protection and enforcement of rights. This supervision takes two forms: one is primarily political and is the responsibility of the OHCHR and the mechanisms associated with it, such as special rapporteurs for countries including Afghanistan and Cambodia, or on themes such as extrajudicial killings, disappearances and violence against women. The other form of supervision is more judicial., the task being performed by specialist, independent bodies set up under human rights treaties.

Most major treaties provide for periodic reports to these bodies; this is the principal means of supervising a state's performance of its treaty obligations. But some treaties also provide for a complaints mechanism, either at the insistence of another state or of a person who alleges that his or her rights have been violated. Even when there is a complaints procedure, the decision of the body is not strictly enforceable, although it provides a valuable opportunity for the body to elaborate the provisions of the treaty and explain the scope of rights protected by it and the permissible derogations.

This has been a particularly valuable aspect of the work of the United Nations Human Rights Committee, set up under the International Covenant on Civil and Political Rights. However, the potential of the supervisory role of the international system has yet to be realised. Until now meagre resources have been provided to the United Nations and the treaty bodies, many of whom can only meet once or twice a year for a fortnight or so and have inadequate secretariat support and virtually no follow-up machinery. This state of affairs is ample evidence of the low priority accorded to human rights by the international community, as is the fact that the international supervisory system is highly fragmented, incoherent and largely ineffective.

Supervision is also exercised at the regional level for states that are members of regional systems, and also at the national level. Some national human rights commissions may be required to produce an annual report but more often this task is performed by national and international NGOs. Of the latter, Amnesty International and Human Rights Watch are well known. It is also worth mentioning that the United States Department of State produces an annual report on the state of human rights in other countries which is an important aspect of its foreign policy.

ACTORS AND INSTITUTIONS

The preceding subsections have given some account of the actors and institutions that form part of the human rights system. Here it is sufficient to recapitulate that actors exist at various levels and include official and unofficial bodies. There has been considerable emphasis on strengthening national institutions for the protection of rights since the World Conference on Human Rights, held in Vienna in 1993. The OHCHR has played an important role in the promotion of human rights commissions. As discussed in the upcoming subsection on Democratization: The record, considerable foreign assistance has been given for the strengthening of judicial and legal institutions.

A significant set of actors are civil society institutions, which operate nationally and internationally. The framework of human rights has provided a powerful basis for their growth and networking, and they have played an important role in popular mobilization and aggregating demand. In authoritarian states, they have kept alive the demand for democratization, and brought violations of rights to world attention. They are an important lobby for the protection of human rights, and play a significant supervisory role. They were once seen as troublemakers by governments and international agencies, but now enjoy considerable legitimacy in official circles, and are accepted as an indispensable partner in the pursuit of human rights.

BENEFICIARIES OF RIGHTS

The beneficiaries of rights are human beings. However, most legal systems extend human rights to corporations and other entities at least to the extent that they are capable of exercising them. It used to be that rights were traditionally restricted to citizens, and many constitutions still so restrict their scope. International instruments are ambiguous; they speak as if rights belong to everyone., with only the political rights being restricted to citizens, but they do not seem capable of enforcing the wider view of entitlement to rights. However, an increasing number of states extend non-political rights to all residents, although some still discriminate against immigrants in civil, economic and social rights. In a globalizing world, the restriction of rights to citizens, especially when citizenship is conceived of in narrow racial or ethnic terms, is a serious limitation on people's exercise of rights.

So long as rights were attached to citizenship, there was a notion of a uniform set of rights. After the international covenants on civil and political, and on economic, social and cultural rights were adopted, available to everyone., the international community turned its attention to specific groups of people. Conventions for the protection of vulnerable groups racial minorities, women, children, indigenous peoples and migrant workers were adopted. For the most part, they reiterate the rights that these groups allegedly already enjoy under the two Covenants, but provide a basis for affirmative action, special policies and protective institutions, and networking. These developments were in some cases presaged in national systems for example, India, which adopted special constitutional protection of historically disadvantaged minorities.

The concern with vulnerable groups, particularly minorities, has promoted the concept of group rights. In the classical traditions of human rights, only individuals had rights; those who adhere to this approach are uncomfortable with rights of groups and newfangled ideas such as the right to development. But the notion of group rights has assumed a particular importance in multi-ethnic societies, where it has in some cases become the organizing matrix of society.

INTERNATIONALIZATION OF HUMAN RIGHTS AND STATE SOVEREIGNTY

From the perspective of the Declaration and the prospects of international action, the degree of internationalization of human rights is a significant factor. The expression internationalization of human rights refers to the process whereby human rights are encapsulated in international instruments, most of which have become binding on signatory states. The process encompasses the elaboration of human rights, binding states to respect and enforce these rights, and setting up an international system of supervision and enforcement of the obligations of states in respect of human rights. Internationalization of rights also refers to the norms by which states conduct their relations with other states and which international organizations must follow in their work, and it is deemed to have established a new international morality. Because international human rights have been established in what passes for a consensual process, it is often assumed that they are universally valid, as opposed to, for example, democracy, where it is conceded that there is no uniform, universal form. The result is that states may be more willing to intervene to promote or protect rights than to support democracy or criticize political systems that look authoritarian.

The process has resulted in the translation into international instruments of human rights originally developed in national systems and adopted in several state constitutions. The inscription of these rights in international instruments has expanded the scope of the operation of human rights, bringing an important change in the character and purpose of international law and making individuals and their rights its central concern.

The manner in which a state treated its citizens used to be regarded as an internal affair; it was no business of other states or international organizations. The concept of state sovereignty provided a shield for states against external intervention and even external comment. State sovereignty and non-intervention in the domestic affairs of a state are still the cornerstone of the international order under the United Nations Charter. But the notion of what is domestic has changed under the Charter's imperative to promote and protect human rights. International instruments have placed special responsibilities on the state with regard to minorities and indigenous peoples, and other vulnerable communities or groups. This change in international law has been reinforced by international and regional instruments, which have placed obligations on states to respect human rights and to account to the international community for the performance of this responsibility. A number of institutions and procedures have been established since the United Nations was founded to address the question of the violation of human rights by a state. The right of states, regional organizations and the international community to criticize states that violate the human rights of their nationals is increasingly recognized. The eruption of civil wars, often centring on ethnic conflicts, has increased the involvement of the international community in the affairs of states; this involvement is most dramatically manifested in humanitarian intervention, but also takes the form of mediation and conciliation, strengthening national capacity for the promotion of and respect for human rights, monitoring the observance of treaty obligations, and imposing sanctions. The lack of immunity for heads of state for torture and similar crimes, and the establishment of an international criminal court, reinforces this trend.

However, it is important to note that this qualification on state sovereignty is not universally accepted. A number of states, among them those that have been victims of imperialism, argue that state sovereignty and a strong state is essential for the protection of the rights of citizens. Foremost among the proponents of this view is China. Sometimes this pragmatic argument is combined with a doctrinal view of state sovereignty, drawing its inspiration from pre-UN days. Russia has, for example, tried to fend off criticism of its conduct in unleashing a brutal war on the Chechens on the grounds that what it does to its own citizens is its own business, squarely within its sovereignty.

The Association of South-East Asian Nations refused to condemn Indonesia for the atrocities that its troops perpetrated in East Timor. The resistance of states to the notion that human rights anywhere is a matter of international concern, justifying international action, is a serious impediment to the enforcement of human rights. It prevents speedy remedial action by or through the United Nations Security Council. Sanctions or interventions follow only upon brutal repression of groups, resulting in great loss of life. An international consensus on the grounds and modalities for intervention is necessary to prevent extreme violations of human rights. Hesitation about a forthright commitment to the role of the international community in the enjoyment of rights, particularly humanitarian intervention, is no doubt induced by anxieties about the hegemonic power of some states, and the fear that interventions will be selective to serve the interests of powerful countries like the United States.

THE HUMAN RIGHTS INDUSTRY

Despite the complex structure of the human rights system, those involved in the propagation and promotion of human rights form a small group. At the unofficial level, there are a handful of international NGOs that dominate the scene, enjoy a favoured status with the United Nations and receive most of the media publicity. National NGOs are frequently dependent on them as interlocutors for fundraising and for guidance on tactics and organization.

There are also a small number of Western foundations that sustain this movement and thus exercise a disproportionate influence on the orientation and even the possibility of the human rights movement and a small number of official international, regional and national organizations with human rights mandates. There is a considerable circulation of personnel between these NGOs, foundations and organizations, and a strong bonding. The term human rights industry is often used, pejoratively, to refer to the self-interest of the aforementioned groups and the way they organize the production, dissemination and implementation of rights. It suggests that their primary commitment is to their own organizations and their dominance of the system, not the protection of rights.

There is no need to buy into all of this cynicism, but there is little doubt that the human rights movement has become highly bureaucratized, hierarchical, even narrow. The industry having become highly legalistic due to the proliferation of rights, and the mushrooming of the jurisprudence of courts, tribunals and committees, the leadership has passed to lawyers, who for the most part are less concerned with mobilizing mass social movements around rights than with advocacy and lobbying.

The framework of human rights will serve the agenda of the Social Summit only if it is carried to the people, if they believe that their own oppression is clearly linked to the violation of rights, and if they are organized to claim their rights and to base their agenda and organization on them. It is ironic that the people in whose name the legitimacy of rights is claimed are for the most part isolated from participation in human rights movements.

DIFFERENCES AND CONTROVERSIES OVER HUMAN RIGHTS

Early differences surrounded the relative claims of civil/political and economic/social rights, and led to their bifurcation and separation into two covenants. The water that has since flowed under the bridge has done little to dilute the opposition of the United States to economic and social rights. At the same time, many governments in Africa and Asia justify their resistance to civil and political rights on the grounds that they are less important and urgent than economic and social rights. The separation does little to strengthen arguments for the indivisibility of rights and freedoms, or for the equal attention of the world community to them. It laid the foundation for continuing controversy about priorities, sequence and legitimacy of rights. Since then other controversies have come to the fore.

COMMUNICATOR CHANGE TO RIGHTS

The statement in the Declaration, which proclaims rights as universal, indivisible, interdependent and interrelated., is now the official United Nations view of human rights. Powerful cultural and intellectual arguments have been marshalled against this proposition. The very approach, which gives primacy to human rights, is being contested. Various government leaders in Africa and Asia claim that the traditions of their societies place, and have always placed, special importance on duties, as opposed to the Western preoccupation with rights. The same emphasis, it is said, is explicit in all the world's major religious and spiritual beliefs. Variations of this argument are espoused by communications in Western countries; they favour social organization and engagement on the basis of responsibilities, not rights to which some communicators attribute many ills of contemporary society. The argument that rights promote individualism, selfishness and litigiousness, and undermine the cohesion of the community, brings these two groups together. Although these groups seriously misunderstand the nature and dynamics of rights, which are increasingly concerned with peace and justice, and underrate the extent to which the regime of rights incorporates notions of responsibility and the collective good, their opposition to human rights can undermine the goals reflected by human rights.

CULTURAL RELATIVIST CHALLENGE TO HUMAN RIGHTS: ASIAN VALUES

Closely connected to this approach is an even more formidable objection to the idea of universal human rights the objection of cultural relativism. The essence of this argument is that human rights are based on culture and, since cultural values vary, there cannot be any universal human rights. A version of this approach that has received a great deal of public attention is what has been called Asian values.. The strongest proponents of this approach are a few leaders in Southeast Asia, who argue that the values of Asian, particularly Confucian, culture have provided political stability and economic development, and that these values are oriented to the community.

They claim that Asian values emphasize harmony, unlike the confrontation that arises from the exercise of rights. These leaders were able to persuade Asian governments assembled in Bangkok in April 1993 prior to the World Conference on Human Rights in Vienna to endorse a declaration that is often taken to represent the Asian view of rights, although it did not support all doctrines connected with Asian values. Once one gets past the ritualistic homage to human rights, there are four major purposes of the 1993 declaration made in Bangkok encompassed by the overarching objective of placing the question of rights within an international relations framework:

- To emphasize the rights of states. It reaffirms the principles of respect for national sovereignty, territorial integrity and non-interference in the internal affairs of states and the importance of the right to development, which the proponents of Asian values see as premised on the sovereignty of states.
- To condemn practices associated with the West and the imbalance in the world system. The references to colonialism and apartheid are clearly directed at the West. Asian states such as China, Indonesia or Myanmar with colonies or other forms of foreign occupation, are fully absolved of any wrongdoing. The 1993 declaration deplores Any attempt to use human rights as a conditionality for extending development assistance or as an instrument of political pressure.. The West is also targeted indirectly for creating an unjust international economic order and, presumably, poverty, which are the primary causes of the violation of rights.
- To establish that the state is the appropriate framework for the definition and enforcement of rights. The clearest statement appears in paragraph

9, which recognizes that states have the primary responsibility for the promotion and protection of human rights through appropriate infrastructure and mechanisms., and that remedies must be sought and provided primarily through such mechanisms and procedures..

- To establish a framework for the analysis of rights themselves. On one hand, it suggests that, all the talk of universality and indivisibility not with standing, rights are to be understood in the context of national or regional particularities and various historical, cultural and religious backgrounds, and condemns the imposition of incompatible standards.. On the other hand, it draws attention to the contribution Asian states can make to the World Conference with their diverse and rich cultures and traditions. Second, it hints at the priority of economic development for the enjoyment of rights, and states that economic and social progress facilitates the growing trend towards democracy and the promotion and protection of human rights.

There is little evidence that Asian economic success is due to family or community structures or to any other aspect of Asian values. Instead it is the resources and structures of the state that have played a decisive role in private accumulation and production. Those of us who live in the more economically successful parts of Asia are not struck by the cohesion of the community, or by the care that the community or family provides, or by benevolent governments, or by a public disdain for democracy. Instead we notice the displacement of the community by the pretensions and practices of the state. Far from promoting reconciliation and consensus, the state punishes its critics, suppresses the freedom of expression without which dialogue is not possible and relies on armed forces rather than persuasion. The doctrine of Asian values thrives on the perception of those who are perched on the higher reaches of the state and the market.

The 1993 NGO Declaration on Human Rights may be contrasted with a statement issued at the same time by Asian NGOs in Bangkok, which was subsequently elaborated in the Asian Human Rights Charter. First, the NGOs emphasize the international provenance of rights and contend that, since rights are universal in concern and value, they override national sovereignty. They state: We are entitled to join hands in solidarity to protect human rights worldwide. International solidarity transcends the national order, to refute claims of State sovereignty and non-interference in the internal affairs of State.. Second, the NGOs believe in the universality and indivisibility of rights. This conclusion is drawn partly from their views on the purpose of rights the promotion of human and humane development and peace. Development should be informed by rights and democracy so as to ensure a harmonious relationship between humanity and the natural environment.. NGOs strongly support democratization at national and international levels, and favour a broad meaning of self-determination in the national context. For this and other reasons, they deplore the increasing militarization through the region., which is incompatible with peace and human rights. Like the states, the NGOs see a relationship between rights and culture, but they see cultures enriching our experiences and understanding of rights, producing a cosmopolitan and hence truly universal view of rights, rather than retreating behind the barricades of relativism.

They see the empowerment of people as a function of rights, particularly the vulnerable groups, including indigenous peoples, whose right to self-determination has been systematically denied; women; children, whose welfare should be a paramount concern of every state, regardless of considerations of state capacity and security; internally displaced people and refugees, whose rights are violated as a direct result of militarization and armed conflict.; and peasants and workers, who all too often endure the worst cases of human rights abuses in the region.

THE FUNDAMENTALIST CHALLENGE

Religion occupies an ambiguous position in relation to human rights. Some people claim that it constitutes the foundation of rights and that without the religious notion of the sacredness of the individual, there cannot be a concept of inalienable human rights. Others, preferring a secular and humanistic justification for rights, attribute the violation of rights to religious beliefs and indeed there is much historical evidence that religions have acquiesced to or justified slavery, massacres, intolerance and other forms of oppression. In contemporary times, a fundamental challenge to human rights comes from fundamentalists of all kinds, who deny the equality of all human beings and support many practices that violate principles, norms and procedures of human rights.

This is most obvious in the case of Muslim fundamentalists., who have based the organization and laws of their states on Islamic principles. A number of Muslim states, which have ratified international human rights conventions, have entered blanket reservations that subordinate these conventions to religious teachings. However, a number of Islamic scholars and Islamic organizations have used religious texts for interpretations that make Islam compatible with human rights, and have employed that compatibility to mobilize support for human rights. But it is at the ideological level that religions have posed the major challenge to human rights. Like cultural relativism, religion juxtaposes an alternative normative framework for the organization of society and authority.

Cultural and religious relativism rules out both common action and the criticism of the mores and practices of a society by reference to standards external to the society; and hence the project of universal rights. This approach has a static and unjustified view of culture and ignores the commonality between and the interaction of cultures. It misunderstands the purpose of contemporary human rights, which it conceives of as the ideology underpinning privilege and hierarchy instead of promoting change. But it does respond to a sense on the part of many people in poorer regions of the world of an economic and intellectual hegemony of stronger states, and of their own marginalization. It is essential to engage with rather than dismiss cultural and religious relativism if human rights are to provide a common framework of interaction and policy, even though many more people in poorer countries are attracted to the egalitarian and redistributive dimensions of human rights, on which the Copenhagen Declaration builds its programme of action.

IDENTITY POLITICS

The United Nations version of human rights as universal and indivisible has come under attack from what has been called identity politics.. Identity politics are an attack on what is assumed to be the mores of the dominant group in society, masquerading as the universal. The attack has come from ethnic as well as social minorities, such as women and homosexuals. Women point to many aspects of the regime of rights that merely reflect patriarchy and the interests of men, and homosexuals argue that many of the values of society are grounded in a particular view of sexuality that ignores their own orientation. The recognition of differences of this kind is not necessarily a challenge to the orthodox view of human rights, and indeed the rights of women and homosexuals can be, and in many jurisdictions have been, accommodated within that view. However, there is one version of the recognition of difference that does not sit so comfortably with that orthodox view, and it has to some extent inspired international conventions on the rights of indigenous peoples. It has also gained some currency in Canada and is particularly associated with the writings of Kymlicka and Taylor.

Their arguments start from the premise of the autonomy and authenticity of the individual under liberal theory. Liberalism regards the individual as the centre of society. There are two aspects of individualism that seem to deny special measures for minorities. The first is the equality of all individuals, or at least of all citizens, who must be equal bearers of rights and obligations under the law or, at least in the public sphere, must meet as equals. The second aspect is that, in order for the individual to find his or her authenticity and exercise his or her autonomy, the public sphere should be neutral in terms of values, culture and religion. Kymlicka and Taylor challenge the conclusion that is drawn from the liberal premise of the centrality of the individual. They argue that individuals do not develop their values or identity in isolation from others, but in association with them.

Taylor contrasts the ideal of equality with the politics of difference, based on the modern notion of identity:

- With the politics of equal dignity, what is established is meant to be universally the same, an identical basket of rights and immunities; with the politics of difference, what we are asked to recognise is the

> unique identity of this or that individual or group, their distinctiveness from every one else. The idea is that it is precisely this distinctiveness that has been ignored, glossed over, assimilated to a dominant or majority identity. And this assimilation is the cardinal sin against the ideal of identity.

Kymlicka considers that culture is absolutely essential to the feeling of belonging and participation, and that is the most important of all bearings that a person needs to negotiate his or her way through life. He says, Cultural membership affects our very sense of personal identity and capacity.. The authenticity of one's culture cannot be replaced by other cultures, even if one is given the opportunity to learn its language and medium.

The broader position taken by Kymlicka has been influential and controversial. He regards culture as the most important defining feature of a community; he assumes a consensus within the community on the values of the community; he regards culture as unchanging; and he seems to believe in conflicts between cultures. In all these assumptions he is wrong. There are serious implications of recognizing the isolation of communities and entrenching their cultures in this way. What justifies discrimination against other cultures that are implicit in this approach? How do we define culture? Can we say that the cultures of Hindus and Muslims are different and antagonistic, when so many customs, habits and much of history unite them, and give them a common identity? Nor does Kymlicka's model acknowledge multiple identities that are so characteristic of the contemporary period. It would seem better to build on this overlapping of identities and values than to foster separation and antagonism, which are the inevitable result of Kymlicka's approach.

INDIVISIBLE AND INTERDEPENDENT

Nor can it be said that rights are indivisible and interdependent, except as a rhetorical device. As the scope of rights and freedoms has expanded, the tensions and even contradictions between different sets of rights or at least the tensions surrounding the achievement thereof have become obvious. These tensions do not arise only between civil and political rights, on one hand, and economic, social and cultural rights, such as between the right to private property and the right to education or shelter, on the other. They also arise within each set of rights, for example the tension between the freedom of expression and the protection against hate speech or incitement to war. Nor must we ignore the varying interests, national and corporate, that are served by different rights. There is no agreement among scholars on the effect of civil and political rights on economic development, or vice versa. This has cast doubt on the interdependence of the two sets of rights. A simplistic or high-minded approach that ignores these tensions and contradictions is unlikely to produce an effective policy on human rights that has the capacity to reconcile the various goals of social development.

SEARCH FOR CONSENSUS

Such agreement as there is has been secured through a variety of compromises. Sometimes it is done by putting together seemingly incompatible claims and propositions. A version of this strategy appears in the Declaration where the commitment to human rights is bracketed with full respect for the various religious and ethical values and cultural backgrounds of people. Another strategy is to pair the traditional bundle of rights with the right to development. This strategy was endorsed at the 1993 World Conference on Human Rights, where the West withdrew its objections to the right to development in return for the acceptance by Asian states of the hallowed formula of universal, indivisible, and interdependent.

At an earlier stage, the right to self-determination played a similar role in the rapprochement of liberal rights and decolonization. It now plays a somewhat different role, as the foundation for democracy. The right to development, which can also be central to the Copenhagen aspirations, is still problematic, conceptually and practically. Attempts to reconcile different approaches and interests have been made by scholars, who emphasize the common values of different cultures and religions, and attempt a synthesis where values differ. It is clear that, despite the formulations in the Declaration and these efforts, there is no effective consensus on human rights and democracy that can be counted on to underpin the strategy of the Declaration.

DEMOCRACY

THE RIGHT TO DEMOCRACY: THE LEGAL FOUNDATIONS

One of the great achievements of the United Nations in the field of human rights was to bring colonial empires to an end. The primary foundation for its work was the principle of self-determination. Both the Covenants contain the right of all peoples to self-determination by virtue of which.. they freely determine their political status and freely pursue their economic, social and cultural development. Despite this broad promise, self-determination did not lead to democracy; it protected against foreign, but not domestic, tyranny. Once colonial rule ended, state sovereignty trumped democracy. However, in recent years self-determination has been revived as a principle for the internal organization of a state based on the right of a people to choose their form of government and to elect and participate in it. Self-determination has been linked to article 25 of the ICCPR.

This article guarantees all citizens, without discrimination, three kinds of rights that are important for the Copenhagen agenda:

- The right and the opportunity to take part in the conduct of public affairs, directly or through freely chosen representatives;

- To vote and to be elected at genuine periodic elections which shall be by universal and equal suffrage and shall be held by secret ballot, guaranteeing the free expression of the will of electors; and
- To have access, on general terms of equality, to public service in [their] country.

The basis of this right was stated more forthrightly in the Universal Declaration of Human Rights: the will of the people shall be the basis of the authority of governments.. The ICCPR also contains a number of rights that are essential to democratic politics, such as freedom of expression, the right of assembly, the right of association, freedom of belief and conscience, and the protection of the rule of law.

Article 25 was not always considered the basis of democracy. The word democracy itself is not used. There is no reference to pluralism, which is deemed to be an essential attribute of democracy. It has been argued that elections under single party systems could satisfy the requirements of the object. In any case, even free elections should not be equated with democracy, which also includes notions of continuing accountability, the rule of law and respect for human rights, especially those of minorities.

However, with the collapse of the Soviet Union it has been possible to read a broader meaning into the object. But it needs to be emphasized that, while today's interpretation favours the broader view, it does not justify intervention by the international community to enforce democracy on a recalcitrant state.

Regional and bilateral sanctions can be imposed if a state's conduct in denying democracy is strongly disapproved of. In combination with regional declarations, it has also been used to require a degree of democratization as a precondition of the membership of an organization. One may compare this approach with that in Asia, where ASEAN clearly repudiated democracy as a criterion of membership when it welcomed Myanmar and Viet Nam to its ranks.

RIGHTS OF MINORITIES TO POLITICAL PARTICIPATION

The orientation towards democracy has been reinforced by the favourable development of the rights of minorities from the low point of the ICCPR, which only grudgingly recognized the existence of linguistic, religious and cultural minorities and imposed no positive obligations on the state towards them. When the United Nations began work on an international regime of rights, it emphasized individual rights and carefully avoided giving rights, particularly political rights, to groups. There are trends now, however, towards a greater recognition of cultural and ethnic bases of autonomy. Article 27 of the ICCPR, until recently the principal United Nations provision on minorities, was drafted to exclude collective rights and was narrowly interpreted. However, in recent years the United Nations Human Rights Committee has interpreted the article in a more positive way, using it to develop collective rights of minorities., including a measure of autonomy, and some positive obligations on the states.

In a series of decisions, the Committee has interpreted the article as a basis for collective rights as a basis for the preservation of the culture and way of life of a minority group, and as a basis for protecting and developing traditional ways of life. Efforts have also been made by that Committee and others to interpret the right to self-determination to mean, where relevant, internal autonomy rather than secession. This broader approach is reflected in the United Nations Declaration on the Rights of Minorities adopted by the General Assembly in 1992.

Unlike the ICCPR, it places positive obligations on the state to protect the identity of minorities and encourage conditions for the promotion of that identity. The Declaration states that persons belonging to minorities have the right to participate effectively in public life and the right to participate effectively in decisions on the national and, where appropriate, regional level concerning the minority to which they belong or the regions in which they live. It does not go so far as to require autonomy for minorities, but it lays the foundation for it by recognizing community rights and the importance of identity.

Several initiatives have been taken in Europe, through the OSCE, the Council of Europe and the EU to promote the concept of autonomy and the right of minorities to political participation, although its impact is so far restricted to Europe. This is manifested both in formal declarations and, where appropriate, interventions to solve ethnic conflicts in Europe. Article 35 of the Declaration on the Human Dimension of the CSCE recognizes appropriate local or autonomous administrations as one of the possible means for the promotion of the ethnic, cultural, linguistic and religious identity of certain minorities.

The principal instrument of the Council of Europe is the Framework Convention for the Protection of National Minorities, which protects various rights of minorities, obliges the state to facilitate the enjoyment of these rights, and recognizes many rights of identity.. It obliges state parties to create the conditions necessary for the effective participation of persons belonging to national minorities in cultural, social and economic life and in public affairs, in particular those affecting them.

There is no proclamation of a right to autonomy, but the exercise of some of these rights implies a measure of autonomy. The Declaration and statements of principle by the Council of Europe, although not strictly binding, have been used by the OSCE High Commissioner for Minorities and other mediating bodies as a basis for compromise between contending forces, and have thus influenced practice, in which autonomy has been a key factor. The European Community, now EU, has also used conformity with the Declaration as a precondition for the recognition of new states in Europe. The ability of existing states to confer recognition on entities, especially break-away states, can be a powerful weapon to influence their constitutional structure. When various republics were breaking away from the Federal Republic of Yugoslavia and the Soviet Union split up, the EC issued a Declaration on the Guidelines on the Recognition of New States in Eastern Europe and in the Soviet Union, although it was not applied in all cases.

Among the conditions a candidate had to satisfy before it would be recognized was that its constitution contain guarantees for the rights of ethnic and national groups and minorities in accordance with the commitments subscribed to in the framework of the CSCE.. Entities requesting recognition were asked to submit evidence that their constitutions conformed to the guidelines and recognition was granted only if the evidence satisfied an EC constitutional tribunal set up for this. Similar principles have been used for admission to the Council of Europe and the EU.

The greater involvement of the United Nations or consortia of states in the settlement of internal conflicts has also helped to develop the concept of self-determination as implying autonomy in appropriate circumstances, such as in Bosnia, Eastern Europe and Kosovo. However, the birth of new states, following the collapse of the communist order in the Soviet Union, Eastern Europe and the Balkans, has removed some taboo against secession, and the international community seems to be inching towards some consensus that extreme oppression of a group may justify secession.

This position has served to strengthen the internal aspect of self-determination, for a state can defeat the claim of separation if it can demonstrate that it respects political and cultural rights of minorities. A further, and far-reaching, gloss has been placed on this doctrine by the Canadian Supreme Court, which decided in 1999 that Quebec had no right under either the Canadian Constitution or international law to unilateral secession, but that if Quebec were to decide on secession through a referendum, Ottawa and provinces would have to negotiate with Quebec on future constitutional arrangements.

Such a view of self-determination has some support in certain national constitutions, indicating no more than a trend at this stage. Often constitutional provisions for autonomy are adopted during periods of social and political transformation, when an autocratic regime is overthrown or a crisis is reached in minority-majority conflicts, or there is intense international pressure. Propelled by these factors, a number of constitutions now recognize some entitlement to self-government, such as the Philippines in relation to two provinces, one for indigenous peoples and the other for a religious minority; Spain, which guarantees autonomy to three regions and invites others to negotiate with the centre for autonomy; Papua New Guinea, which authorizes provinces to negotiate with the central government for substantial devolution of power; Fiji, which recognizes the right of indigenous peoples to their own administration at the local level; and recently Ethiopia, which gives its nations, nationalities, and peoples the right to seek wide-ranging powers as states within a federation and guarantees them even the right to secession.

In the wake of the break up of the Soviet Union, the Russian Constitution of 1993 provides for extensive autonomy to its constituent parts, whether republics or autonomous areas. The Chinese Constitution entrenches the rights of ethnic minorities to substantial self-government, although in practice the dominance of the Communist Party negates their autonomy. In other instances, the constitution may authorize, but not require, the establishment of autonomous areas, with China again an interesting example, in order to provide a constitutional basis for One Country Two Systems.

INDIGENOUS PEOPLES

The International Labour Organization Indigenous and Tribal Peoples Convention adopted in 1989, represented a reversal of paternalistic and assimilationist approach followed in the 1957 Indigenous and Tribal Populations Convention. Convention No. 169 recognizes the aspirations of these peoples to exercise control over their own institutions, ways of life and economic development and to maintain and develop their identities, languages and religions, within the framework of the States in which they live.. It notes that their cultural and religious values, institutions and forms of traditional social control are to be preserved.

The system of land ownership and the rules for the transmission of land rights are to be protected. The Draft United Nations Declaration on the Rights of Indigenous Peoples goes even further and proclaims their right to self-determination, under which they may freely determine their political status and freely pursue their economic, social and cultural development. The principle of self-determination gives them the right to autonomy or self-government in matters relating to their internal and local affairs., which include social, cultural and economic activities, and the right to control the entry of non-members.

It recognizes their collective rights and the right to maintain and strengthen their distinct political, economic, social and cultural characteristics. These ideas have already formed the basis of negotiations between indigenous peoples and the states in which they live, giving recognition not only to their land rights but also to forms of autonomy although African and Asian governments deny the existence of indigenous peoples in their states and the instruments have had little impact there.

Indigenous peoples, particularly in North America, also base their claims on other legal bases:

- Their inherent sovereignty, which predates colonization and
- Treaties with incoming powers.

The United Nations and the international community have shown a concern for the fate of vulnerable communities that was not envisaged in the United Nations Charter. Then the preoccupation was with decolonization, as reflected in the establishment of the Trusteeship Council. Once a major UN department, its role has diminished. It has been suggested that the change in the emphasis of the United Nations should be registered by transforming the Trusteeship Council into a Council on Diversity, Representation and Governance, with major responsibility for minorities and indigenous peoples.

DEMOCRATIZATION: THE RECORD

There is no doubt that more countries enjoy democracy now than, say, a decade ago. A number of Eastern and Northern European countries turned to constitutional democracy after the collapse of communism, with considerable assistance from Western Europe and the United States. South Africa achieved a miraculous transition to democracy and a regime of rights; Mozambique put both civil war and authoritarianism behind it; and the largest African state, Nigeria, saw the end of a particularly obnoxious military regime. Northern Ireland is having an uncertain transition to peace, stability and power sharing. Even the United Kingdom, with a long and cherished tradition of parliamentary supremacy, has devolved significant power to Scotland and Wales, and has adopted a Bill of Rights.

Fiji overcame a military regime and its racist successor to achieve a constitution strong on political stability, power sharing, rights and social justice. But in general the picture is less rosy in Africa, Asia and Latin America and, even when there are elections, there is no particular commitment to pluralism, rights, transparency or accountability. Governments are headed by powerful presidents with few limitations on their power.

Constitutional limits on the number of terms that a person may be head of government are ignored or repealed. Restrictions continue on rights, often spuriously in the name of national security or public order. What is particularly depressing is that China, the only permanent member of the Security Council from Asia, Africa and Latin America, has neither democracy nor respect for rights and is a vigourous defender of its authoritarianism. Another member of the Security Council, Russia, has wreaked terrible suffering on the Chechens, committing gross violations of fundamental rights with impunity.

There has been great progress in civil and political rights at the level of constitutions and laws no modern constitution is without an elaborate bill of rights, there are increasing numbers of institutions for the promotion and protection of rights; judicial bodies have developed new doctrines and jurisprudence to strengthen rights; and there are many more meetings on rights, regionally and internationally. But experience also shows that democracy, in the narrow sense of elections and the operation of parliamentary institutions, does not ensure respect for human rights. It also often coexists with corruption, the lack of accountability and the persecution of minorities.

In the area of ethnic difference traditionally the source of great conflict, instability and oppression there has been some progress. Concepts and rules have emerged or are emerging that recognize group identity and confer collective and political rights on minorities. Several ethnic and other civil wars have been brought to an end through negotiated settlements, although many continue and cause great suffering to numerous peoples. Indeed it must be acknowledged that ethnic conflict, or what passes for ethnic conflict, is still the greatest cause of the violation of rights, political instability and oppression.

EXTERNAL ASSISTANCE FOR DEMOCRACY AND RIGHTS

It is not my purpose to draw a balance sheet of democratization. The Copenhagen Declaration on Social Development is directed importantly to international assistance and cooperation towards its goals, and I want to focus on these efforts for democratization. The end of the Cold War, which to an extent freed major powers from the need to buttress their client states and to destabilize unfriendly states, encouraged the West to invoke the international democracy norms to mount a democratization campaign.

The propping up of dictators became an embarrassment to them, and the people they had oppressed for so long felt emboldened to demand democracy and accountability. It would be wrong, however, to assume that the foreign policy interests of major powers took second place to democracy and human rights; even today foreign interests dominate their policies. Assistance has also come from private foundations and international NGOs, as well as from associations of states, such as the EU, and lately from the United Nations and other international organizations. Only a handful of states are involved in these efforts the most active being Denmark, the Netherlands, Sweden, the United Kingdom and the United States.

External involvement has taken several forms ranging from pressure and sanctions on, or incentives to, recalcitrant dictators; encouragement and support to democratic forces, particularly NGOs; to technical assistance and equipment. To a large extent, the forms of assistance have reflected the West's experience with democracy. The development or invigouration of civil society has been a major aim, to raise public awareness of rights and entitlements, to raise a sense of responsibility, and to strengthen the capacity of civil society to put pressure on governments to adhere to public morality. Typical forms of assistance to civil society are the establishment or granting of support to NGOs, particularly women's groups; the provision of assistance to professional groups, such as the legal profession and human rights organizations; the strengthening of the media as a vehicle for public debate; and the promotion of freedom of expression and scrutiny of government. A key role is envisaged for NGOs in the strategy of establishing or mobilizing civil society. When a government decides to democratize, it is offered assistance To frame a national constitution consistent with a state's prerogative to devise its own constitution. These states have been encouraged to follow a participatory form of constitution making. Most new constitutions contain guarantees of human rights, provide for independent institutions and many other features of constitutionalism. Several constitutions provide for the diffusion of power, in the form of devolution or decentralization.

International assistance has focused particularly on the holding of elections, less so on the electoral system itself. Many official and private groups, local as well as international, are recruited or offer to act as election monitors to ensure the fairness of the process. For a while, democratization was equated to holding elections. It is now being recognized that, while free and periodic elections are a necessary ingredient of democracy, they are far from being sufficient. So assistance has been provided for the strengthening of institutions, particularly those of accountability, including the legislature.

Bilateral and multilateral assistance has been forthcoming for human rights commissions and similar bodies. Major programmes have been undertaken with the help of foreign aid to modernize and strengthen the legal system. This assistance has taken the form of rebuilding courts, especially in states where they were destroyed in civil war; computerizing court facilities; training judges and legal practitioners; promoting the professional association of lawyers; up-grading legal libraries; making legislation and law reports easily available; legal aid; and reform of law and procedure. This approach is motivated by the belief that the rule of law is central to the exercise of democracy, control of corruption and other abuses of power, and the protection of rights.

FRAGMENTED ASSISTANCE FOR HUMAN RIGHTS AND DEMOCRACY

The current system of assisting democratization and the protection of rights is fragmented. A considerable number of programmes have been undertaken by the]Organization for Economic Cooperation and Development countries, principally on a bilateral basis; there is some co-ordination through the EU mechanisms.

The efforts of international bodies are even more uncoordinated and lacking in direction. The principal economic institutions, the International Monetary Fund and the World Bank, have until recently claimed to be non-political and thus desisted from aiding progressive political initiatives while at the same time supporting other kinds of capitalist-oriented, political policies.

Their recent concern with good governance is connected less with democratic reform than with providing legal and economic conditions for opening markets to foreign capital. United Nations Secretary-General KofiAnnan has taken some lead in centring UN work on human rights. The OHCHR has provided some co-ordination, with the present High Commissioner attempting to play a leading role in the promotion of rights.

Of the UN agencies, the United Nations Development Programme has made the clearest commitment to mainstreaming human rights in its programmes. The more specialized agencies have reviewed their policies to reflect greater engagement with human rights, but the results so far are unimpressive.

ASSESSMENT OF EXTERNAL ASSISTANCE TO DEMOCRATIZATION

It is too early to pronounce a verdict on external assistance to democratization since these efforts are beginning to be evaluated to determine what methods and institutions work, but some tentative conclusions can be stated. Perhaps the most important point is that external assistance can play only a facilitative role. It can use aid conditionalities to put pressure on the national government, but unless there is overwhelming local demand for democracy backed by effective institutions and popular mobilization, these external pressures are unlikely to yield lasting progress. Rights and democracy have to be struggled for. One reason that South Africa is off to such promising start is that the struggle for democracy was the people's struggle, and the politicization of civil society enables the electorate to put pressure on the government to honour the commitment to democracy and fairness. Foreign governments and international organizations cannot really play a significant role in persuading reluctant presidents to democratize that task has to be left to the people.

Within the scope of assistance that foreign donors can provide, the record is mixed. NGOs, which are the primary engine for change in the face of official resistance, have generally failed, or often have not tried, to mobilize the people. They are essentially lobbying groups, without a mass base of their own, and are excessively dependent on external donors for funding.

Thus strategies and projects that appeal to external donors are taken up by the NGOs, often without critical evaluation of their usefulness or effectiveness in the national context. They are accountable to foreign donors as part of their contractual relationship with them and therefore lay themselves open to the charge of being instruments of foreign governments. It has become fashionable to criticize NGOs for the self-interest of their staff, but there is no doubt that NGOs have made valuable contributions and attracted competent and dedicated people, and there is clearly a role for them as human rights watchdogs. However, it does mean that the mobilization functions tend to be ignored. Nor do foreign governments keep faith with NGOs. They are more interested in working with governments, and if they have a chance to do so, tend to shift funds away from NGOs. Indeed an astute government can greatly weaken support for NGOs, and the NGOs themselves, by seeming to espouse human rights and democracy.

The limitations of elections for democratization have already been commented on. The broadening of aid to overcome the limitations of elections has had an impact, but not enough to significantly deepen democracy. The media, even where responsible and professional, have not always had the expected results. One example is the press in Kenya, which has been very critical of the president, alleging the most serious corruption and violations of rights, but it does not seem to have embarrassed him or eroded his support among those who have traditionally voted for him basically his ethnic vote. The same can be said about the press in Cambodia.

Reform of the legal system has also had mixed results. The process may have increased the professionalism of the system, but not access to courts and lawyers. Traditional systems of dispute resolution have been downgraded and, while these are not without their own problems, they did provide easy access to the system, the system was understood by the people, and for the most part accepted by them. Professionalization increases the costs of the system of justice; affects different groups access unequally, particularly favouring corporations that are able to hire the best lawyers; increases the time lag between the filing and hearing of cases; and makes the system alien and intimidating to most people. Legal reform has tended to focus on changes that favour the market mechanism and the integration of the national economy into the global, which frequently affects poorer sections of the population adversely.

The context of efforts to promote democratization determines their orientation. The collapse of communism was welcomed as a triumph of liberal democracy. But many more saw it as the triumph of the market. It is not easy to distinguish support for democracy from support for markets in the efforts of individual or collective Western states to promote rights and democracy abroad. Indeed, it can be said that the support for markets is stronger; the rationale for that support is more powerfully presented than for democracy. The IMF and the World Bank have hijacked democracy and rights through the advocacy of the narrower concept of governance., which is at the bottom of the charter of political and legal institutions for capitalism. In this way, political rights of participation and accountability are not only subordinated to the market, but are actually undermined. Another weakness of the external support for democratization has been inadequate attention to reinforcing strengthening of economic and social rights. Democracy is often justified by the benefits it brings to the people, through political stability and economic development. Unless people see economic advantages for themselves, their enthusiasm for democracy is likely to wane; economic betterment is what confers legitimacy on a democratic order. External assistance is, of course, provided for health, water, agricultural development and so on, but it is not clearly tied to individual or group entitlements, and is often not enough to improve the lives of most people. Experience has shown that with democratization there is no automatic change for the better in the economy.

Donor-recipient relationships are always difficult, but they are particularly sensitive in the context of assistance for democracy and human rights. They involve an element of pressure, if not direct coercion, at least the coercion that comes from the recipient's knowledge that other forms of assistance by the donor may be at stake if overtures on democratization are not accepted. In some cases, of course, human rights conditionalities have been imposed by the donors. The evidence suggests that donors who provide assistance across a range of areas are more effective in influencing the recipient's human rights and democracy policies than those who tend to focus principally on rights and democracy. Assistance in this area touches on many points that are closely connected to a state's sovereignty., the election and operation of government, the workings of the legislature, judicial reforms and modernization of the legal system. It also involves the donor's engagement with and assistance to, and sometimes management of, civil society.

Moreover, it is all too easy for the recipient to dismiss rights and democracy as foreign ideas, and to feel or feign particular irritation at the disregard of its own cultural, historical and political traditions. This active and extensive engagement of donors in the politics of the recipient state is likely to cause great tensions, and therefore the extent and modalities of external engagement need to be handled with great care and delicacy, but also firmness when appropriate.

WHAT MAKES FOR SUCCESS OR FAILURE

In summary, external assistance can play a useful, but supplementary, role in promoting democracy and respect for rights. It can strengthen the status and resources of civil organizations and state bodies committed to democratization and rights. But the role that external assistance can play is limited and contingent on a firm commitment of the people or government, or both, to democracy and rights. In the end, the establishment and deepening of democracy depends on the people and government of a state; it has to be endogenously driven to be sure of lasting success.

SOCIAL JUSTICE: ECONOMIC, SOCIAL AND CULTURAL RIGHTS

THE LEGAL FOUNDATIONS

In adopting the framework of human rights, the Copenhagen Declaration, in conformity with United Nations orthodoxy, places equal importance on all human rights. But realistically, it is economic and social rights that are essential to the Copenhagen agenda. Civil and political rights are undoubtedly important in organizing demands for greater equity, and in themselves for facilitating an open and accountable society.

But the evidence that these rights also lead to economic and social development is not conclusive. So economic and social rights that directly provide housing, food, education and clothing are crucial. Unfortunately, economic and social rights are so far the Cinderella of rights; they are attacked, conceptually, for lacking the qualifications to be called rights, as the beneficiaries and providers are not easily identified, and even when identified the legal process cannot enforce rights. They are also attacked politically, as increasing state power, and interfering with the autonomy, and assets, of individuals. Thus in so far as economic and social rights are central to the achievement of the Copenhagen agenda, considerable research and lobbying will be necessary to transform these rights into clear and enforceable targets and standards. This will require some intellectual ingenuity and political will, but that it can be done is clear from countries, such as Sri Lanka, that have been able to provide many of these rights despite a relatively poor economy.

The United Nations Charter committed its members to promote higher standards of living, full employment, and conditions of economic and social progress and development and solutions of international economic, social, health and related problems, and international cultural and educational cooperation. The Universal Declaration of Human Rights contains a number of economic, social and cultural rights: the right to social security, and economic, social and cultural rights indispensable for the individual's dignity and the free development of the individual's personality; the right to work, free choice of employment, just and favourable conditions of work and protection against unemployment, including the right to join trade unions; the right to rest and leisure; the right to a standard of living adequate for family health and well-being, including food, clothing, housing, medical care and necessary social services; the right to education; and the right to participate in the cultural life of the community, to enjoy the arts and to share in scientific advancement and its benefits.

These rights formed the core of the ICESCR, but the formulation is too broad to provide sufficient guidance on implementation and the machinery for implementation and supervision is much weaker than for the ICCPR, typified by the omission of any complaints procedure. These rights also find their way into conventions for the protection of women, children, indigenous peoples and migrant workers, and form one of the core components of the Declaration on the Right to Development in the following expression:

- States should undertake, at the national level, all necessary measures for the realization of the right to development and shall ensure, inter alia, equality of opportunity for all in their access to basic resources, education, health services, food, housing, employment and the fair distribution of income. Effective measures should be undertaken to ensure that women have an active role in the development process. Appropriate economic and social reforms shall be carried out with a view to eradicating all social injustices.

Several national constitutions require or urge the state to provide similar services, although for the most part they are mandatory only for disadvantaged groups. India and South Africa are two outstanding examples, where the obligations on the state are based on the moral and political recognition of past injustices to particular ethnic or social groups. The recent Fiji Constitution imposes a legal obligation on the government to institute schemes for preferential policies for poorer communities and groups. Several other countries such as Australia, Canada, Malaysia and the United States, as well as Northern Ireland, also have preferential policies. However, these policies have not always helped the really disadvantaged the resources having been appropriated by the better-off in the various communities, and used for political and patronage purposes. In any case, the resources allocated for these policies are too limited to make a major impact on poverty.

THE RECORD

These provisions have not been used to provide assistance for economic, social and cultural rights in the post-Cold War era in the way political rights in the ICCPR were seized on to promote democracy. A 1998 UNDP report notes that fifty years after the adoption of the Universal Declaration of Human Rights, one third of the developing world's people are enslaved by a poverty so complete that it denies them fundamental human rights... Nearly 12 million children die each year before their fifth birthday. More than 800 million people go hungry.. It also notes that 30 per cent of all children under five are malnourished and that 38 per cent of all adult women are illiterate. Another report observes that nearly 100 million people are homeless, and the number of those without adequate housing exceeds one billion.

It is often claimed that economic, social and cultural rights are different from other rights in that they are not justiciable and cannot be enforced in courts. State obligations under the ICESCR or national constitutions are not enforceable rights of the people. Moreover, because the ICESCR commits member states to take steps, individually and through international assistance and cooperation, especially economic and technical, to the maximum of its available resources, with a view to achieving progressively the full realization of the rights recognised in the present Covenant by all appropriate means, some national courts have taken the view that the Covenant is not directly applicable in their states but requires national legislation. However, the United Nations Committee on Economic, Social and Cultural Rights has declared that at least some rights in the Covenant were intended for and are capable of immediate and direct application. Most arguments advanced about the difficulties of making social and economic rights enforceable are not persuasive, nor is it productive to think of rights only in terms of judicial enforcement. It is more valuable to focus on the obligations of states; as has been pointed out, a state's obligation in relation to all categories of rights may be seen as involving different types of obligations that can be fulfilled variously by positive action, by refraining from acting, or by creating an environment in which rights can be achieved. There is no reason why the beneficiaries of these rights should not be involved in the planning and implementing of programmes for achieving the rights, or why their access to the appropriate institutions responsible for implementing rights should not be guaranteed.

The fact is that the non-enforceability of economic and social rights springs from the low regard in which these rights are held by dominant national and international groups. Philip Alston has pointed to the low priority given to these rights and the limited resources devoted to their implementation. He says that denials of the most fundamental economic and social rights continue on a massive scale that affects hundreds of millions of people and offers various explanations for the neglect of economic, social and cultural rights:

- Preeminent among them was the impact of the Cold War and of the ideological struggles between communism and capitalism. This factor changed what was a rational and balanced debate between 1944 and 1947 into a struggle that encouraged the taking of extreme positions and prevented objective consideration of the key issues raised by the concept of economic and social rights.

Another reason is that the implementation of these rights requires skills and expertise that are alien to what has been termed the normative-judicial model of human rights implementation. The result is that the human rights lawyers, the diplomatic representatives, the secretariat officials and the NGO representatives who have come to dominate human rights discussions will feel distinctively ill at ease and ill-equipped to deal with many of the most pressing issues arising from a concern wiTheconomic, social and cultural rights. Finally, the proposition that minimum core economic and social rights ought to be accorded to every individual is still automatically made subject by decision makers to an economic calculus that will often culminate in various economically compelling reasons as to why such rights simply cannot be recognised. Little attempt has been made to establish criteria for measuring the success of the progressive implementation of these rights.

However, in recent years increasing attention has been paid to economic and social rights as a result of a series of world conferences such as those on women, children and social development. The 1973 Human Rights Conference endorsed the right to development. The current United Nations Secretary-General, KofiAnnan, has tried to make human rights a core concern of the United Nations and its agencies, which has stimulated thinking about the means of mainstreaming human rights into development. The High Commissioner for Human Rights has entered into agreements with UNDP and other agencies to promote human rights in their work. The World Food Summit of 1996, convened by the Food and Agriculture Organization of the United Nations, noted the appealingly low standards of nutrition of millions of people, particularly children and women, and the terrible consequences of malnutrition and hunger, observing that the problem was not so much the lack of food as the access to it. The governments of the world pledged themselves to achieving food security for all and as an immediate objective to reducing the number of undernourished people to half the 1996 level by 2015. The OECD has a commitment, together with member states, to reduce the level of poverty by half by 2015.

A number of recent national constitutions have incorporated social and economic rights. National courts had already begun to develop jurisprudence facilitating litigation on these rights. Important impetus to their realization was given with the establishment of the United Nations Committee on Economic, Social and Cultural Rights in 1986, which has done valuable work to clarify and elaborate the provisions of the Covenant, and is developing a system of reporting and supervision. A number of NGOs have been formed to promote these rights.

Courts are now more willing to read ICESCR-type rights into the more justiciable provisions of the ICCPR-type rights. Thus the Indian courts have given a wide definition to the right to life. In one case the Indian Supreme Court held that the right to life includes the right to live with human dignity and all that goes with it, namely, the bare necessities of life such as adequate nutrition, clothing and shelter over the head and facilities for reading, writing and expressing oneself in diverse forms, freely moving about and mixing and commingling with fellow human beings. In another case the Supreme Court explicitly used Directive Principles of State Policy to interpret the scope of the right to life giving it a broad meaning to include protection of health, provision of education, and just and humane conditions of work. A recent Indian Supreme Court decision has declared that the right to life guarantees access to medical services, especially in an emergency.

The Court said that the state cannot ignore its constitutional obligation to provide adequate medical services to preserve human life on account of financial constraints, which it must take into account in allocating funds for medical services. The Bangladesh Supreme Court has decided that the right to life is not limited to the protection of life and limb necessary for the full enjoyment of life, but also includes, among other things, the protection of the health and normal longevity of ordinary human beings. Despite these bold moves, the judiciary is neither particularly qualified nor willing to establish entitlements to economic and social benefits and, particularly in Bangladesh or India, unable to enforce judgments that do recognize social and economic rights. The right to non-discrimination has also provided the basis for the enforcement of social and economic rights. The Canadian Supreme Court has declared that hospitals that run government schemes for health care are in breach of section 15 of the Charter of Rights if they do not provide sign interpreters for deaf patients, for lack of de facto equality. The Court said that the principle that discrimination can accrue from a failure to take positive steps to ensure that disadvantaged groups benefit equally from services offered to the general public is widely accepted in the human rights field. The Court reiterated its earlier view that a government may be required to take positive steps to ensure the equality of people or groups who come within the scope of section 15 The United Nations Human Rights Committee has declared that the rights to equality under the ICCPR extend to all rights guaranteed in the ICESCR.

National jurisprudence on economic and social rights will, in conjunction with the General Comments of the United Nations Committee on Economic, Social and Cultural Rights, help to establish or refine details of these rights, which in both the Covenant and national laws tend to be rather general. Hopefully this clarification and standard setting will increase pressure on governments and international organizations to implement these rights. It is partly with this view that the Committee has undertaken interpretations of key social rights; it has so far issued guidelines on the rights to housing and food, and is well advanced on the guidelines on education. In 1991 it provided an explanation of what constituted the right to adequate housing as guaranteed in article 11(1) of the Covenant. The Committee defined the right to housing as not only having a roof over one's head, but also the right to live in security, peace and dignity.

It then outlined the following features of the right:

- Legal security of tenure;
- Availability of services, materials, facilities and infrastructure;
- Affordability;
- Habitability;
- Accessibility;
- Location; and
- Cultural adequacy.

In 1999 in Comment No. 12, the Committee issued its guidelines on the right to food, which, it said, is not merely a minimum package of calories, proteins and other specific nutrients.. It defined the right to adequate food as consisting of the availability of food in a quantity and quality sufficient to satisfy the dietary needs of individuals, free from adverse substances and acceptable within a given culture; and the accessibility of such food in ways that are sustainable and that do not interfere with the enjoyment of other rights.

The Committee also provided useful guidance on the obligations of states for the provision of social and economic rights, and the ways in which these obligations may be discharged. The state of country's development is not an excuse for not providing these rights; a state must do what it can within its means, and must justify any lack of priority given to its legal obligations. It must also adopt appropriate development strategies for the different sectors to which these rights pertain.

Measures can be legislative, administrative or facilitative, and may include a mix of public and private initiatives. Similarly, remedies can be judicial as well as administrative. An essential step towards progressive implementation is monitoring, with reference to standards and benchmarks. The Committee has also drawn attention to the role of the international community helping states without adequate resources to ensure that their basic needs are met; this role is stipulated in article 56 of the United Nations Charter and article 23 of the Covenant.

These initiatives and developments augur well for the realization of social and economic rights. However, it must be recognized that the dominant economic force of our times globalization runs counter to them and will probably undermine them. It is therefore important to turn to the nature of globalization and to its impact on these rights.

GLOBALIZATION

Globalization is a compendium of ideas, practices, institutions, directions of change and ideologies. Some of these diminish rights, others promote them, and some do both simultaneously: for example, the Internet and other forms of technology provide more opportunities for both freedom of expression and access to information, and uncover new possibilities for networking, but, at the same time, they greatly increase the influence of corporations and the opportunities for hate speech, pornography and sexual trafficking. That makes it particularly difficult to distinguish between the positive and negative consequences of globalization for rights.

However, even though they are intertwined, it may be possible to distinguish the economic processes of globalization from the more political and social processes. This paper focuses on the negative consequences for rights, which I believe are dominant, but it would be unwise to ignore the positive potential of globalization. The economic processes are connected with the development of national market economies and their integration globally on market principles. The market system is driven by the search for profits, which replace older values of reciprocity and social solidarity by the morality of profits. In order to increase profits, more and more objects, which previously were communal or in other ways inalienable, are brought within the domain of the market as commodities. Historically, this has had the effect of converting commons into private property and breaking up the cohesion of communities.

This is all too evident in areas where the market frontier has moved in recent decades, such as in Africa and Asia: migration to cities, the anomie of urban life, the collapse of the extended family, and the replacement of sentiment by money as the basis for human motivation. Throughout history, societies have tried to combat or moderate the natural consequences of the market. The development of trade unions and their politics and the democratization of the state have provided a counterbalance to the predatory tendencies of the market. In the West, the balance between the market and democratic politics produced the welfare state. Global capitalism is relatively unfettered by regulations. On the contrary, it enjoys the support of powerful capitalist states, most notably of course the United States and the member countries of the EU. A number of international economic institutions especially the IMF, the World Bank and the World Trade Organization share and reinforce the ideology of global capitalism. These states and institutions have taken it upon themselves to create the political and legal conditions for the global market they favour: removal of barriers to international trade and services, the movement of capital, the global protection of property rights, the privatization of state companies, the deregulation of business activities and the phasing out of welfare services.

All these developments have diminished the capacity of states to provide essential social services to the people. The effects of structural adjustment policies in Africa and the South Pacific, imposed by the IMF and the World Bank, have been little short of disastrous; they have reduced the access of all but the most privileged groups to education, health and nutrition. Even in Europe, where the welfare state was born, there have been severe cutbacks. In East Asia, where welfare was often provided by commercial corporations, benefits have been phased out allegedly because of the corporations inability to compete in the international economy if they have to absorb the costs of welfare. Several of the negative social and political consequences of globalization are to do with its asymmetries. The obvious asymmetry is that between capital and labour the former may move freely, but not the latter. It is therefore possible for capitalists to move, or threaten to move, their enterprises as a way to negotiate economic concessions from the host state, or to negotiate with workers for low wages and non-unionization. Labour is at a considerable disadvantage in what is clearly an unequal situation.

Likewise, capital is entitled to national treatment wherever it chooses to go, but not migrant workers, who are subject to considerable legal and practical discrimination in host countries. Global capital relies increasingly on part-time or informal forms of labour, which means that workers have little security of employment, and that wages and rates of unionization are low. The result is also that the workforce consists increasingly of women who are more prepared, able or compelled to accept these terms.

To a significant extent, several states are also becoming captives of global capitalism. They dare not impose high taxes for fear of scaring away foreign as well as domestic capital. In some countries there has been little attempt to enforce industrial safety standards for the same reason. In free economic zones that many countries have established to attract foreign capital, large portions of the national legal and fiscal systems are suspended. States that wish to engage with the international economic system and few think that they can afford not to have to accept complex legal and administrative regimes, granting extensive rights to foreign capital and prohibiting discrimination to support domestic entrepreneurs. The result is that these states are unable to provide basic welfare services to their people. China's experience is a good illustration of what happens to social and economic rights when the market becomes the dominant matrix of economy. Despite its general economic backwardness, China used to ensure its people equal and decent standards of education, health and shelter. With the spread of market practices and ideology, these services are being phased out, and becoming commodities that must be purchased on the market. The result is that basic needs are beyond the capacity of millions of people. South Africa is finding that, despite pressures from the historically disadvantaged groups for the satisfaction of basic needs and the constitutional requirements to do so its social policies are effectively governed by its commitment to engage fully with the international economic system.

GLOBALIZATION AND HUMAN RIGHTS

The effects of globalization enable us to gain fresh insights into the nature of rights. Certain kinds of rights are important for globalization property, association, independent judiciary and the rule of law. But globalization does not conceive of social and economic rights it thinks in terms of social and economic benefits as outcomes of markets, not as any kind of preconditions. It points to various weaknesses of the regime of rights: in an age of mass migrations many rights are restricted to citizens; the human rights regime provides no redress against the violation of rights by non-state institutions, despite the overwhelming power of transnational corporations to determine our life chances; and the basic framework for the protection and enforcement of rights is still the state, while the obligations to protect human rights are international. The international system is vigourous in elaborating norms, but lacks the jurisdictional basis and often the political will to enforce them. However, most states lack resources to protect human rights, especially economic and social rights. Globalization has sharpened the distinction between civil and political rights, which it needs, and economic, social and cultural rights, which threaten its dominance. Clearly, rhetoric is less powerful than material forces.

CONCLUSION AND RECOMMENDATIONS

ANALYSIS

The World Summit for Social Development adopted a human rights framework as part of its strategy to eradicate poverty. The observance of human rights facilitates peaceful co-existence and consequently social and political stability. A democratic society is predicated on respect for human rights. This much is generally recognized. Somewhat more controversial is the third proposition underlying the Social Summit strategy that a society that wants to achieve social justice also has to implement social and economic rights. There is a powerful school of thought that argues that social justice is the outcome of the market economic system, and not a contrivance of the state. This school of thought, associated with globalization and the hegemony of the United States, is a principal obstacle to the implementation of social justice. But there are other obstacles too.

Although human rights norms covering key areas of human existence have been negotiated through international collaboration, the machinery for their enforcement at the international level is rudimentary and grossly under-resourced. In most states as well, the system for the enforcement of rights is highly inadequate. Even though a majority of states profess a primary commitment to human rights, in practice their governments do not wish to encumber their diplomatic relations with the inconvenience of holding other governments accountable for human rights violations the more so if their own economy might suffer from demanding such accountability. For the most part, the so-called human rights and governance conditionalities are little more than blackmail to force states to develop and open their markets to outside investors.

At home, many governments are reluctant to rule by the logic of human rights, and their police and security forces are often implicated in serious violations of rights. Despite the ideology and rhetoric of human rights, human rights activists are looked upon as troublemakers and subjected to harassment and persecution. The truth is that human rights too often threaten powerful vested interests.

RECOMMENDATIONS

If human rights are to become the framework for social development, fundamental reforms in and strengthening of the human rights regime are necessary. The first and the hardest is to accept the implications of the universality of human rights. The concept of universality has been discussed largely in terms of the relevance of a common core of human rights to all societies. But it also has another dimension the responsibility of the world community to ensure that all people, wherever they might be, are guaranteed their rights. Similarly, the concept of the interdependence or indivisibility of rights has to be placed in the context of global responsibility for the promotion of rights.

The West has insisted on the indivisibility of rights because it is suspicious of many governments that have argued that civil and political rights should be postponed until there is a higher level of economic development. If the West is serious about the indivisibility of rights, then it is obliged to ensure that sufficient funds are transferred to poorer countries for the satisfaction of the basic needs of their people. However, it has so far refused to accept the logic of this position, and has shown a marked reluctance to engage in serious negotiations on the implementation of the Declaration on the Right to Development; foreign aid has fallen to 0.22 per cent of gross national product, despite the formula agreed to long ago of 0.77 per cent.

In order to make human rights the framework for social and economic policies, it is necessary to build a genuine international consensus on their value and importance which is hard to do. The more concrete the issues such as child labour, environment, terms of international trade, intellectual property rights where rights really matter, the more differences seem to divide West and the rest. Many international differences are played out in the language of rights; paradoxically this delegitimizes rights, as was the case in Kosovo and East Timor intervention became possible only when President Clinton criticized Indonesia.

Both the West and the East are guilty of double standards. Consensus requires both intellectual effort in uncovering values that unite different religions and cultural traditions, and a willingness to incorporate values that have animated non-Western societies in the international regime of rights. It also requires political will, which is harder to establish for reasons already discussed.

Mainstreaming human rights in development, which should be a special responsibility of multilateral financial and development institutions, in conjunction with state policies and initiatives, is a prerequisite of the Copenhagen Programme of Action. Mainstreaming means that the elimination of poverty should be the principal aim of development projects and, before a project is undertaken, there should be a study of human rights implications.

United Nations agencies have shown some interest in mainstreaming human rights, but it is the Bretton Woods institutions, which wield greater economic clout, that need to be persuaded of the value of social and economic rights. Consideration should be given to establishing a world development fund for social and economic rights., to be financed directly from tax revenues worldwide on specified luxury products.

Social and economic rights must be given the priority that has been denied them. Considerable research and imagination are needed to provide the practical underpinnings of economic and social rights, the modalities for enforcement, and standards and benchmarks for monitoring progress. This will require more funding for this enterprise, the establishment of networks and the commitment of governments.

Together with regional organizations, the United Nations must devote more resources to human rights work more human rights experts should be trained and recruited, more human rights missions should be organized, and more field offices of the OHCHR should be established. The international machinery for the supervision of the observance of human rights should be strengthened. All states should sign protocols that give their nationals the right of direct access to international committees and tribunals this aspect of their work has proved more fruitful than periodic reports by governments.

Furthermore, the United Nations and other international organizations should increase their capacity for dealing with civil conflicts and wars, which today are a major source of suffering and oppression. This suggests the need for better protection of minorities, and a mechanism for swift response to mass violations of rights.

The regime of human rights should be extended to cover the policies and conduct of large private economic corporations. They have power without responsibility. The human rights of millions of people depend on the policies of these corporations.

Neither the state nor the international system is likely to support the struggles of the oppressed which are essentially attacks on the present state and international systems. Therefore the revolutionary potential of rights is likely to remain dormant for the foreseeable future. Popular support for human rights will not be secured so long as poverty is not seen as a concern of the rights regime. But this in turn will not happen until the concept of rights is used to mobilize society to demand greater equity.

Unless there are pressures from civil society, in both the rich and the poor countries, for social justice and respect for human dignity, little progress will be made. A major weakness of the human rights movement has been the inability to involve the masses as subjects rather than objects of rights. In this lies the most fundamental challenge to human rights scholars and activists. The agenda of the World Summit for Social Development has little prospect for success unless there is this transformation in the regime of rights.

13

Disability and Human Rights Approach to Development

THE SOCIAL MODEL OF DISABILITY

As set out in more detail in the first briefing note, the social model of disability provides an understanding that is substantially different from the traditional view that disability is essentially about physical or mental deficit or abnormality. Within a social model paradigm impairment is seen as normal for any population. What disadvantages and disables people with impairments is a complex web of discrimination made up of negative social attitudes and cultural assumptions as well as environmental barriers, including policies, laws, structures and services, which result in economic marginalisation and social exclusion. Of course, this social model analysis is not limited to disability. It has been used to describe the experience of invalidation, inequality and injustice for all groups that face discrimination. Essentially, the social model offers an analytical framework for understanding why and how this discrimination occurs.

WHY DISABILITY IS A HUMAN RIGHTS ISSUE AND IN TURN A DEVELOPMENT ISSUE

Human rights are a twentieth century phenomenon developed in response to the atrocities of World War II. They set out an internationally accepted moral code by which the intrinsic humanity of every individual is recognised and protected. Human rights are the fundamental, universal and indivisible principles by which every human being can claim justice and equality. As disability describes the barriers faced by people with impairments to achieving equality and justice, and because disabled people are human beings too, it is axiomatic that disability is a human rights issue. And as with all groups who face discrimination and disadvantage it is the recognition of that intrinsic humanity that is essential to reaching outcomes that result in the full implementation and protection of human rights. As the 24th Special Session of the UN World Summit for Social Development and Beyond declared, 'The ultimate goals of development are to improve living conditions for people and to empower them to participate fully in the economic, political and social arenas.' This development must be achieved for all people. However, as has been repeatedly documented, access to full and equal participation has been denied to disabled people in almost every country, helping to create conditions that result in them being among the poorest of the poor.

At the same time, being poor is not only about being socially excluded but also makes people much more vulnerable to contracting a whole range of disabling impairments. Poverty and disability are in this sense locked in the embrace of a real dance of death. This is made far worse in developing countries in the South, where the failure of economic and social development is characterised by widespread and seemingly intractable poverty associated with wars and civil unrest, malnutrition, poor sanitation, lack of immunisation, inadequate health care, few safety provisions and pollution. Such is the music, which gives the dancers no respite.

Human rights are indivisible and universal. Continuing to leave disabled people out of mainstream systems of development by perpetuating discrimination and exclusion violates these rights. From a human rights perspective, development programmes can, therefore, no longer make excuses for not addressing disability, particularly as many development agencies now claim to be working within an explicit human rights framework.

A HUMAN RIGHTS APPROACH TO DEVELOPMENT

Since the 1990s many multi-lateral and bilateral agencies have adopted a human rights approach to development. This approach seeks to ensure that each person is seen as having an equal right to freedom, dignity, non-discrimination and protection from the state against abuse of these rights, together with access to economic, cultural and social rights. It is argued that only by empowering all people to be able to make decisions about their lives will it be possible to reduce poverty and achieve the Millennium Development Goals. The UK Department for International Development has been one of the leaders in developing this approach, which was set out forcefully in White Papers it produced in 1997 and 2000, and in a number of other major documents, including the 2000 target strategy paper, Realising human rights for poor people.

While there are a great many strands to DFID's approach, the main, cross-cutting principles are:

- 'Participation: enabling people to realise their rights to participate in, and access information relating to, the decision-making processes which affect their lives.
- Inclusion: building socially inclusive societies, based on the values of equality and non-discrimination, through development which promotes all human rights for all people.

- Fulfilling obligations: strengthening institutions and policies which ensure that obligations to protect and promote the realisation of all human rights are fulfilled by states and other duty bearers.'

DISABLED PEOPLE'S ROLE AND STATUS

Although disabled people are mentioned in DFID's 2000 target strategy paper on poverty, the way in which their human rights are compromised and the connection between this and poverty is not spelt out. Only by understanding disability from a social model viewpoint, that is with disability being the result of systematic discrimination rather than impairment itself, can the link be made in such a way as to establish a framework for tackling the human rights abuses and poverty which continue to blight the lives of the vast majority of disabled people in the developing world. And, as many prominent commentators have observed, unless this is done it will prove impossible to achieve the poverty reduction targets set out in the Millennium Development Goals. Disabled people have been fostering progressive social change by putting a human rights approach to development into practice, often many years before such an approach was adopted by international agencies.

While disabled people's organizations are keenly aware of human rights issues and/or have explicitly adopted the social model as their guiding ideal, generally the projects and organizations have developed through a more prosaic route, people simply trying to understand the oppression they experience and struggling against it at a local or national level. As is often the case, it is only through this kind of struggle that a broader and more socially transforming understanding is achieved.

NOTHING ABOUT US WITHOUT US

It is not surprising that different local circumstances mean there is considerable variation with respect to how a human rights approach has evolved. Nonetheless, there is one defining characteristic: all such interventions based on this approach have been controlled by disabled people themselves. This in turn accords with a key observation made in DFID's target strategy paper that: 'Human rights provide a means of empowering all people to make decisions about their own lives rather than being the passive objects of choices made on their behalf'. For disabled people this is of particular significance since traditionally they have been seen as a group which needs to be looked after by others, not one that can act on their own behalf. 'Nothing about us without us' was the slogan promoted by Disabled Peoples' International at its founding in 1981 and has been used by disability rights activists every since. It has been particularly effective in capturing a key idea of disabled people's struggle for human rights–self determination is essential for achieving equality. This in turn has helped to unite groups from countries throughout the world in common cause. It has, for example, informed their message to governments taking part in the UN process of elaborating a convention on protecting the rights of disabled people: that in doing this they must listen to the voice of disabled people.

DISABILITY AND HUMAN RIGHTS IN ACTION

There are a considerable number of long-term projects developed by disabled people which exhibit implicitly or explicitly a human rights approach, as well as conforming to the DFID's three principles–participation, inclusion and fulfilling obligations–with regard to disabled people.

There are local organizations of disabled people who run income-generating projects such as chicken farms or crafts, operate loan schemes for small businesses, run local community based rehabilitation services and work cooperatively with local elders to raise the status of disabled people in their village and to ensure greater access and self determination. These groups are often linked to regional and national organizations who provide them with leadership training, capacity building and the most essential information needed to take action on these rights-based activities. It is crucial that both the local and national organizations or groups do not only take part in specific income generation or CBR projects, but are also involved in:

- Ensuring that all policies and programmes that affect disabled people involve disabled people
- Raising the status and opportunities for self-determination of disabled people both locally and nationally
- Cooperating with the local community and thereby changing attitudes to disability

And last, but by no means least:

- Spreading the word–telling other disabled people and the wider community that disability is a human rights issue, how to achieve those rights, giving examples of good practice and how to overcome the obstacles to inclusion and participation.

Two of these projects are briefly outlined in order to show how a human rights approach grew organically out of struggles against the systemic oppression and denial of basic human rights experienced by disabled people and the transforming power of this approach. We also consider an example of how this same approach has been applied at a higher level by disabled people seeking to build a disability dimension into Poverty Reduction Strategy Papers.

SELF-HELP ASSOCIATION OF PARAPLEGICS, SOWETO, SOUTH AFRICA

In the 1980s black disabled people in South Africa had little chance of survival in such an inaccessible and hostile environment, let alone the chance to achieve a decent standard of living. In 1981 a group of eight disabled individuals, many of whom had been disabled in the fight against apartheid and unhappy with the prospect of being forced into institutional care, decided to set up a self help association. They wanted to enjoy the simple dignity of being in control of their own lives but realised this meant having to support themselves.

They decided to do this by opening a factory, employing only disabled people, doing sub-contract work for industry. With start-up funding from corporations and trust funds the first SHAP Centre opened in 1983, the second in 1989. From the outset SHAP has been managed by disabled people and after the initial employment initiative, SHAP expanded its programmes to include transport, sport, education, training, advice and peer support. By doing this it has provided a liberating example to other self-help groups in South Africa who are, in differing circumstances, seeking to follow their lead. One of the crucial elements of SHAP was its economic selfsufficiency. After an initial injection of start-up aid funding, SHAP functioned and grew as a non-profit making business. This has also set an example to many disabled people's organizations both in the South and North who, without that economic self-sufficiency, can be constrained in their self-determination by funding criteria and the objectives of aid and development funders. Within the context of a human rights approach, the SHAP example is instructive because their initial motivation was about achieving economic independence, not human rights. As Jerry Nkeli, explained: 'In the early 1980s a few of our colleagues in South Africa attended an international conference organized by Rehabilitation International.

The few people who attended that conference were quite privileged and all were from the white community. They came back with a lot of excitement. They had the theory, they knew that it is proper to reject charity and welfare, but they didn't have the numbers. They met the self-help group in Soweto, who did not know how to philosophize, who didn't know how to contextualize their struggle, but who in a very simple way understood that they did not want charity and wanted to run their own life and who had the numbers.' In other words, the founders of SHAP had grasped the importance of self determination, a central element in the current human rights discourse, 20 years before it was taken up by the aid agencies. The linking of the two groups of disabled people, from Soweto and those with international experience, the example of the black liberation struggle in the US and the continuing battle against apartheid was the heady mixture out of which the South African disability movement was forged. It is interesting to note that the same meeting of Rehabilitation International, which was to have such a strong impact on SHAP, also prompted the birth of Disabled Peoples' International.

In fact, over 200 disabled people returned to their own countries after that conference and set up national organizations of disabled people whose primary demand was for 'full participation and equality in our society wiThequal rights and responsibilities'. The leaders of SHAP went on to the leadership of Disabled Peoples' South Africa and then on to the world arena of disability rights, creating effective role models for disabled people everywhere.

ANDHRA PRADESH RURAL POVERTY REDUCTION PROGRAMME, INDIA

A pilot programme in Andhra Pradesh for reducing poverty, which was funded mostly by the World Bank, contained a 'disability component'. David Werner, one of the founders of the Projimo Project in Mexico, was brought in as an advisor. The work done in India bears many of the hallmarks of Projimo's participatory approach, essentially involving disabled people in leadership roles and at all stages of the process, including initial planning and the feasibility survey.

The first part of the project was extremely important, because having disabled people leading the local poverty surveys boThencouraged disabled villagers to get involved and offered empowering role models. The survey was designed around a rights-based approach and drew heavily on Paulo Freire's pedagogy of liberation, based on having people describe their world and then through a grounded participatory process arrive at ways to transform it. One of the outcomes of the survey was the setting up of disability 'sangams' at village level so that disabled people could work together to improve their situation, both socially and economically.

In the sangams disabled people are able to define their own needs, the barriers that exist and collectively take action to overcome them. They also organise demands for legal certification and entitlements. Another major goal has been getting disabled children into schools, as well as obtaining the necessary medical care, surgery and assistive devices they need.

Werner writes: 'Within the self-help disability sangams in Mahabubnagar, the interest and potential exist to improve health and rehabilitation services at the village level. Such an empowerment approach could help meet an urgent need for the most vulnerable people. It would also increase respect and opportunities for disabled people. And reduce poverty.' One of the biggest accomplishments the members say they have made is 'to be treated with respect'. 'Now people don't call us "the lame boy" or "the blind girl" but address us by our real names'. The disabled people who initiated this project are not yet fully involved in India's national disability rights agenda, but because of the size of the country and the cultural and political scene, the disability movement has not been able to coordinate nationally with any real coherence. They have, however, had considerable influence on the regional and local environments. In 2003, the World Bank agreed further to support the APRPRP with a credit of US$150 million. Judith Heumann, the World Bank's Advisor on Disability and Development, said: 'The inclusion of the disability community into this project will enable us to reach a group from the poorest of the poor, who are usually forgotten. The efforts of this project should be duplicated in other states'.

DPOS ENGAGE IN FORMULATING POVERTY REDUCTION STRATEGY PAPERS

Project work on disability and development remains important, but over the last decade or so, an increasing proportion of aid for the poorest countries has been delivered through World Bank/International Monetary Fund budget support programmes built around Poverty Reduction Strategy Papers and related aid instruments. On the whole, disability and other cross-cutting issues have fared badly in this new aid regime.

On the face of it this may appear somewhat surprising, as a key element in the process of putting together a PRSP is supposed to be consultation with civil society as well as the development of propoor growth strategies. With disabled people clearly being both part of civil society and among the poorest of the poor it might be expected that they would be a key constituency. However, a recent World Bank survey concluded that the coverage of disability within PRSPs was limited and a '...patchwork of fragmented and uncoordinated interventions'. It was also clear that in PRSPs most references that there are to disability are about social protection, not social inclusion. Because development and spending plans are set out in the PRSPs, if disability fails to get included as a mainstreamed consideration it is likely that the needs of disabled people will continue not to be met. This is why it is so vital that DPOs have a strong voice at every stage of the consultation process.

If this was to happen anywhere in the developing world, Uganda was the most likely country, as it has perhaps one of the strongest disability movements and disabled people are integrated at all levels of government. Nonetheless, it was not until the third PRSP that this was to happen and then not without a concerted political effort by disabled people. The National Union of Disabled Persons of Uganda is the national umbrella Organization for Ugandan DPOs. It was set up in 1987 to give a unified voice to disabled people. It now has almost 70 member groups and works closely with national, regional and local government.

The Organization promotes the social model and sees disability as a human rights issue. The alleviation of poverty is a principle goal of NUDIPU and this is why they lobbied the government so strenuously to become included in developing the Poverty Eradication Action Plan, as the PRSP is known in Uganda. Supported by the Danish Council of Organizations of Disabled People and Action on Disability and Development, NUDIPU developed a detailed submission, the result of research and a broadbased

But, despite having a nominal place at the table, NUDIPU had all kinds of problems. Technical capacity was a major one, as the PRSP process is extraordinarily complex. There was also pressure from donors and government to get the PRSP settled quickly so that the aid would flow. 'As a result, the PEAP process, in which civil society had been meaningfully involved, became constricted into a six month PRSP process from which they found themselves, to some extent, squeezed out'. Many people also considered that the government, as well as the World Bank and the IMF, were using DPO involvement as a way of legitimising the PRSP process, rather than out of any genuine interest in the rights or needs of disabled people.

CONCLUSION

A great many more examples could be given of DPOs involved in innovative, human-rights based projects of empowerment and poverty alleviation. Most of these have undoubtedly made a considerable difference to the disabled people they have touched, the problem is that overall they have not succeeded in touching the vast majority who continue to be actively and passively excluded from the mainstream of society. As David Werner writes of the poverty reduction project in Andhra Pradesh: 'Clearly, to substantially reduce poverty in India–or anywhere else–will require transformation of unjust socioeconomic and political structures that go far beyond the village-based health and rehabilitation measures.

But in the meantime, such measures can help the most vulnerable villagers cope a bit more successfully. By coming together to solve their problems in time a critical mass of "people who care for one another as equals" will be reached so that, collectively, they can begin to demand and work for more far-reaching change.' In theory, the PRSP process should be one way to help bring about this 'far-reaching change' as it provides the opportunity for a more democratic formulation of governments' economic policies and a greater opportunity to get disability on the mainstream development agenda. However, as yet this has not happened.

The example of Uganda points to the need for more sustained donor capacity-building support for DPOs so they can take part on equal terms, consult and inform their members and hold their governments to account. It also points to a need for donors and governments to take more seriously as well as genuinely value the contribution from civil society organizations. Donors especially must be more assiduous in discovering methods within the new aid paradigm to encourage governments to do this. Unless this happens, a human rights approach to development will be, as many critics have claimed it is, little more than empty rhetoric to deflect public attention from the resource-draining, poverty engendering political economy of globalisation.

14

Human Rights and the Social Construction of Sovereignty

The principle of sovereignty is widely considered the grundnorm of international society, and evolving human rights norms are seen as a compensatory international regime, the purpose of which is limit the inhumane consequences of the sovereign order. The principle of sovereignty grants states supreme authority within their territorial borders and denies the existence of any higher authority beyond those borders. Human rights norms, in contrast, place limits on how states can treat their peoples, compromising sovereignty in the name of universal standards of legitimate state conduct. Sovereignty and human rights are thus considered two separate regimes, that stand in a zero-sum relationship—the stronger the principle of sovereignty, the weaker norms of human rights, and vice versa.

There is a fundamental tension, Hedley Bull argues, between the principles that sustain international order—foremost among which is the mutual recognition of sovereignty—and the demands of human justice articulated in human rights norms. 'The basic compact of coexistence between states, expressed in the exchange of recognition of sovereign jurisdictions, implies a conspiracy of silence entered into by governments about the rights and duties of their respective citizens.'

It is this silence, and the atrocities it masks and permits, that have fuelled calls for the qualifying of sovereignty, for the building of a 'global consensus that state sovereignty is conditional upon the protection of at least basic human rights ...' This object takes issue with these views about the institution of sovereignty and the international human rights regime. Treating these as separate, mutually contradictory regimes obscures the justificatory role that human rights principles have performed in the constitution of the modern sovereign order. The organizing principle of sovereignty has never been a self-referential value; it has always been justified with reference to particular conceptions of legitimate statehood and rightful state action.

In the twentieth century, sovereignty has been increasingly justified in terms of the state's role as guarantor of certain basic human rights and freedoms, supplanting the politically impotent legitimating principle of divine right. This is more than a conceptual nicety. Without recognizing the justificatory role that human rights have played in the constitution of the modern sovereign order, we cannot explain key moments in the expansion of that order. Emergent human rights norms provided the moral resources for the delegitimation of colonialism and the subsequent proliferation of new sovereign states in the developing world, and they have played a similar role in the growth of international society since the end of the Cold War.

While these norms have so far failed to prevent many states from systematically violating the human rights of their inhabitants, by defining the terms of legitimate statehood they have been crucial in defining the contours of international society's postwar expansion. In what follows, I argue that the principle of sovereignty and human rights norms are best conceived as two normative elements of a single, distinctly modern discourse about legitimate statehood and rightful state action.

The protection of basic human rights is integral to the moral purpose of the modern state, to the dominant rationale that licenses the organization of power and authority into territorially defined sovereign units. The tensions that exist between sovereignty and human rights stem not from their separateness, from their status as parallel and antagonistic regimes, the latter instituted to civilize the former, but from the inherently contradictory nature of the modern discourse of legitimate statehood, a discourse that seeks to justify territorial particularism on the grounds of ethical universalism. I demonstrate this discursive connection by showing how appeals to emergent human rights norms delegitimated the institution of colonialism, provided the moral foundations for the norm of self-determination, and thus licensed the proliferation of post-colonial states in Africa and Asia. Here I directly contest a prominent line of argument, articulated by Robert Jackson and others, that sees the development of the international human rights regime as a response to decolonization and the spread of 'ramshackle states' in the Third World.

SOVEREIGNTY AND HUMAN RIGHTS: A TALE OF TWO REGIMES

Sovereignty is traditionally understood in highly categorical terms. Sovereign states are said to enjoy supreme decision-making authority within their territorial boundaries, while being under no political or legal obligation to observe any overarching authority outside those boundaries. Sovereignty, F. H. Hinsley contends, is 'the idea that there is a final and absolute political authority in the political community ... "and no final and absolute authority exists elsewhere"'. Realists treat sovereignty as an empirical attribute of the state, an assertion that states make about their territorial authority backed by military power, economic resources and perhaps the consent of the people.

Rationalists, in contrast, treat sovereignty as an institution of international society, a deeply embedded organizing principle that licenses the organization of political authority into centralized, territorially demarcated political units. The former emphasize the role of war-fighting and military competition in the rise of the modern international system, the latter stress the emergence of norms of mutual recognition, non-intervention, and self-determination. Both, however, view sovereignty as an absolute, an empirical or institutional fact that cannot be qualified without nullification. 'Human rights', John Vincent argues, 'are the rights that everyone has, and everyone equally, by virtue of their very humanity'. In holding such rights, all humans are entitled to make claims against other individuals, national communities, and humanity as a whole for the respect and satisfaction of certain civil and political freedoms and social and economic needs.

At times these rights have been grounded in reason, need, custom and contract, but in all cases they have been seen as universal and inalienable. While the idea of universal human rights was first articulated in the seventeenth and eighteenth centuries as a defence against the excesses of monarchical rule, the systematic codification of such rights at the international level has largely, though not exclusively, been a twentieth century development. Shocked into action by the Nazi genocide of Europe's Jewish population, and cajoled by diverse non-state actors, states have progressively 'legislated' an 'international bill of rights', comprising the Universal Declaration of Human Rights and the two International Covenants on Human Rights, augmented by a web of 'right-specific' treaties, conventions and declarations, spanning everything from worker's rights to the rights of indigenous peoples. The emergence of the sovereign order and the development of the international human rights regime are usually seen as connected only by way of their mutual incompatibility.

Not only are their generative dynamics thought to be distinct, with war-fighting and strategic competition driving the development of the former and liberal idealism propelling the latter, but the sovereign order is thought by sceptics to stand inviolable against the universalist challenge of the human rights regime and by optimists to be fundamentally compromised by that regime. Taking the first of these positions, Stanley Hoffmann argues that although the post-1945 development of international human rights norms 'has questioned two sacred elements of sovereignty: the right to wage war, and the right to do what you like to your citizens', these norms have had little impact on the realities and dynamics of international politics. Adopting the rival position, Kathryn Sikkink claims that the 'doctrine of internationally protected human rights offers one of the most powerful critiques of sovereignty as currently constituted, and the practices of human rights law and human rights foreign policies provide concrete examples of shifting understandings of the scope of sovereignty'. Both of these positions view sovereignty in highly categorical terms, and differ only over the corrosive potency of the independently constituted international human rights regime.

THE PROBLEM OF EXPLAINING INTERNATIONAL SOCIETAL EXPANSION

The tension between absolute state power and individual freedom makes this tale of two regimes intuitively plausible, yet this analytical separation is heuristically unhelpful in a number of regards. My concern here is with the obstacle this poses for understanding international societal expansion in the late modern era. Such expansion occurs when the basic organizing principle of international society remains constant—where sovereignty, heteronomy or suzerainty continue to structure the distribution of political authority—but where the number of recognized political units within that society increases.

In the history of the modern international society, societal expansion has been an ongoing process, with postwar settlements, imperial breakdown, and state fragmentation fuelling constant, if erratic, growth in the number of sovereign states. There have, however, been several great moments of societal expansion, where there have been rapid and significant expansions in the membership of international society. In the twentieth century, three such moments stand out: the post-Versailles reconfiguration of the European political order, the decolonization of the European empires in Asia and Africa, and the post-Cold War proliferation of states, primarily in East Europe but also elsewhere, wiTheast Timor being the most recent addition to international society. Treating sovereignty and human rights as clearly differentiated, mutually antagonistic regimes obscures one of the crucial dynamics that have propelled late modern international societal expansion—the central role that human rights norms have played in the constitution of the dominant discourse of legitimate statehood, and the importance of this discourse in licensing the proliferation of sovereign units. The limitations of this analytical separation are clearly apparent in Robert Jackson's otherwise insightful writings on decolonization, writings that have sought more nuanced understandings of sovereignty, statehood and the expansion of international society.

Jackson advances a modified rationalist account of the institution of sovereignty, arguing that since the Second World War there has been a fundamental change in the norms governing which political entities are entitled to recognition as fully independent states. Prior to the late 1950s and early 1960s only those countries which demonstrated 'empirical sovereignty'—'the wherewithal to provide political goods for [their] citizens' —were accorded sovereign status. The so-called 'standard of civilization' was used to determine such achievement, and the European powers ensured that membership of international society was an exclusive, jealously guarded right. This old 'positive sovereignty' game, Jackson argues, has since been supplanted by a new 'negative sovereignty' game, under which weak states have been granted 'juridical sovereignty' without exhibiting any of the trappings of empirical statehood. Only through reference to this change in the meanings attached to the sovereignty regime, Jackson concludes, can we explain the nature and speed of European decolonization.

It was the triumph of the central principle underlying the new negative sovereignty regime—the right to self-determination—which spurred this dramatic expansion of international society. 'Anti-colonialism', he writes, 'looks more and more like a sea change in international legitimacy'. Jackson's thesis that the speed of decolonization can best be attributed to a shift in the institution of sovereignty and the salience of the new international norm of self-determination is not in question here. Three main alternative explanations of decolonization exist, but Jackson persuasively argues that each fails to explain adequately why the process took place when it did, why it happened so quickly, or why it was a system-wide phenomenon spanning all imperial powers and colonies.

The first of these emphasizes how national liberation movements made stable imperial rule increasingly difficult, raising the political, military and economic costs of empire. The problem with this argument is that the strength of these movements varied across empires and colonies, never posing a general threat to the institution of colonialism. As Holland argues, 'Western Europe's status and capacity...was clearly on the wane for most of the twentieth century, and violently so after 1945, but whether that status fell in relation to Upper Volta or the Gold Coast/Ghana is very doubtful.'

The second explanation stresses how the war-ravaged European powers, faced with new demands for domestic social welfare expenditure, could no longer bear the economic costs of empire. Such pressures are undeniable, but it is not certain that they were the main consideration in European decisions to disengage. John Darwin argues that it 'is far from clear that...the economic argument turned decisively against empire and global commitments in the 1940s and 1950s.

Indeed, it seems likely that the economic repercussions of the Second World War encouraged a revival of British interest in parts of their colonial empire and in imperial economic integration generally.' The third explanation focuses on international pressures, particularly the rise of two superpowers both strongly opposed to colonialism. Once again, though, these pressures were not decisive.

As the Cold War escalated, the Americans toned down their anti-colonialist rhetoric, becoming more sympathetic to British imperial concerns than their wartime lobbying would have suggested, and in any case there is little evidence that pressure from Washington ever significantly swayed British calculations, let alone those of other imperial powers. Undoubtedly, these nationalist, economic, and international factors contributed to decolonization, but Jackson is correct to argue that the generalized nature and speed of

European disengagement can be explained only by introducing a fourth, normative factor—the system-wide shift in the sovereignty regime governing international society. Jackson's work flounders, however, when it comes to the relationship between the negative sovereignty regime and international human rights norms.

Jackson claims that the construction of a comprehensive human rights regime was a direct response to the advent of the negative sovereignty game and its attendant right of selfdetermination. In the age of high imperialism, the gradual spread of constitutionalism limited the excesses of power within metropolitan Europe, and the imperial powers granted sovereignty to only those polities that demonstrated a dictated level of 'civility'. The new sovereignty game changed all of this. European colonies now enjoyed a categorical right to self-determination, a right to constitutional autonomy free from external political, economic and normative constraints. In short, they were accorded 'juridical sovereignty' without having to demonstrate 'empirical sovereignty'.

Jackson argues that this led to the proliferation of weak states with neither the empirical capacities to meet the needs of their peoples, nor rulers with the political will to maintain adequate constitutional brakes on the exercise of power. This has resulted in a dramatic increase in human rights violations, an increase that 'is particularly evident outside the West where citizenship often is scarcely more than a nominal status with little or no real purchasing power.' The construction of international human rights norms, Jackson contends, was a direct response to this change in the membership of international society and associated decline in 'civility'. He writes that the 'new sovereignty game is ... complicated by the emergence of a cosmopolitan regime which seeks to establish the legal status of humans in international relations against the sovereign Leviathan. This norm is not part of the sovereignty game but is a reaction to it: human rights are intended to curb sovereign rights' [my emphasis]. The idea that the right to self-determination ushered in a negative sovereignty regime that bestowed unequivocal rights to rule is widespread. In his classic work on international law, George Schwarzenberger writes that the right to selfdetermination rests on 'pristine sovereignty in the form of lawlessness'. In a similar fashion, Jack Donnelly claims that self-determination meant 'a right of colonial territories to recognition as sovereign states within colonial borders.

Considerations of justice were thus banished from decisions on membership of international society.' Few scholars go as far as Jackson in arguing that the international human rights regime was a specific response to the advent of the right to self-determination, the rise of the negative sovereignty regime, and the proliferation of weak Third World states. Yet it is commonplace for the development of the international human rights regime to be seen as a discrete process, driven largely by Western states, that evolved parallel to, and in conflict with, the politics of self-determination that transformed the meaning of sovereignty. In a clear statement of this position, Donnelly argues that the 'death of the classic standard of civilization was accompanied by the entrenchment of a Hobbesian conception of sovereignty. ... The decades following the Second World War, however, also saw the development of an extensive body of international human rights law that recaptured, in a substantially purified form, the morally appealing idea of adherence to shared standards of justice as a condition for full membership in international society.' Jackson's argument about the rise of negative sovereignty regime, decolonization and human rights suffers from two serious weaknesses.

With regard to the first of these, although he provides a painstaking description of the apparent revolution in the rules of the sovereignty game and how this delegitimated European imperialism, he provides no explanation for this transformation. The construction of a new sovereignty regime around the right to self-determination may well have spurred the single most dramatic expansion of international society, but why did these norms emerge when they did and with such salience? This explanatory weakness is compounded by a number of crucial empirical anomalies in Jackson's account of the relationship between the new sovereignty regime and international human rights. First, he ignores the fact that the most important international human rights instruments—including the relevant provisions of the United Nations Charter, the Universal Declaration, and the two international covenants—were negotiated before or during the most intense phase of decolonization and the proliferation of 'quasistates', not after. Second, he overlooks the crucial role that 'first wave' post-colonial states—such as India and Pakistan—played in the initiation and negotiation of these instruments, a role in which they strongly supported the importance, and at times even the primacy, of civil and political rights in addition to economic, social and cultural rights.

Third, he obscures the heavy reliance that these states placed on the discourse of human rights in their formulation and advocacy of the right to selfdetermination. The remainder of this object presents an alternative, constructivist account of the international societal expansion that attended decolonization, an account that treats international human rights as integral to the discourse of legitimate statehood that licensed that expansion, not simply a response to the excesses of the post-colonial states it generated.

This account not only explains the phenomenon that Jackson merely describes, it accommodates the significant empirical anomalies in his historical account.

COMMUNICATIVE ACTION AND THE CONSTITUTION OF SOVEREIGNTY NORMS

To understand processes of international societal expansion it is necessary to abandon the prevailing, highly categorical conception of sovereignty and to treat it instead as a variable, practically constituted institution. This is the view first advanced by critical theorists and taken up more recently by constructivists. In an early statement of this position, Richard Ashley argues that 'sovereignty is a practical category whose empirical contents are not fixed but evolve in a way reflecting the active practical consensus among coreflective statesmen' It is all else a set of norms concerning the legitimate organization of political authority, the content and implications of which vary from one historical and practical context to another.

For those wishing to study sovereignty, therefore, the challenge is not to arrive at a universally valid definition that fixes its meaning and content, but rather, as Thomas Biersteker and Cynthia Weber observe, to explore 'the constitutive relationship between state and sovereignty; the ways the meaning of sovereignty is negotiated out of interactions within intersubjectively identifiable communities; and the variety of ways in which practices construct, reproduce, reconstruct, and deconstruct both state and sovereignty'. An exploration of this sort must begin with the recognition that sovereignty is a social norm, subject to the same constitutive processes as all other norms, rules and principles.

Like their domestic counterparts, international norms, rules and principles are social artifacts, the normative products of moral debate and dialogue between states about legitimate statehood and rightful domestic and international conduct, products that are reproduced through routinized communication and social practice. Norms, rules, and principles thus have histories, they emerge out of complex processes of communicative action, and they are maintained through the conscious, and at times unconscious, application of taken-for-granted canons and repertoires of appropriate state conduct.

The communicative processes that surround international norm formation vary from one issue and context to another, but they also exhibit a common dialogical structure. When seeking to establish a new norm, rule or principle, or to give an established one new meaning, states will seek to justify their moral claims. As theorists of communicative action observe, actors engaged in such projects usually try to associate their prescriptions with values that are already accepted as normative within the relevant speech community. As Agnes Heller observes, '[c]ontestants enter the discourse with different values, and they all try to justify their values (as right and true). They do so by resorting to values higher than those which they want to justify, by proving that the latter are but an interpretation of higher values, or that they can be related to these higher values without logical contradiction'.

Specialists on international norm formation have termed this process 'issue-resonance', 'nesting', or 'grafting'. In her study of the rise of developmentalism in Latin America, Kathryn Sikkink argues that '[n]ew ideas are more likely to be influential if they 'fit' well wiThexisting ideas and ideologies in a particular historical setting.' And in seeking to explain the recently enshrined norm against the manufacture, deployment and use of land mines, Richard Price shows how 'moral entrepreneurs' successfully 'grafted' their claims to established elements of just war doctrine, namely the dictates for civilian discrimination and against unnecessary suffering.

In the communicative processes that generate new international norms, rules and principles, not all 'higher values' have the same justificatory power. Theorists of communicative action have shown that 'identity' values are particularly persuasive, as they define the meaning and nature of legitimate social and political agency. Such values lie at the heart of what Jürgen Habermas calls the 'lifeworld', the 'storehouse of unquestioned cultural givens from which those participating in communication draw agreed-upon patterns of interpretation for use in their interpretive efforts'.

Within domestic society, the best way to further a moral claim is to 'graft' it to prevailing views about what constitutes a fully realised human being, or to beliefs about the ideal community of such beings. At the international level, moral claims that are shown to be consistent with intersubjective beliefs about the behaviour and goals of ideal states, or to foster the development of such states, carry the greatest weight. Historically, the identity values defining ideal individuals and states have been closely linked, with the latter usually being cast in the service of the former. Furthermore, domestic and international identity values have changed over time— Renaissance Italian ideas about the ideal individual and state differed markedly from those that prevail today. These insights into communicative action and norm formation are of crucial importance in understanding the social construction of sovereignty regimes.

Sovereignty is an intersubjective organizing principle, a principle that licenses the arrangement of power and authority into territorially-demarcated, centralized and autonomous political units. As John Ruggie observes, it is a principle that specifies 'the basis on which the constituent units are separated from one another'. Like all social norms, the principle of sovereignty has a history, a history that has involved the same sort of communicative processes that surround the production and reproduction of other social norms.

Just as the construction of issue-specific norms has entailed the grafting of new principles to pre-existing social values, so too has the principle of sovereignty. When sovereign states were constructed in ancient Greece, when they were championed again in Renaissance Italy, when absolutist states were carved out of the declining heteronomous order of medieval Europe, and when the age of revolutions spurned the development of modern nation-states, the idea of sovereignty did not emerge in a moral vacuum; it had to be justified, and that justification has always taken the form of an appeal to higher-order values that define the identity or raison d'être of the state, whether they entail the pursuit of justice, the achievement of civic glory, the protection of a divinely ordained social order, or the advancement of individuals' rights and the celebration of the nation.

Contrary to conventional wisdom, therefore, sovereignty should be viewed as a dependent or secondary principle—an historically contingent prescription about the distribution of power and authority that needs to be grounded in more fundamental existential values. It is mistakenly assumed that sovereignty is the most basic international institution, the normative bedrock of the society of states. Even constructivists have failed to understand the communicative processes that generate sovereignty regimes, often writing as though sovereignty were a self-referential value that could be upheld without reference to other social values, particularly those pertaining to the 'good' served by centralizing authority within territorially-defined bounds.

Building on Aristotle's observation 'that every state is an association, and that every association is formed with a view to some good purpose', the principle of sovereignty is best understood as but one part of larger complexes of normative values that undergird international societies, complexes that elsewhere I have termed 'constitutional structures' At the heart of these structures lie hegemonic beliefs about the 'moral purpose' of the state, beliefs that define 'the reasons that historical agents hold for organizing their political life into centralized, autonomous political units' These beliefs provide the justificatory foundations for the organizing principle of sovereignty and inform systemic norms of procedural justice.

They define the raison d'être of the sovereign state, and specify the terms of legitimate statehood and rightful state action. Their content varies, however, from one historical context to another. Ancient Greeks tied the moral purpose of the state to the cultivation of bios politikos, a distinctive form of communal life; Renaissance Italians defined it in terms of the pursuit of civic glory; Europeans in the age of absolutism linked it to the preservation of a divinely ordained, rigidly hierarchical social order; and in the modern era, the rationale for the state has been increasingly tied to the protection of individuals' rights.

HUMAN RIGHTS, THE RIGHT TO SELF-DETERMINATION, AND DECOLONIZATION

The communicative processes are most palpable at great moments of international societal expansion, when the existing political order is challenged by new claims to sovereignty, grounded in revolutionary, reconfigured, or redeployed ideals of legitimate statehood. At such moments, the prevailing international organization of political authority is portrayed as inconsistent wiThexistent or ascendent conceptions of the moral purpose of the state, thus demanding the dismantling of established sovereign or imperial units to permit the construction of new sovereign states. This is what occurred at Versailles, with decolonization, and after the Cold War. With regard to the second of these, with which we are concerned here, a conception of the moral purpose of the state that has been ascendent since the middle of the nineteenth century, and which ties legitimate statehood to the protection of individuals' basic human rights, was mobilized by 'first wave' postcolonial states to discredit European imperialism, establish the right to selfdetermination, and license wholesale decolonization.

THE ASCENDENT MORAL PURPOSE OF THE MODERN STATE

During the seventeenth and eighteenth centuries the legitimacy of European states rested on the divine right of kings, a right that God supposedly bestowed on monarchs giving the authority to ensure the preservation of a divinely ordained, rigidly hierarchical social order. By the latter half of the eighteenth century, the ideological foundations of this rationale were beginning to erode. Mirroring shifts in scientific thought, political and economic theorists abandoned holistic conceptions of society, championing new ideas of political and economic individualism.

The impact of these ideas was profound, with political individualism fuelling the American and French Revolutions, and economic individualism providing the ideological resources for the Industrial Revolution. In the ensuing 50 years, European politics was riven by protracted conflicts over the terms of legitimate rule, compounded by the economic dislocation of traditional patterns of social organization and affiliation. The ancien régime won a temporary reprieve at the end of the Napoleonic Wars, invoking the constitutional metavalues of absolutism at the Congress of Vienna to shape a new international order. By the middle of the nineteenth century, though, the tide had turned. Justifying state power and authority by appealing to monarchical right and the need to preserve a divinely ordained social order became more and more untenable, and legitimate statehood and rightful state action were increasingly tied to the representation of individuals' political interests and the protection of their inalienable human rights. This new conception of legitimate statehood was not immediately expressed in the development of an international human rights regime, and the embedding of that regime is still under way.

Constitutionalism and the rule of law had spread to most European states by the end of the nineteenth century, but these changes were primarily the result of domestic political processes, not the consequence of internationally legislated norms. The 'moral purpose' of the modern state filtered into international society in two phases, structuring the external institutional practices of states first, and prescribing the internal relations between governments and their citizens second. In the first phase, stretching from 1850 to 1945, the influence of modern principles of legitimate statehood and rightful state action on international politics was largely architectural, affecting the nature and functioning of basic institutional practices.

The revolutionary principles that only those subject to the law have the right to legislate, and that laws must apply equally to all of society's members, informed the development of multilateralism and positive international law, resulting in a huge increase in the number of multilateral treaties and associated organizations. Clearly evident in the development of universal conferences of states and the evolution of the International Court of Justice, modern ideals of selflegislation and reciprocally binding rules of conduct became the structuring norms of international governance, ultimately producing the United Nations and the growing edifice of contractual law between states.

Throughout this period, though, the moral gaze of international society was primarily external, with states celebrating the new principles of rule in their relations with one another but shying away from the articulation and codification of international norms concerning the application of such principles within states. To be sure, the state was no longer seen as the monarch's domain, but the emerging idea of the state as the political manifestation of the nation, and state policies as the political expression of the national interest, encouraged the assumption that when the principle of national self-determination is upheld, the state and society stand in a symbiotic embrace. This focus on international institutional construction, paired with a tragic faith in the pacific benefits of racially defined national self-determination, found their clearest and most problematic expression in Wilsonian internationalism and the Versailles peace settlement.

Nazism put an end to this first phase, pushing the society of states to enshrine modern ideals of legitimate statehood and rightful state conduct in a comprehensive international human rights regime. The Holocaust exposed in stark relief the pathological consequences of an international system that sanctioned a racially-defined principle of national self-determination, and since 1945 the international community has championed, if not adequately defended, the ideal of the ethnically and racially neutral democracy, a democracy in which the civil and political and economic and social rights of citizens and non-citizens are protected and promoted. While the society of states had moved to protect human rights in the past, with tentative steps made in the areas of minority rights, workers rights, and the rights of women, after the Second World War legitimate statehood was more explicitly tied to the protection of basic human rights.

This connection has been articulated in an ever expanding battery of international human rights instruments. These instruments are elaborations on the principles laid down in Articles 55 and 56 of the Charter of the United Nations, which commit member states 'to take joint and separate action' to provide 'higher standards of living, full employment, and conditions of economic and social progress and development', and to cultivate 'universal respect for, and observance of, human rights and fundamental freedoms for all without distinction as to race, sex, language, or religion'. Further articulating these principles, the 1948 Universal Declaration of Human Rights defines the simultaneous satisfaction of individuals' economic rights (such as the rights to work and to social security) and civil and political rights (such as the right to vote, to free speech, and to due process) 'as a common standard of achievement for all peoples and all nations...' These obligations were given formal legal status by the International Covenants on Civil and Political Rights and Economic, Social, and Cultural Rights signed in 1966 and brought into force ten years later.

The progressive development of these human rights instruments has formally enshrined modern ideals of legitimate statehood in the normative fabric of international society, extending the influence of such values from the constitution of basic institutional practices to the prescription of statesociety relations.

'FIRST WAVE' POST-COLONIAL STATES AND THE INTERNATIONAL HUMAN RIGHTS REGIME

It is widely assumed that the development of the international human rights regime was a Western project, and that developing countries have consistently and vigourously defended their domestic jurisdictions against such norms. In Donnelly's words, 'these newly independent states (understandably) emphasized their sovereign equality, understood in radical legal positivist terms, and met efforts to hold them to minimum standards of humane behaviour towards their own citizens with charges of neo-colonialism'. While this view correctly captures the general attitude of developing states once decolonization had been achieved, it seriously misrepresents the position of newly independent states in the early stages of the international campaign against colonialism.

Though small in numbers, developing states from Asia and Latin America played a prominent role in the drafting of both the Universal Declaration and the two International Covenants. In fact, states such as India, Pakistan, Brazil, the Philippines, Chile, and Columbia represented an important force in the alliance with several Western states that successfully thwarted attempts by South Africa and Soviet bloc countries to derail international human rights initiatives. It is also common wisdom that developing states have consistently favoured economic and social rights over civil and political rights. The satisfaction of economic entitlements has certainly become a prominent, if not predominant, feature of the developing world's diplomatic agenda, but this has not always been the case. It was initially intended that there would be only one international covenant, but states disagreed about whether it should include economic as well as civil and political rights. The Soviet Union and its clients argued that the proposed covenant should not only include economic rights, but that these rights should have priority. While other states generally accepted these rights, they vigourously opposed their inclusion in a single covenant along with civil and political rights. This was partly on the grounds that different categories of rights demanded different implementation mechanisms, but some states—including the leading developing countries—argued that civil and political rights should have priority. In 1951, India and Lebanon argued that 'the two groups of rights were not of equal importance, the full enjoyment of economic, social and cultural rights being ...dependent on the assurance of civil and political rights.' Together with leading Western states, they managed to overturn a former UN decision and force the drafting of two separate covenants.

Throughout the negotiations on the Universal Declaration and the two International Covenants, leading developing countries consistently argued that the protection of human rights was an international concern which circumscribed the state's domestic jurisdiction. In the debate by the Third Committee of the General Assembly on the draft Universal Declaration, the Pakistani representative stated that 'it was imperative that the peoples of the world should recognize the existence of a code of civilized behaviour which would apply not only in international relations but also in domestic affairs'. In a prophetic statement, the Chilean representative told the General Assembly that 'no one could infringe upon the rights proclaimed in it [the Universal Declaration] without becoming an outcast from the community of states'. These attitudes were reflected in the position that developing states took on the question of implementation and enforcement, an issue that focused on whether individuals and non-governmental organizations should have the right to petition the United Nations directly on human rights violations by their states.

While Sovietbloc countries opposed all implementation measures on the grounds that they violated the state's domestic jurisdiction, and the United States and Britain argued that only states should have the right to petition, leading developing states insisted that individuals and NGOs must have direct access to the United Nations. After unsuccessfully trying to have the right to petition enshrined in the Universal Declaration, a coalition of Western and developing states (including Denmark, India, and Mexico) pushed to have the International Covenant on Civil and Political Rights recognize such a right. Whatever their subsequent human rights records, if it were not for the early efforts of these states, the Covenant's Optional Protocol— the compromise instrument which allows individuals experiencing human rights violations in signatory states to petition the United Nations Human Rights Committee directly—would probably not exist.

GRAFTING THE RIGHT TO SELF- DETERMINATION TO HUMAN RIGHTS NORMS

Until the late 1950s and early 1960s the world was divided into a hierarchy of political forms, with the system of sovereign states at the pinnacle surrounded by a range of dependent colonies, protectorates, and mandates. In addition to the economic and military gulf separating these entities, the division was based on the European application of a standard of civilization which distinguished between civilized, barbarian, and savage peoples. This standard consisted of two principal criteria: one political, the other economic, scientific and technological. As we have seen, the former ranked peoples just as to their perceived capacities for civil government. Several British Colonies, wrote John Stuart Mill, 'are composed of people of similar civilization to the ruling country; capable of, and ripe for, representative government: such as the British possessions in America and Australia.

Others, like India, are still at a great distance from that state.' This ranking was reinforced by the idea that European states surpassed all others in material achievement, a prejudice apparently vindicated by the glories of the industrial revolution. Having placed themselves at the top of the civilizational hierarchy, European states assumed a paternalistic attitude towards other peoples, shrouding their domination in a veil of moral responsibility. This civilizing mission is still apparent in the Charter of the United Nations which reaffirms the colonial powers' 'sacred trust' to cultivate their dependencies' 'political, and educational development' and 'to assist them in the progressive development of their free political institutions, just as to the particular circumstances of each territory and its peoples and their varying stages of advancement'.

Within the space of two decades this hierarchy was levelled into a radically expanded system of juridically equal sovereign states. Neither the speed nor the generalized nature of this revolution can be explained solely through changes in the balance of material power between the colonizer and colonized—a shift in the norms governing the membership of international society also played a crucial role.

The old sovereignty game, and its associated moral defence of hierarchy, were systematically discredited and supplanted by a new principle that 'all peoples have the right to self-determination' irrespective of their levels of political, economic, and social development. Jackson thoroughly documents this normative revolution, but he fails to recognize that the right to self-determination only triumphed because developing states skilfully grafted it to pre-existing international human rights norms. While the Charter of the United Nations upholds 'the principle of equal rights and self-determination of peoples', this principle only became a serious threat to the institution of colonialism after it had been mobilized by newly independent states in early negotiations over the two International Covenants.

These countries strongly supported the development of the human rights regime, and their campaign for full decolonization explicitly portrayed self-determination as a prerequisite for the satisfaction of such rights. The right to self-determination is plagued by a central ambiguity: it is unclear which communities are entitled to claim or exercise such a right. In the history of modern international society there have been two resolutions to this problem. The first—embodied in the Versailles settlement—emphasized the rights of racially and ethnically defined nations. As Rupert Emerson observes, 'the peoples involved in the Wilsonian period were ethnic communities, nations or nationalities primarily defined by language and culture ... '. Like Mill, Wilson believed that democracy could function properly only where the population of a state was bound together by linguistic and cultural affinities. Believing that communities with such affinities could be determined by measuring their 'objective' ethnic characteristics, he and his fellow Americans argued at Versailles that 'their team of experts could provide better evidence of the lines of national divisions and affiliations than could be obtained from plebiscites of the populations concerned'.

This cultural understanding of 'peoples' and 'nations' informed the standard of civilization that the colonial powers invoked to justify their tutelage. The division of the world into civilized, barbarian, and savage peoples was at heart a racial categorization. Western dominance rested on the supposed superiority of European culture, and the primacy of Britain, France, and Germany was attributed to their extraordinary racial qualities. At the bottom of the hierarchy were the 'dark races' of Africa who were seen as lacking all civilizational achievement and potential, a condition that licensed ongoing European oversight and control. Somewhere in the middle fell the barbarian peoples of Asia, who were considered educable, long-term candidates for political and economic achievement. By the end of the Second World War two factors had undermined this initial resolution. Nazism made world leaders fearful of encouraging a resurgence of ethnic nationalism and provided the single most important impetus for the development of international human rights norms. Second, most of the parties interested in claiming self-determination after 1945—the European colonies of Africa and Asia—had multi-ethnic or multi-racial populations.

For these reasons, anti-colonialist movements and their allies in the United Nations made little reference to the integrity of ethnically defined nations in their campaign for decolonization. As Emerson observes, 'in the era of decolonization, ethnic identity [was] essentially irrelevant ... '. Instead, self-determination was portrayed as a necessary prerequisite for the satisfaction of individuals' basic political and economic rights. This connection between the right to self-determination and human rights was first articulated in 1950 by Afghanistan and Saudi Arabia in the United Nations negotiations that eventually produced the two International Covenants. Laying the groundwork for the eventual inclusion of the right to self-determination in Article 1 of both Covenants, they successfully moved a motion calling on the Human Rights Commission to study 'the right of peoples and nations to self-determination'.

Frustrated with the Commission's failure to launch such a study, in 1951 the representatives of Afghanistan, Burma, Egypt, India, Indonesia, Iran, Iraq, Lebanon, Pakistan, the Philippines, Saudi Arabia, Syria and Yemen, among others, called for the General Assembly to insert an article on the right to self-determination into the draft Covenants. They argued that this inclusion 'would give moral and legal support to peoples aspiring to political and social independence and would be a valuable contribution to international peace and security. No basic human rights could be ensured unless this right were ensured ... '. This call was reiterated in a February 1952 General Assembly resolution, which explicitly placed self-determination in the service of two higher order values: the need 'to save present and succeeding generations from the scourge of war' (which prefaced virtually all United Nations resolutions), and the need 'to reaffirm faith in fundamental human rights' Later that year developing states escalated their claims, passing a General Assembly resolution that not only asserted the right to self-determination, but also the obligation of European states to decolonize. 'The right of peoples and nations to self-determination', it clearly states, 'is a prerequisite to the full enjoyment of all fundamental human rights'.

These efforts culminated in two victories: the enshrining of the right to selfdetermination in the opening articles of both International Covenants, and the 1960 Declaration on the Granting of Independence to Colonial Countries and Peoples. The positioning of the right to self-determination at the very beginning of the Covenants clearly signalled its status as a prerequisite for the realization of basic human rights. 'All peoples', Article 1 of both Covenants declares, 'have the right to self-determination.

By virtue of that right they freely determine their political status and freely pursue their economic, social and cultural development'. The 1960 Declaration is generally considered the crucial United Nations resolution on decolonization. It not only begins by reaffirming 'faith in fundamental human rights, in the dignity and worth of the human person, in the equal rights of men and women and of nations large and small', its opening declaration states that the 'subjection of peoples to alien subjugation, domination and exploitation constitutes a denial of fundamental human rights'. By linking self-determination to the basic rights and freedoms of all individuals, developing states successfully undermined the paternalism of the European colonial powers. 'Inadequacy of political, economic, social or educational preparedness', the Declaration asserts, 'should never serve as a pretext for delaying independence'. Far from being a categorical right with no strings attached, therefore, the post- 1945 right to self-determination was deliberately and explicitly tied to the satisfaction of basic human rights. What is more, it was 'first wave' post-colonial states, as well as nationalist elites in colonial territories, who bound the two together, quite deliberately placing the former in the service of the latter. Given prevailing ideals of legitimate statehood and rightful state action, and the international community's new-found interest in applying these to internal state-society relations, this was an immensely rational strategy, a strategy that artfully appealed to higher order values of political legitimacy to discredit colonialism and establish a right to immediate independence.

The so-called 'third generation' or 'solidarity' right of selfdetermination was self-consciously constructed upon the normative foundations of prior 'first' and 'second' generation political and economic rights of individuals. As Jackson observes, juridical sovereignty became the right of all colonies, producing and protecting an array of empirically weak states, but this right was granted on the grounds that it was a necessary precondition for the satisfaction of basic human rights. That many developing states have since sought to separate their right to independence from the observance of human rights, or to invoke non-Western values to deny the universality of liberal civil and political rights, does not alter the fact that the campaign against colonialism championed such rights and used them to justify the right to self-determination.

CONCLUSION

In contrast to the prevailing assumption that sovereignty and human rights constitute separate, mutually antagonistic international regimes, this object has argued that they are better understood as two normative elements of the inherently contradictory modern discourse of legitimate statehood. Lying at the heart of prevailing ideals about the moral purpose of the state, human rights have increasingly provided the justificatory foundations for sovereignty. This connection is clearly apparent in the communicative processes that have surrounded key moments of late modern international societal expansion. And as the case of decolonization indicates, such expansion is inexplicable without reference to the grafting of the right to selfdetermination, and in turn sovereignty, to emergent international human rights norms. In advancing and demonstrating this argument, two other widespread assumptions have been challenged.

Where it is generally assumed that the construction of the international human rights regime was a Western project, we have seen that 'first wave' post-colonial states played a prominent role in the negotiation of both the Universal Declaration and the two International Covenants, a role in which they frequently gave priority to civil and political rights over social and economic rights, and in which they backed stronger rather than weaker mechanisms of accountability and enforcement. All of this challenges the assumption made by Jackson and others that the international human rights regime was a reaction to the proliferation of 'ramshackle states' in the Third World.

While the excesses of these states have certainly fuelled the development of the regime, especially since the 1970s, their very existence as recognized, independent polities can only be attributed to the successful mobilization of emergent human rights norms. In contrast to the constructivist argument advanced here, realist and rationalist approaches struggle to explain late modern international societal expansion. For realists, expansions or contractions in the number of sovereign states are driven by the material capacities that states can marshal to defend or expand their sovereign jurisdiction, territorial integrity, and overseas holdings.

Increases or decreases in the number of states are attributed to the struggle for power, usually expressed in violent conquest, armed secession and major wars. Without denying the potential of such dynamics to produces changes in the membership of international society, they cannot account for the type of large scale expansion that attended decolonization. The type of generalized, militarily potent, armed struggle that would have been necessary to dismantle all of the European empires in the space of twenty-odd years simply did not exist, and Jackson is correct to argue that this transformation could only have come about through the wholesale delegitimation of colonialism as an institution. Rationalists fare no better in explaining international societal expansion of this magnitude.

Despite the considerable effort that Bull and others devoted to describing the expansion of modern international society, and despite Jackson's focus on decolonization, rationalists lack the conceptual and theoretical resources to explain such expansions. Like constructivists, Bull considers sovereignty to be an institution, but he assumes that its meaning is fixed, which makes his conceptual framework ill-suited to explaining the type of changes in the sovereignty regime that accompanied decolonization. More than this, though, because rationalists treat sovereignty as a discrete institution, not embedded in other constitutive norms and values, they have no way of comprehending the communicative processes that produce transformations in the sovereignty regime. This is where Jackson's argument fails. Although he departs from other rationalists in seeing change in the meaning of sovereignty, by failing to see how sovereignty and human rights are bound together within a single discourse of legitimate statehood, he can only describe, not explain, the direction of that change.

The perspective on sovereignty and human rights advanced here differs from that adopted by other constructivists, but it is by no means incompatible with their positions. While others have not gone so far as to conceive of sovereignty and human rights as components of a single discourse of legitimate statehood, many of their arguments imply such a move.

Constructivists view sovereignty as a variable, practically constituted institution, its precise content and political implications varying with time and context. Constructivists concerned with human rights often attribute some of this variance in the meaning of sovereignty to the articulation and institutionalization of international human rights norms, suggesting that the discourses of political authority and rights are in dialogue, a dialogue about legitimate statehood. Perhaps the most significant difference, then, between the perspective advanced here and most constructivist work on human rights concerns analytical focus. Where I have focused on the connection between human rights and international societal expansion, others have focused on the impact of international rights norms on domestic state practices. The first of these projects illuminates the normative dynamics configuring the membership of international society, the second exposes the complex connections between international human rights norms, international organizations, non-states actors, and state compliance. The obvious challenge is for constructivists to bring these two analytical foci together, to produce an holistic and complete understanding of the relationship between international human rights norms and sovereignty.

15

European Chapter of Human Rights-Amnesty International

INTRODUCTION

The fact is that human rights are as much a global as a national concern. Countries across the world recognized this when they became a party to the International covenant on civil and political rights. In doing so, they undertook legal obligations to the international community to observe and protect human rights. Not only did they make a unilateral declaration against Torture saying that they would comply with the UN Declaration against Torture, they even initiated the resolution of the UN General Assembly that introduced these Declarations.

AMNESTY INTERNATIONAL

Amnesty International itself is an expression f the idea that human rights are of international concern. It is an independent organization funded by voluntary contributions from its members in over 150 countries in all regions. It does not accept funds from governments. It does not take any position regarding aid donors making the provision f aid conditional on human rights performance.

Its task is strictly limited to the human rights field. It works for the release of prisoners of conscience who have not used or advocated violence, for fair trails for all political prisoners; and against torture, the death penalty, extra judicial executions and disappearance. It relies upon and appeal to, the moral power of informed public opinion. In working to protect human rights, Amnesty International primarily addresses government, because it is governments that are responsible under international law for side guarding such rights.

However, it also condemns and opposes torture, deliberate and arbitrary killings and hostage taking by armed political opposition groups, and it has repeatedly done so public regarding groups committing such abuses in Punjab, Jammu and Kashmir and Assam. Most recently, in June1992 it issued a statement in which it against condemned the recent deliberate and arbitrary killing by armed groups in Punjab, calling on these and other armed groups around the world to stop such killings of civilians, including hostages, and to live up to basic humanitarian standards.

In carrying out its mandate, it is politically impartial. It has monitored the protection of human rights in India and elsewhere since the late 1960s and have reported human rights violations under each administration regardless of political persuasion. In its report it not only addresses it self to government authorities at the central level. But equally to all state government, a number of whom are led by political parties opposed to the ruling party at the centre.

On a global basis, it is also committed to impartiality in its work and the application of a universal standard to all governments. Its latest annual report covers over 140 countries despite several press reports across nations alleged that it is a part of an anti to a countries propaganda campaign.

In Britain and the USA it fought against the aid Pakistan. In fact, for may years it has urged the UK Government to independently investigate a range of human right issues, including shoot to kill allegations in Northern Ireland, and last year it submitted information about the UK to the UN committee against Torture. It has repeatedly criticized the USA for its extensive use of the death penalty which it believes to be arbitrary and racially biased and which included the execution of juvenile offenders.

Another recent Indian press article said that it had nothing to say about human rights violations in Pakistan and china. In fact last year it had published a report on torture and deaths in custody in Pakistan and worked to stop violations against religious minorities there. Human rights violations in China cover virtually the full range of concerns in this mandate and it regularly reported on prisoners of conscience, torture and the high rate of executions there. It is currently campaigning to end torture and arbitrary detention in Tibet. It hopes that Indian will join then in applying the pressure of public opinion on all these governments.

In raising the question of human rights protection in India one is motivated by the desire to help end the violations and promote those human values and standards which are universally recognized as applying to all people at all times. It is now widely recognized that all human rights are indivisible and interdependent.

It is sometimes argued that development, the rights to food, housing and other economic rights are more important than freedom of expression, the rights not to be arbitrarily detained or even the right not to tortured. It rejects the view that it is difficult to accept so far as civil and political rights on the one hand, and economic, social and cultural rights on the other, as of equal importance.

To safeguard the independence and impartiality of its work, Amnesty International members in any one national section must work only on cases and campaigns in countries other than their own. The European section of

Amnesty International has therefore had no involvement whatever in this report.

This report was compiled by the Research Department of its International Secretariat. Although the Governments, in their reaction to the publication f the original version of the report said the report was based on mere hearsay and that it consisted of conjectures and general allegation details of over 400 individual cases of deaths in custody that were given in the second half of this report. The amnesty have carefully cross checked the information in this report drawing on information provided by various Government officials, on official inquiries and on reports in the Newspapers of these countries. It has relied as far as possible on court records, sworn statements and other first hand information from witnesses themselves.

During the last three years members of amnesty international have written to government officials, in the various countries to ask specified questions about the people listed in this report as having died in custody after torture or ill treatment. They have asked whether investigations have been carried out and whether anyone has been brought to justice for the crimes apparently committed. They have received no substantive replies. Nor has Amnesty international been allowed to carry out research, to investigate these or other human rights concerns or discuss them in any substance with any Government for more than a decade; the last time they were allowed to do so was sometime in 1978.

The Ministries in their statements, made out that the Amnesty International had given it no more than one week to respond to the text of this report, whereas, the they had asked for six weeks. In fact those who delivered the text of the report to the leaders of countries disagree with this.

Today thee are more than 250,000 members, subscribers and supporters in 151 countries or territories with national sections in 40 there are 2560 adoption groups, of from three to sometimes more than 50 members batch group is allocated responsibility for two or three prisoners of conscience or possible prisoners of conscience. The cases are balanced politically and geographically to reflect impartiality.

If a case is still under investigation, because there is not enough evidence to determine whether the prisoner is a prisoner of conscience, the group seeks further information and urges the government to supply details of the charges against the prisoner. With a prisoner of conscience, the group puts its energy into writing letters, circulation petitions, publicizing the case and calling on the authorities for the prisoner's immediate and unconditional release. The group may also raise money to send relief assistance, such as money, medicine or clothing, to the prisoner and the prisoner's family.

A unique aspect of Amnesty International's casework placing the emphasis on the need for international protection of human rights is the fact that each group works on behalf of prisoners held in countries other than its own.

Group members also take part in national and international campaigns that attract wide publicity some join the special network set up to respond with a minimum of delay in case where torture or executions are feared. Some are organized into groups of members of the same profession, for example layers or medical doctors.

Doctors intervene on behalf of prisoners in need of medical treatment, or threatened with torture; on Amnesty International missions they examine alleged torture victims; and medical groups assist the rehabilitation of torture victims. Organizations like churches and trade unions and individuals like artists, parliamentarians and government officials are approached at national and local level to exercise influence on behalf of prisoners within their own spheres of activity.

Group members, as well as the individual members and affiliates, participate in decision making meetings at the national level which vary with the differing organizational structures in each country. Delegates from national sections then go forward to an annual International council, attended by some 200 participants. The council is the supreme governing body of the movement; for example, the statue of Amnesty International can be changed only by a two thirds vote of all the delegates. The council determines the international budget the decides on main policy questions. The council also elects members to the International Executive Committee, a nine member's body responsible for carrying out the decisions of the council and supervising the international Secretariat. The committee approves all missions sent to a country to meet government officials, investigate allegations of human rights abuses and interview former prisoners. All amnesty International Publications are issue under the committee's authority.

This structure ensures that the vital decisions of the movement are controlled by the membership and its elected representatives. The role of the International Secretariat is to collect information on the human rights questions of concern of Amnesty International, evaluate it and make recommendations for policy and action. The secretariat, with a staff of 150 people of some 30 nationalities, has to compile details about prisoners, answer the numerous queries about them, and keep the members groups and sections up to date on cases, campaigns and new projects. The funds to sustain these activities are raised by Amnesty International members themselves. At its council meeting in September 1980 Amnesty International reaffirmed its policy of relying for finances on the efforts of members and donations from the public Amnesty International does not accept government money for its international budget.

It will accept such funds only for its programme of humanitarian relief assistance, provided that these are distributed under the sole control of Amnesty International. This financial independence is essential to keep the movement free from interference by governments, funding agencies or pressure groups and to keep it true to its original spirit. Despite the range of activities undertaken by Amnesty International members, much of the work was frustrating and difficult. For Amnesty International members the challenge remains two fold; to combat political, religious and racial intolerance internationally, and to overcome the indifference to human rights issues that they confront all to often in their own communities.

The promotion and protection of human rights is an international responsibility, which has been recognized by the United Nations (UN) and other international organizations, and is the very foundation of Amnesty International's work. Amnesty International gives great importance to working through and strengthening international mechanisms for the protection of human rights, and has encouraged and supported the establishment and implementation of international standards.

It has consistently worked with the UN, whose charter pledges member state to work for universal respect for and observance of human rights and fundamental freedoms for all without distinction as to race, see language or religion.

Amnesty International has consultative status (Category II) with the Economic and Social Council (ECOSOC) of the UN which allows it to participate in the work of ECOSOC and its specialist sub bodies on human rights matters within its expertise. The commission on Human Rights is a functional commission of ECOSOC composed of 43 member states elected by the council. It is the principal body dealing with human rights with the UN. The commission is serviced by the sub commission on prevention of Discrimination and Protection of Minorities composed of 26 individuals elected by the commission who serve in a personal capacity.

The committee on Crime Prevention and Control, a body of 25 individuals elected by ECOSOC is responsible for the preparatory work for the UN Congress on the prevention of Crime and the Treatment of Offenders, which takes place every five years. These congresses have adopted major international human rights standards, for example the first in 1955 drew up the UN Standard Minimum Rules for the Treatment of Prisoners; the fifth in 1975 the UN declaration against torture the Declaration of the Protection of all persons from Torture and other cruel, Inhuman or Degrading Treatment or Punishment.

16

Human Rights Commission-Minorties Commission Remedies against violation of Human Rights

INTRODUCTION

The commission on Human Rights and minority commission (hereafter "The Commissions") are subsidiaries of the Economic and Social Council. The Charter of the United Nations specifies that the Council "shall set up Commissions in the economic and social field and for the promotion of human rights". In its first meeting in 1946, the Economic and social Council established tow functional commissions, one on human rights and other one the status of women. It was decided that these commissions would be composed of State representatives. The Commission on Human Rights is now composed of 53 states elected by the Economic and Social Council.

Immediately following its creation, the Commission established a subsidiary body that is now known as the Sub Commission on the Promotion and protection of Human Rights (hereafter "the Sub Commission"). The Sub commission, which is composed of 26 experts who are elected by the States members of the Commission, has interlaid a mandate to undertake studies authorized by the Commission and to make recommendations.

The Commission meets annually for six weeks in Geneva in March April. The sub Commission meets or three weeks in August, also in Geneva. The office of the High commissioner for Human Rights acts as secretariat to the Commission and the Sub Commission. Similarly the report of the High Commissioner 28 February 2-3 Complies and analyses information concerning the rights of persons belonging to minorities through the lens of conflict prevention. The report notes that the 1992 Declaration on the Rights of persons belonging to National or Ethnic, Religious and Linguistic Minorities the Declaration is the only UN instrument addressing exclusively the rights of persons belonging to minorities. The report states that the linkage between minority protection and the prevention of conflict has been recognized and highlighted in the basic UN documents reports of the Secretary General, the Millennium Declaration, reports of the High Commissioner. The High Commissioner stated that the OHCHR will continue to collect information and analysis of problems related to minorities with a view to providing input to the UN's work on conflict prevention. Thus, the minority commissions are working for the betterment of human society, avoiding conflicts of all types.

HUMAN RIGHTS COMMISSION-AN OVER VIEW

The National Human Rights Commission was constituted in October 1993 under the Human Rights ordinance of 28 September 1993, which was soon after enacted as the protection of Human Rights Act, 1993,(hereinafter referred to as the Act). It is a fully autonomous body; its autonomy derived out of the method of appointment of the members, their fixity of tenure, and statutory guarantees thereto, the status they have been accorded, the manner in which the staff responsible to the Commission would be appointed and would conduct themselves; as also the autonomy it enjoys in terms of its financial powers.

COMPOSITION OF THE COMMISSION

- A chairperson who has been a chief justice the Supreme court;
- One member who is or has been, a judge of the Supreme Court;
- One member who is, or has bee, the Chief Justice or a High Court;
- Two members to be appointed from amongst persons having knowledge of, or practical experience in, matters relating to human rights.

The Chairperson of the National Commission for Minorities, the National Commission for the Scheduled castes and Scheduled Tribes and the National Commission for women shall be deemed to be members of the Commission for the discharge of certain functions. The shall be a Secretary General of the rank of the Secretary to the Government of India who shall function as the Chief Executive Officer of the Commission. The Headquarters of the Commission shall be at Delhi and there is an enabling provision in the Act to establish offices at other places in India with the previous approval of the Central Government. The method of appointment envisaged in the Act is unique inasmuch as it is made by the president on the recommendations of a high powered Committee consisting of the following.

- The Prime Minister-Chairperson
- Speaker of the House of the people Member
- Minister in charge of the MHA in the Government of India-Member
- Leader of the Opposition in the House of the people member
- Leader of the opposition in the Council of states-Member
- Deputy Chairman of the Council of States-Members

However, no sitting judge of the Supreme Court or a sitting Chief Justice of a High Court shall be appointed without consultation with the Chief Justice of India. The Chairperson or any other Member of the Commission can only be removed from his office by an order of the President on the ground of proved misbehaviour or incapacity after the Supreme Court has, on an inquiry held in this behalf recommended such removal.

The term of office of the Chairperson and members will be five years from the date of assumption of office or until the age of 70 years, whichever is earlier. On ceasing to hold office, the Chairperson and Members shall be ineligible for further appointment under the Government of India or under the government of any State. The act provides that besides the Secretary General, the Central Government shall make available to the commission such police and investigative staff and an officer not below the rank of Director General of police and such other officers and staff as may be necessary for the efficient performance of the functions of the Commission.

The commission may appoint other administrative, technical and scientific staff considered necessary in conformity with the Rules made by the Central government in this behalf. In terms of Section 2 of the Act, "Human Rights" means the rights relating to life, liberty, equality and dignity of the individual guaranteed by the constitution or embodied in the International covenants and enforceable by courts in India. "International Covenants" means the International Covenant on Civil and political Rights and the International Covenant on Economic, Social and Cultural Rights adopted by the General Assembly of the United Nations on 16 December 1966.

The following functions devolve on the Commission under the Act:

- Inquire, on its own initiative or on a petition presented to it by a victim or any persons on his behalf, into complaints of
  - I. Violation of human rights or abutment thereof; or
  - II. Negligence in the prevention of such violation
- Intervene in any proceeding involving any allegation of violation of human rights pending before a court with the approval of such court;
- Visit, under intimation to the state Government, any jail or any other institution under the control of the state Government, where persons are detained or lodged for purposes of treatment, reformation or protection to study the living conditions of the inmate and make recommendations thereon;
- Review the safeguards provided by or under the constitution or any law for the time being in force for the protection of human rights and recommend measures for their effective implementation;
- Review the factor, including acts of terrorism that inhibit the enjoyment of human rights and recommend appropriate remedial measures;
- Study treaties and other international instruments on human rights and make recommendations for their effective implementation;

- Undertake and promote research in the field of human rights;
- Spread human rights literacy among various sections of society and promote awareness of the safeguards available for the protection of these rights through publications, the media, seminars and other available means;
- Encourage the efforts of non governmental organization and institutions working in the field on human rights; and
- Such other functions as it may consider necessary for the promotion of human rights.

The complaint are expected to be self contained. They may be in Hindi, English or any language included in the Eight Schedule of the constitution. No fee is charged complaints. The commission may ask for further information and affidavits to be filed support of allegations whenever considered necessary. The commission may, in its discretion accept telegraphic complaints and complaints conveyed through FAX.

Ordinarily, complaints of the following nature are not entertained the commission:

- In regard to event is which happened more than one year before the making of the complaints;
- With regard to matters which are sub-judice;
- Which are vague anonymous or pseudonymous;
- Which are frivolous nature;
- Those which are outside the purview of the Commissions; and
- Which pertain to service matters.

The commission is vested with the wide ranging powers relating to inquiries and investigation under the Act. While inquiring into complaints under the Act, the Commission could exercise a the powers of a civil court trying a suit under the code of civil procedure 1908 and in particular in respect of following namely;

- Summoning and enforcing the attendance of witnesses and examining them on oath;
- Discovery and production of any document;
- Receiving evidences on affidavits;
- Requisitioning any public record or copy thereof from any court or office;
- Issuing commissions for ht examination of witnesses or document;
- Any other matter which may be prescribed.

The commission has its own investigating staff for investigation into complaints of human rights violations. Under the Act, it is also open to the Commission to utilize the service of any officer or investigation agency of the Central Government or may state Government. In addition, the Commission envisages the association in appropriate cases of outsiders as Investigators or observers. The commission, while inquiring into complaints of violations of human rights, may cal for information or report from the central Government or any State Government or any other authority or organization subordinate thereto within such time as may be specified by it. If the information or report is not received within the time stipulated by the commission, it may proceed to inquire into the complaint on its own on the other hand, if, on receipt of information or report, the commission is satisfied either that no further inquiry is required or that the required action has been initiated or taken by the concerned Government or authority, it my not proceed with the complaint and inform the complainant accordingly.

The commission may take any of the following steps upon the completion of any inquiry:

- Where the inquiry discloses the commission of violation of human rights or negligence in the prevention of violation of human rights by a public servant, it may recommend to the concerned government or authority the initiation of proceedings for prosecution or such other action as the commission may deem fit against the concerned person or persons;
- Approach the Supreme Court or the High court concerned for such directions, orders or writs as that Court may deem necessary; and
- Recommend to the concerned government or authority for the grant of such immediate interim relief to the victim or the members of his family as the commission may consider necessary;
- Subject to the provisions (5) below, provide a copy of the inquiry report to the petitioner or his representative;
- The commission shall send a cop of its inquiry report together with its recommendations to the concerned. Government or authority and the concerned government or authority shall, within a period of one month, or such further time as the commission may allow, its comments on the report, including the action taken or proposed to be taken thereon, to the commission.
- The commission shall publish its inquiry report together with the comments of the concerned government or authority, it any, and the action taken or proposed to be taken by the concerned government or authority on the recommendations of the commission.

The term 'armed forces' for purposed of the Act means the naval, military and air forces and includes any other armed forces of the union. The Act envisages the procedure with respect to armed forces which is at variance with the procedure set out for complaints of violations of human rights by any other public servant.

- The commission shall notwithstanding other provisions of the Act, adopt the following procedure while dealing with complaints of violations of human rights by members of the armed forces.
  - It may, either on its own motion or receipt of a petition, seek at report from the Central Government.

- After the receipt of the report, it may either not proceed with the complaint or as the case may be, make its recommendations to that government.

- The central Government shall inform the commission of the action taken on the recommendations within three months or such further time as the commission may allow.
- The commission shall publish its report together with its recommendations made ot the central government and the action taken by that government on such recommendations.
- The commission shall provide a copy of the aforesaid report to the petitioner or his representative.

Responsibility of the Central Government/State Government/Authority to which report/recommendations have been sent. The Central government/ state government/authority has to indicate its comments/action taken on the report/recommendations of the commission within a period of one month in respect of complaints relating to armed forces.

Annual and Special Reports of the Commission

The commission is required to submit an Annual Report to the Central Government well as the State Government concerned. Besides, the commission may at any time submit special reports on matter which, in this opinion, is of such urgency or importance that it should not be deferred till submission of the Annual Report. It is enjoined on the Central Government as well as the concerned State Government to lay before each House of parliament or the State Legislatures respectively the Annual and Special Reports of the commission along with a memorandum of action taken or proposed to be taken on the recommendations of the Commission and the reason for non acceptance of the recommendations, if any.

State Human Rights Commission

There is an enabling provision in the Act for state Human Rights Commission to be constituted by the respective State Governments. The State commission shall consist of;

- A Chairperson who has been a Chief Justice of a High Court.
- One member who is, or has been, a judge of a High Court;
- One Member who is, or has been, a District Judge in the State;
- Two members to be appointed from amongst persons having knowledge of, or practical experience in, matters relating to human rights.

There shall be secretary who shall be the Chief Executive officer of the State Commission and shall exercise such powers and discharge such functions of the State Commission as it may delegate to him.

The headquarters of the State Commission shall be at such place as the State Government may, by notification, specify.

Constitution of the State Commission

The Chairperson and other members of the Commission shall be appointed by the Government after obtaining the recommendations of a Committee consisting of

- The Chief Minister Chairperson
- Speaker of the Legislative Assembly Member
- Minister in charge of the Department of Home in the State members
- Leader of the Opposition in the Legislative Assembly Members

Where there is a Legislative Council in a state, the Chairman of that Council and the Leader of the Opposition in that Council shall also be members of the Committee. No sitting judge of a High Court or a sitting District Judge shall be appointed except after consultation with the Chief justice of the High Court of the concerned State. The Chairperson or any other Members of a State Commission can only be removed form his office by an order of the President in accordance with the procedure envisaged for the National Commission.The term of office of the Chairperson or Member will be five years from the date f assumption of office or at the age of 70 years, whichever is earlier. A member is however eligible for reappointment for another term of five years subject to the age limit of 70 years. On ceasing to hold office, the Chairperson or a member are ineligible for appointment under the Government of the State or under the Government of India.

Officers and Staff of the State Commission

The concerned State Government shall make available to the State Commission an officer not below the rank of a secretary to the State Government who shall be the secretary of State Commission and such police and investigative staff under an officer not below the rank of an Inspector General of Police and such other officers and staff as may be necessary for the efficient performance of the functions of the State Commission. The State commission may appoint such other administrative, technical and scientific staff as it may consider necessary.

Functions of the State Commission

A State Commission may inquire into violations of human rights only in respect of matters relating to any of the entries enumerated in List II Concurrent List) in the seventh Schedule of the Constitution. However, if any such matter is already being inquired into by the National Commission or any other Statutory commission, the State Commission shall not inquire in to the said matter. Subject to this, the powers, the procedure of investigation, inquiry and steps to be taken thereafter are comparable to those of the National commission.The State commission shall submit Annual Report to the respective State Governments and may, at any time, submit special reports on any matter which in their opinion is of urgency or importance. It is enjoined on the State Governments to cause to lay on the Table of the respective State Legislature the Annual and Special Reports of the State Human Rights Commission.

Human Right Courts

The act envisages that for the purpose of providing speedy trial of offences arising out of violations of human rights, State Governments may with the concurrence of the Chief Justice of the concerned High Court specify for each District Court of Sessions to be inhuman Rights Court to try such offences. For every Human Rights Court, the State Government shall specify a public prosecutor or appoint an advocate of at least seven years standing as a special public Prosecutor for the purpose of conducting cases in that Court.

Finance, Accounts and Audit

The Central Government and the concerned State Government shall, after due appropriation made in this behalf, apy to the National Commission and the concerned State Commission respectively by way of grants necessary funds for being utilized for purposes of the Act. The accounts f the Commission will have to be maintained in an appropriate form devised in consultation with the Comptroller and auditor General of India and are subject to audit by the latter or any person appointed by him. The accounts of the Commission as certified by the Comptroller and Auditor General or his appointee together with the Audit Report shall be laid before each House of Parliament by the Central Government in the case of National Commission and before the appropriate State Legislature by the concerned State Government in respect of the State Commission.

Miscellaneous

The National Commission as well as the State Commission shall not be inquire into any matter which is pending before a State Commission or National Commission as the case may be or any other statuary commission. If the Goverment considers it necessary, it may notwithstanding anything contained in any other law, constitute one or more special investigation teems consisting of the requisite police officers for purposes of investigation and prosecution of offences arising out of violations of human rights. The Central Goverment as well as the State Government concerned may make rules to carry out the provisions of the Act. The Rules so made are required to be laid before each House of Parliament for a total period of 30 days as regards the National Human Rights Commission and appropriate State Legislature in respect of the State Commissions.

MINORITY COMMISSION: AN OVER VIEW

Minorities Commission Among things noted were the following: the fact that the different claims of persons belonging to minorities required a response specific to each situation: the fact that the appropriateness of measures depends on whether minorities are dispersed and/or concentrated within particular areas of a given country: the dangers of exclusion arising from ethnically based govenments: the importance of providing for the inclusion of all communities and groups in situations where territorial decentralization of governance is pursued: the suggestion that greater focus should be placed on supporting regional strategied for minority cooperation: the suggesion that there is need for further reflection on autonomist and integrative approaches to minority protection in multicultural societies.

The report states that the role of the UN and the internatioanl community is to support national efforts for conflict prevention and to assist in buiding natioanl capacity.

In this context the Secretary-General intends:

- To continue dispatching UN interdisciplinary fact-finding and confidence-building missions to volatile regions;
- To Start submitting periodic regional and subregional reports to the Security Council on disputes that may potentially threaten international peace and security:
- To develop regional prevention strategies with regional partners and with UN agencies:
- To establish an informal network of eminent persons for conflict prevention: and
- To provide the capacity and resources for preventive action in the Secretariat.

The Secretary-General called for the UN to move from a culture of reaction to a culture of prevention and stated that primary focus of preventive action should be to address deep-rooted socio-economic, cultural, environmental,institutional, political and other stuctural causes that often underlie the immediate symptoms of conficts. The report refers to various kinds of initiatives aimed at improving the understanding of situations facing minorities in diverse settings and at devising effective means to address them in luding: the launch in September 2001 of the UN Guide for Minorities (a manual on the Declaration on the Rights of Persons Belonging to National of Ethnic, Religious and Linguiscic Minorities) at the World Conference against racism the convening of regional and expert seminars on various themes-e.g. multiculturalism in Africa, Africa, Afro descendants in Latin America: funding to ensure the partcipation of representatives of minorities in the work of the working Group on Minorities.

The report notes that the 2002 meeting of the working Group was to focus on the partcipation of minorities in public life, including through the purslt of integration of autonomy measures, as well as on addressing group inequalities and the mainstreaming of minority concerns in the develoment process.

The addenda to the Secretaty-General's main report (4, March, 2002) and (8 March 2002) contain the text of replies to an October 2001 note verbale that was sent to governments and intergovernmental and non-government organizations, requesting information related to the better protection of the rights of persons belonging to minorities.

The information provided by the governments of Austria, Bulgaria, Hungary, Lebanon, Madagascar, Russia, Switzerland and Turkey refers to the following matters, inter alia the constitutional protection of equality before the law the constitutional with ethnic grops before laws are adopted: civil and administratibe provisions against publcly expressed prejudices and discriminatory acts against persons on the ground of race, colour, national or ethnic origin or religious belif probisions requiring the non discriminatory treatment of persons by the proce and secrity forces: human rights education aimed at prebenting prejudice and dist riminution and similar training for progessionals: the equal integration of Roma into society: the lack of a universal instrument of a binding character defining the rights of persons belonging to minorities and the need to address this issue dismissal from employment as a result of discrimination and the mistreatment of children belonging to an ethnic minority: criminal and civil cases involving, for example incitement against a community of Roma chidren from the use of a school gymnasium and conducting separate commencement exercise for them, using the excuse of "public hygience". administrative cases related to the election of national minority self-government; provisions in the Europe Framework Convention for the protection of National Minorities; the difficulty of arriving at the definition of "minority" that would receive universal support and the obstacle this could present to the drafting of a legally binding international instrument. The report notes that the responses of government did not reveal a consensus on whether or not a mechanism should be established to draft a convention on the rights of persons belonging to minorities.

Information was also received from the Office of the High Commissioner for National Minorities of the Organization for Security and Cooperation in Europe, referring to, for example, good governance, the possible need for special measured to protect and to allow the further development of distinct cultural identities, promotion of integration, effective implementation of existing norms and standards. The report also notes information that was provided by UNESCO and the UNHCR.

In the discussion on mainstreaming minority rights in development assistance and cooperation as a means of preventing conflict, participants considered the following points, among others; the economic exclusion of minorities and indigenous people and the resulting manifestations of racism and related intolerance, the need to address the use of land and its resources if development policies are to be sustainable in the longer term, participation by minorities and indigenous communities at all stages of the development process nothing that traditional decision making structures might be most appropriate to maximize the participation of communities, the need to ensure equal access to the participation process for women, persons with disabilities, older persons, children and youth, and persons with HIV/AIDS, the need to acknowledge the existence of discrimination and exclusion, to collect better data to understand the causes and nature of such exclusion, and to implement specially targeted programmes for minorities and indigenous people as well the need to integrate the rights of these communities into general programmes for achieving the international Development Goals.

UN Working Group on Minorities

Ensure the wider disseminating of its activities and reports and the widest dissemination of the Declaration on the Rights of Persons Belonging to National or Ethnic, Religious and Linguistic Minorities (the Declaration), as well as the UN Guide for minorities, including by making them accessible in the languages of minority communities.Establish a system for the regular exchange of information on minority issues with regional mechanisms and national institutions, including through the organization of meetings and seminars, particularly on conflict prevention and resolution. Support training programmes for minority communities and groups on utilizing global regional and national human rights mechanisms for the better protection of the rights of minorities. Support the participation of minorities in the drafting of reports authorized by the Working Group. Examine in greater depth the nature extent and dynamics of discrimination against minorities, in cooperation with minority representatives governments and others.

REMEDIES AGAINST VIOLATION OF HUMAN RIGHTS

Over the years, the working of this Commission have changed substantially. Very early on these Commission focused on elaboration various human rights standards including minorities. It drafted the Universal Declaration of Human Rights and the two Covenants, on civil and political rights, and on economic, social and cultural rights and later minority rights. Soon, the main challenge before the Commission came to be how to respond to the human rights violations carried kind including minority rights violations. In 1947, the Economic and social Council passed a resolution stating that the Commission had "no power to take any action in regard to any complaints concerning human rights". So long as those in charge with in the country have not fallen in line with these international covenants.

However, later on the Commission was faced with a number of individual petitions from South Africa and came under considerable pressure to deal with them. This forced it to grapple with the elaboration of procedures to deal with issues connected to Human Rights and minority violations. A taboo was broken soon when the commission established and hoc working group of experts to investigate the situation of human rights and minority violations. The demand to act on the situation in southern Africa led to recognition of the need for public debate on specific countries.

The commission then was able to deal with various other situations, such as coup against a government. By setting up working groups to inquire into the situation of violations of monitories and human rights in this working group was replaced by a special rapporteur and two expers to study such cares later. By 1980, the Commission established the woring group on Disapperarances to deal with the question of enforced disappearances and other violations of Human Rights throughout the world. Since then, there has been less reluctance to establish expert mechanisms to deal with human minorities and rights challenges in various parts of the world. Such mechanisms were progressively applied in a more innovative manner and adapted to an increasing range of violations.

The Commission solicits the help of human rights experts to assist it in the task of examining specific situations including minority rights as can be seen in earlier pass. Over the years, the work of these experts has provided a much needed analysis on how human rights principles are applied in reality. It has formed the basis for an informed and substantive debate at the intergovernmental level. It has given a voice to the often silenced victims and offered a basis for dialogue with Governments on the concrete measures to be taken to enhance protection. Works of the experts is debated during the annual session of the Commission on Human Rights. About one third of the experts also reports to the United Nations General Assembly in New York. Some experts have informally briefed the United Nations Security council. Thus Remedies to Human Rights violations of any kind to day are built in to the institutional structures established. The proceeding paragraphs therefore clearly speaks of these remedies too. The United Nations human rights experts play a vital role in working towards the universal achievement of freedom from fear and want. They are not paid. Their reward is the satisfaction of working towards the realization of human rights, as the highest aspiration of the common people as the Universal Declaration of Human Rights proclaimed.

The system remains seriously under-resource and has yet to achieve its full potentioal, however Efforts are continuing to be made to strengthen the system to enable it to achieve the goal of universal respect for all human rights. With the cooperation of various actors in particular Governments, United Nations bodies, and the non governmental sector, its effectiveness could be considerably enhanced.

Index